Also by Rachel Peden

RURAL FREE

The Land, the People

THE LAND,
THE PEOPLE

࿇࿇࿇࿇࿇࿇࿇࿇࿇࿇

By

RACHEL PEDEN

࿇

Drawings by SIDONIE CORYN

ALFRED · A · KNOPF : NEW YORK · 1966

THIS IS A BORZOI BOOK

PUBLISHED BY ALFRED A. KNOPF, INC.

Macy and BFM, and Walter
(They will know)

The earth is the Lord's, and the fulness thereof;
the world, and they that dwell therein.

Psalm 24

Pre-emption

⋖⋗⋖⋗⋖⋗⋖⋗⋖⋗⋖⋗⋖⋗⋖⋗

I T H A S always seemed to me a book ought not need an introduction, that everything should be contained in the story or come, with O. Henry suddenness, at the end, clarifying the whole dramatic business.

An introduction by any other name is just as delaying, and my reaction has always been, "Get on with the story and let me find out for myself."

On the other hand, if you see a great number of guests at a party, all unlike, you wish to know who they are and why you are all there.

In the four chapters of *The Land, the People*, there are many people, all different. To put them into one book may seem omnivorous, yet they have one thing in common: the land. They all loved the land, lived close to it, and in the end their lives and thinking were shaped by it, and yet at the end, as in the beginning, they were still all different. For all its stern discipline, the land fosters individualism, which is probably one clue to the reason for man's eternal need of a closeness with it.

The farms and the people of this book are all in Indiana. This state, originally an agricultural state whose people were so unsophisticated and independent of thought they acquired a lasting national reputation for those qualities (summed up in the word "Hoosier"), has within late years become a leading industrial state. In the farming community in which I live, as generally in farming communities everywhere, the old patterns are changing almost as swiftly as cloud formations before a storm. The change is felt not only in farming areas but in urban societies everywhere. Writers, speakers, citizens are remembering that man is anciently akin to the earth and needs a close contact with it. The feeling is evident in the increased use of land for parks, in the emphasis laid on conservation of our national resources and wilderness beauty; even, inconsistently, in the trend of people to move into the country and build houses, or to hold on tenaciously to a small farming acreage and live there while working in town for a living income.

To say man is of the earth and that his well-being, even his very survival, depends on an occasional return to it is not enough. It is important to try to find out why this is true. Some people, those most distantly removed from farm living, accomplish the necessary return by going to parks, visiting farm friends and relatives, walking on grass in their own yards, or reading a book about country living.

For others, notably farmers, a mere occasional return to the land is not enough. These lovers have a deep, insatiable passion to be close to the land; they are willing to gamble their strength and ingenuity on its response. Perhaps it is man's inherited, infinitesimally small share of divinity that makes him restless and compels him to keep trying to possess the earth, remold it, dominate it, and, too often, waste it.

The patient earth tolerates these lovers, nourishes, inspires, and comforts them; it disciplines and teaches them and in the end accepts them back tenderly, but never truly surrenders to them nor lets them go free of their obligation.

For man has an inescapable obligation to the land. It is his destiny to touch, observe, and learn from it, in his passionate effort to understand himself. Living close to the land, he sees rules that govern it, and he suspects that a good many of these apply to him also. He suspects also there are rules that apply only to him, or at least apply more acutely to him than to the rest of earth's creatures. He is endowed with a passion to discover what these laws are; now and then, he catches a glimpse of one, and the glimpse changes the shape of his thinking. For when a truth is thus discovered it has to be accepted, no matter what cherished belief or hope it displaces. Man places his hope for eventual harmony on gathering up, piecing together, and understanding these truths.

In the process of understanding the earth and its creatures, man begins slowly to understand himself. And in the
same process, but in reverse, in his passion to reshape and
dominate the earth, he comes near to destroying himself. It
is often said that man has a built-in mechanism for self-
destruction; that if all his great dreams and plans succeeded
as he wished, they would end by destroying him. Fortunately, then, they never wholly succeed. Something inter-
venes, and the pattern of man's behavior never returns to
its origin, completing a static circle, but approaches the
point, swerves above and beyond it, and thus life spirals on
and on. Just as the farm year repeats itself, year after year,

following a pattern but never achieving identical repetition.
A farmer comes to respect the land as much as he loves it,
and when finally he yields to it, it is not defeat any more

than a wheat harvest, yielding to the combine, is defeated. It is a harvest, useful, beautiful, eternally repeated.

From the earth man learns that his values—classifications of good and bad, necessary and dispensable, long and brief— are purely his own arbitrary values, and the earth does not necessarily endorse them. If in the end he learns to combine hope with humility and a kindness and unquenchable gaiety, he has, as farmers say, "made a crop." He has fulfilled his personal obligation to the land.

Chiefly, the farmers in this book are B. F. Mason, my father (who was not a farmer at all but an orchardist); Dakin, a neighbor whose love of his farm almost took the place of all other love; Walter Peden, my father-in-law, who turned to farming as inevitably as cornstalks reach upward in the hot July sun and who presumably handed this inherited love of farming on down to his son Richard, an involuntary heritage that has led Dick and me through some difficult, painful, and also pleasant land experiences. The adult land need of our two children, who have grown up on the Maple Grove farm, remains yet to be fulfilled.

So here, after all, is an introduction, and as Patrick Henry said, if this be treason . . .

R. P.

Contents

High Gap Is the Lord's

THE PEOPLE, chiefly:

B. F. Mason, the orchardist, my father
His wife, Laura, my mother
His daughters, Grace, Miriam, Rachel, Nina, Joie, Kathleen
His son, James

THE PLACE:

A part of Monroe County, Indiana; now a part of the
Morgan-Monroe state forest reservation

❦❧❦❧❦❧❦❧❦❧❦❧❦❧❦❧

"SHALL we stop here a little while?" suggested my sister Nina who was driving. There, from the paved road running gently between flanks of native forest, a little fork went off toward a creosoted pole gateway, beside which the state of Indiana had set a respectful designation, "Stepp Cemetery." In our childhood, living on our father's farm that is now a part of this state-owned forest reserve, we called this place "the Precinct" and we lived in a gaunt, gray, two-story house about six miles from it. The house was originally an inn.

In the Precinct the older graves were marked only by unlettered chunks of stone, or not at all. It is still used, but the more recently set stones are professionally cut and inscribed. Nina and I read a few of them as we walked about looking for the unmarked graves of our grandfather, an uncle, and his small son, buried there long ago.

All around us native Indiana trees—maple, oak, hickory, walnut, tulip poplar, ash, hackberry, sumac, sassafras, wild cherry, beech—lifted their color-filled brushes toward the

3

pale afternoon sky and dripped bright drops of red, yellow, and brown on the ground beside green firs the state had planted when it took over the land from private owners in the 1920's. October was in full cry, but we were in a somber mood. We had just come from a house in a little town to which our mother had moved a few years earlier when she had to begin living alone and in which now she was dying.

Through my mind ran the melody of a ballad people were singing that autumn. My daughter Carol had sung it over and over when she came home from DePauw University the week before for what we all thought would be a final visit with her grandmother: "If you miss the train I'm on, you will know that I am gone; you can hear the whistle blow a hundred miles."

There were seven children in the Mason family when we lived on the orchard farm. By the time my mother moved to the little town, after my father's death, we were all grown and had homes of our own.

Five of us lived at great distances from Mother but all seven went often to the little town to visit her. My sister Nina, who spends much of her time in a Western state and travels a great deal, always came before or after a long trip. She and Mother had gay, bantering visits, and when Nina left, Mother always told her at the very last, "Drive carefully now," and tried not to cry. Nina has driven thousands of miles. When we lived on the orchard farm Mother could harness and drive any of the horses. She took pleasure in hitching up the little fat mule, Martha, to an open-top buggy and driving over the farm to gather apples or peaches from some isolated, self-planted tree, but she never learned to drive a car.

My sister Grace, who lived with her husband, Mirl Lundy, in the country several miles from Mother, went often to visit her and sometimes stayed several days at a time, doing little house-loving chores Mother could no longer do, such as washing and ironing the embroidered pillowslips and treasured old Battenberg doilies, mending Mother's favorite dresses, and just companionably talking.

Mirl, whose own mother died when he was a little boy, was a special friend of Mother's, went to see her almost every week, and liked to tease Grace by saying the real reason he wanted to marry her was so he could have "Laura" for his mother-in-law.

My sister Miriam, who writes children's books, came often also for visits and took Mother out in her car and let Mother lecture her.

I who lived nearest, on a farm, probably went oftenest, and it fell to my lot to make Mother do the hard things she didn't want to do, such as going to the hospital now and then or learning finally to use a wheelchair.

That October afternoon Nina and I had made her as comfortable as possible and left her asleep in the care of Leah, her devoted housekeeper-companion. I don't know which of us suggested going back to the place that had been our childhood home or, in fact, whether it was actually suggested in words at all. Nina and I have always been close in thought and mood, and it may have been just another of the many mutual decisions we have reached simultaneously.

As we walked about the Precinct, from which grass, weeds, and briers were neatly mowed, we noticed that a tall, young persimmon tree had reached out above one grave and dropped an earthy gift of ripe, bright orange persimmons on it. A companionable gesture, I thought, and picked up a few to eat as the farmer lying underneath would undoubtedly have done if he could have.

After a while we got back into Nina's car and drove farther into the Reserve. The state's new, well-paved roads do not follow the routes of our old, dirt roads, and there are few signs remaining of our occupancy. That is to be expected. The land, never completely possessed by any holder, soon forgets its temporary owners. Besides, the state of Indiana, like any private citizen coming into possession of "a piece of property," had begun at once to stamp its own personality on the place. It planted thousands of evergreens, which to former landholders seemed like carrying coals to Newcastle because the hills and ridges were already well forested with native trees, and in time of extreme drought evergreens could be a fire hazard. But the state built a fire tower. It set up a CCC camp. It established picnic areas with tables, fireplaces, shelter houses. It constructed a lake and built a new house for its supervisor to live in, choosing a

6

site just back of the place where our house had burned.

When the orchardist's family moved out of the house, a man who had always worked for my father moved in with his family as caretakers. The hired man's straight black hair, Indian-like profile, and swarthy skin gave support to the accepted belief that he was of Indian ancestry. He had a wife and several children but for some years had carried on an illicit romance with the French-descended wife of a neighbor who was of German ancestry. The German, revolting finally against this international entanglement, angrily set fire to the orchardist's house with the hired man and his family in it. They escaped, but the house burned to the ground and with it all our belongings we had not moved away into the town house. Among these was a large collection of fine Indian arrowheads and hammers that had been picked up on the farm, evidence that Indians once considered this land theirs. Probably they knew its watering places, too —Draper Hollow Spring, Sugar Spring, Cherry Spring, the Big Spring, the Little Spring—but by other names. Probably they, like the orchardist's family, had seen the foxfire on the ground in the woods on damp summer nights and wondered about this mysterious, phosphorescent fungus. There were many earth-covered mounds in the woods, which the orchardist's children implicitly believed were Indian graves and would yield up Indian bones and arrowheads if dug into. Now I realize they were the buried roots of giant trees blown over in a storm and finally covered over and turned back

7

into soil in the thrifty way of nature to feed more plants.

After the Indians there had been a pioneering man who started a little village there, called Stringtown. The orchardist's old house had been this man's inn, with one row of rooms set directly above another identical row and a long "blind" stairway going darkly, without benefit of banister, from the front-door hall to a small upstairs hall. The innkeeper had a store, but his chief business was the tanning of hides in large, square vats dug in the ground at the foot of the slope below the inn.

When we lived there, the floors of the vats were still strewn with bits of old, dry tanbark, so we called that pasture the Tanyard. In the summers when we kept the milk cow there and my sister Nina and I did the milking, we carried the buckets to the pasture and set them under the cows wherever they stood, to milk. I milked Old June, the placid half-Jersey-half-Shorthorn. Nina's hands were smaller than mine so she milked the purebred Jersey, Flower, whose teats were short. Nina was younger than I and more aggressive, always thirsting for adventure and travel, but much more tenderhearted and generous than she wanted anyone to suspect. Her hair was the color of ripe cornstalks, and sunburned because she would never bother with a hat. Years later when I used to read her palm, I was glad to find in it the protective line that looks after some people, and as she grew up it seemed that whenever something of special importance was going to happen, it happened when she was there to see it.

In late summer ironweed grew tall in the Tanyard, offering us its sprangly bouquets of small red-purple flowers; the short grass. was thick and dark green. If we crossed the creek that bordered the pasture we came to a wooded knoll which we called Hillacres.

There we had campfire suppers and gave plays written by my sister Miriam; there we buried our best-loved pets. Miriam baked delicious cornbread in an oversized baking-powder can in the coals and cooked a stew of "meat and potatoes and things" that was so good nobody bothered to ask what the "things" were. We used odd, interesting dishes for these suppers; one of our best was the bone-white, clean-scraped carapace of a box turtle. It looked like a delicately sculptured bowl. In those days Miriam said she wanted to be a doctor and she practiced her healing art on all the sick dogs and cats and broken-legged chickens. Once, when one of her younger sisters had a huge fever blister on the lip, Miriam cut it off with the scissors, and no evil befell either child or the scissors, and the fever blister healed without leaving a scar.

But Miriam had begun writing almost as soon as she learned to talk, and eventually she became a writer of children's books. She created fun and new games and wrote plays wherever she went. She was pretty and had smaller feet than the rest of us had. The unmarried hired men were always in love with her and she was always engaged to them, innocently, two at a time.

The orchardist loved his land, called it "an empire." (In his reading he was devoted to biographies of Napoleon and Lincoln.) Someplace on the farm he discovered little flakes of raw, pure gold; nobody ever knew where. He kept it in a tightly corked little bottle in his "office." (I have it now.) When he bought the farm, seeing already in imagination the orchards and blocks of nursery stock he would plant there, it was known around the locality as "the old Sharp farm." He renamed it High Gap, and we lived there seventeen years before he was injured in an automobile accident and we had to leave the farm sadly and, as we believed, temporarily. In the years he owned it, he added other small farms to it: the Cox orchard, where frosty purple crab apples grew and fell ungathered on the ground, and sometimes in winter, on the way to school, we could find one still edible under the protecting leaves on the ground; the Landrum place, where pungent perfume weed grew rank around the two-room log cabin, and there were two giant oaks beside a well of bitter water, and a sweet-apple tree whereof the apples had a "water core"; the Richards orchard, where strawberries ripened surprisingly early so that on the first exploring trip you seldom had anything but a hat to carry them home in, proudly; the North cherry orchard, that had a little wet-weather pond in the center, and there in spring you heard the first hyla peepers and called them frogs.

My father planted orchards everyplace. He knew the Latin names of plants and trees and called them by those names. He could identify all the peaches and apples. He experimented, was years ahead of his time in horticultural development. He had grafted an apple tree so that it bore sweet apples on one side and sour apples on the other and his children thought this was magic. We believed that if he planted the wooden stove poker with which we poked the fire in the wood-burning stove that heated the dining-living room, the poker would probably take root, blossom, and bear interesting fruit. He said, "I love any kind of a tree, but of course a peach tree most of all." He propagated some new varieties of peach, the most successful being the Shipper's Late Red.

In late May the Shipper's Late Red orchard, just across the Big Spring road, in front of the house, was a cloud of pink bloom. There, in late summer, grew the most delicious peaches I have ever known. Those that were to be shipped by interurban to the Indianapolis market were carefully hand-picked a day or so ahead of complete tree ripeness, packed eighty-five or thereabout to a bushel, and loaded on the wagon in the evening. Early the next morning they were hauled nine miles, as gently as the stony rough roads and the horses would permit, into town. They were large, yellow-fleshed, with velvety pink cheeks, and of perfect peach shape. The ground under those trees was kept free of sod (this was hand-and-shovel work) and deeply cultivated into a fine dust mulch.

On quiet summer nights the tree-ripened big fruits let go and dropped gently, unbruised, upon the ground. In the mornings we could pick them up, break the skin by pinching it between a thumbnail and fingernail, peel it off, thin as paper, and bite into the wonderful juicy richness of peach flavor concentrated there. To be really good, a peach has to be tree-ripened; a peach picked green is still green when it is rotten. People came from many miles to eat and buy the orchardist's spectacular peaches, and he took armloads of blue and red prize ribbons at the Indiana state fairs. The road from town up through Happy Hollow to the orchard farm was steep; in places the earth was washed off completely, leaving a pavement of sheer blue shale. It was a test for the horses we drove over it and a test for the early automobiles in which people came out to buy peaches.

♣   ♣   ♣

That tense October afternoon there was no trace left of the Shipper's Late Red orchard. There was no trace left, either, of the lower barn that had been nearby. "Do you remember that dramatic night storm when we watched it struggle and pull like a living thing and finally collapse in the wind?" asked Nina softly, as if still awed. I did. The old barn had been weakening for years, unrepaired. By that night the huge hand-hewn poplar beams were pulling apart from the handmade wooden pins, the overburdened loft floor sagging badly. The barn loft had been one of our most exciting playhouses. We were strictly forbidden to go into it, so of course we went secretly. It had not been used for hay storage for many years, but in a board-enclosed corner there remained a two-foot depth of old hay, dry and brittle, that made a kind of elevated cushion. The boards on that wall of the barn were loose at the barn-loft floor level. Sitting on the hay cushion, we could push outward against the loose boards with our feet, and let them spring back, somewhat like pumping a foot pedal. For some reason this seemed to us like a pipe organ, and there we "played" the pipe organ and sang, making up hilarious songs to sing as we pedaled.

In the loft also were stacks of troughlike metal burners in which crude oil smudges could be built on cold, late spring nights when frost threatened the peach blossoms. In the barn loft also the fascinating shoes were stored, still in their original boxes.

At one time in his pre-orchard years the orchardist had owned a part interest in a women's shoe store. When the partnership was dissolved he brought his part of the new, unsold stock to the farm and stored it in the barn loft. The shoes had high heels and high button tops; some were red leather with red cloth tops. We loved them, thought they were beautiful, and would gladly have worn them, but they were all too narrow for our feet. We were accustomed to going barefooted. Spring held no happier day than the morning when we could shed the long-legged, one-piece winter underwear that however carefully tightly lapped about the leg still made a bulge under the stocking, and on

that day also one could cast off shoes and run barefooted in sensuous luxury on the grass. Our sister Miriam was the only one of us with feet small enough to get those beautiful red, high-heeled shoes on her feet.

The overflow from the orchardist's former "offices" was stored in the barn loft—many boxes of old business letters that we read, criticized, imitated, and admired. There were bushel baskets grown lopsided and weary from their over-burden of old newspapers and catalogs. There was the orchardist's obsolete business stationery imprinted with red stars and a former address. But our utmost delight in the barn loft was the rolltop office desk. Its drawers were swollen shut and stuck fast, the rolltop likewise unbudgeable. We worked on them for years, confident that if only we could get the drawers open undamaged, great treasures of paper, pencils, crayons, and boxes of paints would be found there. We never succeeded, and playing forbiddenly in the barn loft, we had to be on guard against being seen or heard by anyone passing along the road or by one of the hired men coming into the barn rooms below to get his coat and dinner bucket hanging there. We knew, as the birds of the air know, that the price of freedom is eternal vigilance.

♣   ♣   ♣

Unfortunately, when the state of Indiana took over my father's orchards and other farm land in that vicinity, none of the personnel knew enough about that wild backwoods area to appreciate its valuable landmarks or its distinctively Indiana legends and features. None of them thought to consult old-time residents still living there, who might have told them valuable Hoosieriana.

They could have collected much from Harve, bent, ageless, wrinkled as a potato in late spring, with friendly blue eyes squinted up in a lively smile. Harve's shoes always curled up at the toes because he bought them at rummage sales and they were always several sizes too big for him. Perhaps he thought he would "grow into them." He cut and hauled crossties for Mother, or wove a split hickory seat in an old porch rocker for her, and kept her informed of local news. He hunted the woods for ginseng, which he called "sang," and sold it for his own income. He walked from

Hacker Creek where he lived to Happy Hollow, at least five miles away, to court a widow whose young son worked for the orchardist.

It was Harve who told Mother her house was "ha'anted." The "ha'ant," he said, was a headless woman who stood by the window of an upstairs middle bedroom, holding her head in her hand out of the window and singing "Pass me not, oh gentle Saviour." My mother went ahead and papered the room, laid down clean straw on the floor, and covered it with strips of slick straw matting sewed together and made a bedroom for her four middle children to sleep in. None of us ever did see the "ha'ant."

It was in that room, however, that we saw "Gobby," and watched him come down from the attic for his only and dramatic personal appearance. Gobby was a mythical creature that we learned about from our sister Miriam. She told us news of him and in his name exacted services she never could have exacted for herself. I think probably the idea came to her in some sudden inspiration of the moment. The personality of Gobby gained charm and prestige from her stories until he became so real to us that finally we demanded to see him. This was something Miriam had not anticipated; she put us off as long as possible. Finally she told us if we would swear to sit on the bed in the middle bedroom and not make a sound, she would persuade Gobby to appear. He would come down from the attic through a little trapdoor that had been cut in the ceiling for use in case of fire. We pulled a bureau under the trapdoor and set a chair beside it to make steps for Gobby's convenience.

We had waited a long time, when finally the trapdoor lifted and slowly, silently, while we watched almost without breathing, Gobby began to appear. First one foot, in a high-heeled shoe, reaching around blindly to find the bureau to step on, then a leg, finally a whole body clad only in a suit of tight-fitting long winter underwear with a jaunty hole snagged over one hip. We watched in complete silence. Gobby had long brown braids and freckles on the face exactly like Miriam's, but so strong was the spell we could not be sure. Then suddenly I let out a cry. Without a word, Gobby turned accusing eyes on me and vanished quickly through the little dark hall. But I didn't care. I had just remembered that only Miriam had feet small enough to get into those tiny, high-heeled, red-topped button shoes Gobby had on. We never heard of Gobby again after that.

Two familiar traces remaining that October afternoon were the two giant oaks at the Landrum place, but the road on which we drove ran right over the spot where the sweet-apple tree had stood. There was no trace left of the long rows of blackcap Cumberland raspberries. Gone the goose-berry bushes, the red and the white currant bushes, the plot of ornamental shrubs near the hired man's cabin. On this plot japonicas, unsold, grew too large for transplanting and bore their delicately fragrant red-flecked yellow quinces that were as hard as wood and irresistible to the hired man's thrifty mother. She had gathered a "mess" of those strange-looking fruits to cook, and later demanded angrily of the orchardist, "What is them things, anyway? I cooked 'em all day and they never did get soft."

Gone was the cabin itself and the big weeping mulberry tree the orchardist had planted in its yard and the cherry orchard in front of it. Gone the row of pink roses that ran the full length of the cherry orchard and in June made a rain of sun-warmed pink petals.

In our childhood we gathered these petals by the bucketful for my sister Grace and Mother to make into rose jars and beads. The beads were made of a paste from salt and ground-up rose petals. Formed into cherry-sized balls and dried on a long hatpin so they could later be strung, they turned black and had a pleasant smell, but disintegrated if they became damp. This project was one of many cultural experiments promoted by my sister Grace, who read all the women's magazines she could get and hoarded them for years, and also read all the books in our family's extensive library. She was supposed to ask the orchardist's permission before reading any book, but actually she read first and then asked, for fear he might say no about one of them. My sister Miriam also read most of the books. A volume of Poe's weird tales, in an expensive pale blue and gold binding, so haunted and depressed her that she buried it, and when she dug it up later, it was no longer in a condition for anyone to read.

My sister Grace read catalogs and cookbooks with as much fervor as she read novels, and was fascinated by gourmet recipes and foreign words. Having run across the name "springerle formen" somewhere, she liked the name and gave her own mispronunciation of it, "springery formen," to a drink she prepared for us in spring. It was green onions cut into bits and floating in weakened vinegar (not weakened enough, however) with salt and pepper added. We drank it and liked it as well as the "lemonade" my sister Miriam made from red sumac berries.

Another time, having read about sorrel soup, Grace decided to try it out on the family. She always did these experiments when Mother had gone to town leaving her in charge. Unfortunately, she was not enough of a botanist to identify different kinds of sorrel, and what she used was common sour grass, so the soup was not a real success with the brother, sisters, cousin, and hired men she served it to, although everybody remembered it for years. Her fried radishes met with about the same degree of favor.

We always had these interesting meals when Mother left Grace in charge, but we had a way of getting rid of the evidence without wasting it. Before Mother got back we had a "grab" dinner, in which all leftovers were put on the table and everybody sat down. The rule was you had to take out and eat a serving of anything set in front of your plate, then you could pass it on to anyone you chose, not necessarily the person next to you. It was a much more hilarious, noisy game than "Authors."

Grace was always more interested in reading than anything else when Mother left, however, and once decided to get dinner immediately and get it out of the way so she would have a long time for reading. She cooked the food, summoned the family. Our cousin Ray, older than Grace, was living with us and working there then. He refused to come in from the field, so she angrily said, well then, he could just get along without dinner. But he was within his rights; it was only nine o'clock in the morning when she called us to the table.

Grace took piano lessons, displayed exceptional talent, and gave recitals in town. When the blind piano tuner came to tune the family's upright golden-oak Starr piano, the orchardist paid him in money, my mother paid him with fresh-picked strawberries for dinner, but Grace paid him best to his liking by playing the "Moonlight Sonata," which he said was his favorite music. I still remember the look on his listening face; he looked as if he could see, by moonlight. Grace played classical music and subscribed to *Etude*. My Mother played hymns and sometimes on Sunday afternoons the orchardist sang with her. He did not have a particularly good voice, but he enjoyed it, especially the hymn "Leaning on those everlasting arms"; his best musical performance was on the jew's-harp.

Sunday was not our favorite day. It was restricted. We were not allowed to use tools, such as scissors, needle and thread, sewing machine, hammer, saw or nails, nor to iron. Idleness was never the pure delight that leisure was.

We could read, walk over the farm, ride the work horses. There were, of course, essential daily chores of living that had to be done on Sunday as well as on weekdays, wood and water to be carried in, dishes to wash, floors to sweep, beds to make, livestock and chickens to be looked after. But without scissors we could not cut doll clothes or paper. "Paper Family," a game invented by my sister Miriam, was one of our favorites. For this we cut paper dolls and clothes for them out of the clothing pages of a mail-order catalog. From the furniture pages we cut furniture, dishes, household furnishings, and pasted them into wallpaper-covered magazines to make big houses for the paper dolls to live in. Our paste was homemade of flour and water. It always either molded on top or soured, developing an evil smell.

Workdays were harder, but far more enjoyable. My sister Miriam stayed in the house to help Mother; my sister Grace cleaned the house and did a great deal of ironing. The younger children worked outside. We set out strawberry plants by countless hundreds. At this, one crawled, half-kneeling along the row at the feet of one of the hired men who with a flat-bladed spade made a straight, deep slit in the earth. You set in the plant with its spread-out roots, and the hired man closed the slit by making another one a couple

of inches farther on and pressing the shovel against it. We
also planted apple seedlings and peach seedlings that were
later budded. One year my father planted a quarter of a
million apple seedlings, and to me this seemed like the
largest number to which the human mind could count. We
picked raspberries, strawberries, cherries, and wild blackberries; gathered and hulled walnuts.

In the hot July and August afternoons, if there was no
canning to do or berries to pick, we often gathered in the
"guest room" upstairs to sew. In the absence of guests this
room was occupied by my sister Miriam. It had a big brass
bed and a bird's-eye maple dresser in it, and also the sewing
machine. Mother and all the girls in the family went up there
and sewed. We made school clothes. We mended linens and
clothes. There were always great stacks of things to be
sewed, things to be made over, new things to cut out. It
always seemed to me my turn, for a new dress would never
come. My job was to rip up garments that were to be made
over. I have ripped out thousands of miles of stitching. We
never got everything made, but we did make a great deal.
And in those days only coats and men's clothes were bought
ready-made.

$$\clubsuit \qquad \clubsuit \qquad \clubsuit$$

Sometimes our cousins, the Beebes from Ohio, or the
Masons from nearer home, came for visits, but there were

seldom any children living near enough to be playmates. Playmates were a luxury that went with the six-months' school term. One summer Frank Gose was the hired man living in the cabin above the cherry orchard. He called my brother "Jamesy." He had a daughter Zelma, about my age. That summer it was my particular chore to look after the chickens in the henhouse in the upper plum orchard, which was across the road from the cherry orchard and therefore not far from the hired man's cabin. His wife Huldy had a parlor organ, which to me seemed much more glamorous than a piano. Zelma could play the organ.

We met at the henhouse and went to the cabin where she could "chord" an accompaniment for the ballads she sang. I liked "Oh dear mother, pin a rose on me," wept over the sad story of "Two little children, a boy and a girl, sat by an old church door," but "Red Wing" was my true favorite. My sister Grace, devoted to cultural life and classical music, objected to my singing these ballads, which she called "hoodlum music." My brother James later felt the same way about his sisters singing "Casey Jones."

Once, when I came into the house, I heard the piano giving out what sounded happily familiar to me; I rushed in and accused Grace, "See now, you won't let me sing 'Red Wing' but you're playing it!"

Silently she pointed to the music in front of her. It was "The Happy Farmer." I never cared much for it. In later years when she became a music teacher, my sister Grace taught folk songs in addition to more formal music. She also taught elementary grades and was a superlative teacher. She had the luminous, rare talent of causing a child to discover the joy of learning for learning's sake. She said the most exciting gift you can give a child is an idea. She kept on reading, traveling, collecting magazines and books until finally her house became so filled with them that now when I visit her I feel everybody ought to pitch in, as at an old-time working bee, and get all the books read. She constantly borrows library books, copies out quotations from them, and remembers what she reads. In this, she, more than any other of the orchardist's children, is like him.

He should have been a history professor, specializing in French or American history; he should have directed a horticultural experiment station; he should have held political office; he should have traveled and written books about it. His trouble was simply that he had more talent than he could use. He was impatient of detail or tedious commitments, but in playing checkers was so deliberate that his opponent gladly threw away kings in a fever to get the game over with. He was tall, "straight as a ramrod," as he often said of his mother, intolerant of physical weakness or illness. When his leg was broken in an automobile accident and it seemed he might be crippled, he never gave up. He felt that for him to be lame was unthinkable. He constantly practiced walking, and when he was again able to walk, he was slightly shorter than he had been before, but he did not limp and he was still "straight as a ramrod."

He was sensitive, proud. Insatiably curious about people, he was able to draw conversation out of them and to flatter them years later by quoting them. He had a prodigious memory and "prodigious" was one of his favorite words. He was ten years older than my mother. He loved her dearly and led her a hard life because of the contrast in their essential viewpoints. She wanted the conventional, comfortable things, the small cozy security. He was ambitious, wanting always to reach out for a grasp, however tentative, of some big, exciting thing.

Mother was not a tall woman. She had slim feet and narrow hands and was regularly complimented on her smooth, clear complexion. Tailored suits and dresses were most becoming to her and she could give a look of elegance to any hat she put on. She liked to dress up in pretty dresses, with beads and earrings and perfume. She had pretty legs. I cannot remember a time when she did not have gray in her brown hair that finally became a clear, luminous white, nor can I remember a time when I did not think she was beautiful.

♣   ♣   ♣

The state of Indiana did not buy all of its forest land at one time, and in the beginning did not have, I think, any overall plan for its use, other than the CCC camp; no schedule as a farmer would have, first looking carefully at a farm before buying it. When the state finally got around to looking for a major source of water, it was unable to locate the tumultuous vein of the Big Spring which in our childhood never went dry but sometimes had to be cleaned out in its rock-walled, five-foot-square enclosure. A vein of water as thick as a man's forearm supplied water there for watering all the horses and for all the spraying, and for the big washings Mrs. Adkins did under the beech tree that towered above the spring. She heated water and boiled the white clothes in a galvanized tub over an open fire. She was fat and floppy and amiable and always smelled like soapy water. Usually she ate dinner with us. Sometimes she brought her own dinner and in the afternoons she let us have the cold biscuits, spread with white sugar, that she had left over. We liked them. She had a son and told my mother that his ambition was "to cross the ocean and go to Indy'naplis before he was twenty-one."

The overflow from the Big Spring ran across the road and through the Tanyard and on past Hillacres, eventually reaching Hacker Creek several miles below. At the end of washday Mrs. Adkins walked home along the Hacker Creek Road.

♣   ♣   ♣

The state had not changed the route of the old Hacker Creek Road that passed between the house and the lower barn. Along the yellow clay banks of that road we had found "rattlestones." The hollow, pale brown geodes, dimpled on the outside like a hedge apple, varied in size, but all were light of weight and brittle, easily broken open. Inside they were crystal-lined and there were a few loose crystals that caused the rattle. Along this road and also on down Happy Hollow Road, the orchardist's children found what we called Indian beads, round or oval disks, seldom larger than the salmon bones they resembled, and having a hole in the center, they could be strung for necklaces. Actually, they were the petrified disks of plane lilies that grew there in preglacial times, and were, therefore, even older than the Indian arrowheads and hammers we also found in the fields.

Coming home along the Hacker Creek Road, we passed between a peach orchard on the right and a plum orchard on the left. At the far fence line of the plum orchard the vines of Niagara grapes grew, carelessly twining themselves into the thickety limbs of Lombard and DeSoto plum trees. You could stand on the untrustworthy fence and pick these round, greenly white, sweet grapes and "eat them as a common thing," as the book of Jeremiah says. But you had to be careful not to attract the attention of the black sow that was often kept in the lot on the other side of that fence. She was a good sow, but cross, especially when she had a new litter of pigs. The orchardist called her Clover, but his children, who sometimes had been chased by her, and had heard her eat peach seeds, cracking the hard shells as easily as peanuts between her powerful jaws, spitefully called her "Old Whitenose" and wished she would die.

When she finally did die, painfully, of quinsy, my brother James and I stood around her murmuring in hypocritical mournfulness, "Poor old Whitenose, poor old Whitenose," until finally our sister Nina cried.

There were Concord grapes farther inside the boundaries of the plum orchard, but they were better disciplined. At the front part of that orchard, nearest the house, were the Robinson plums. These were small, bright red, and sour, and made excellent jelly or plum butter. But the glory of them was in the fragrance of their small, whiskery-petaled white bloom. Blooming they literally whitened the tree and scented the air. Going past them to feed the chickens or to carry slop to old Whitenose was an adventure in fragrance. The ripened white petals fell like perfumed snow. But the Lombards in the upper plum orchard near the henhouse were darker green and larger, and when they were the size of large olives they made better heads for the dolls we created by sticking a forked stick into a green plum and dressing it. These dolls required a little more skill than those with corncob bodies but not as much as those with painted eggshell heads. The sturdiest homemade doll was the one made of a clean cornstalk. To make this doll, one peeled off the hard yellow cornstalk exterior, revealing the ridged white pith inside. The head was marked off by biting an indentation about an inch down the stalk and penciling a face on the shorter section. For hair, you could find a wad of sheep's wool snagged on almost any barbed-wire fence. It was gray, washed clean

from a winter's exposure to sun and snow, and was easily fastened to the cornstalk by a small nail. Then also, we had real dolls that we got at Christmas.

I was glad to see the Hacker Creek Road so unchanged; it was along that road that I once gave myself a lesson in self-discipline. When I was a child, my loving and usually practical mother once let me pick out a pair of shoes for myself, by myself. The Mason children always went barefooted joyously as soon and as much as possible, and our unhampered feet widened, so the shoes I selected were too tight. But I thought they were beautiful and knew that when

I had worn them long enough they would stop pinching. Without consulting anybody, I planned how to achieve this quickly.

The Hacker Creek Road ran for a quarter of a mile beyond our house before it was swallowed up in the deep woods. At the side of this road, midway of the clearing, was a volunteer apple tree, one of those planted unintentionally by some passing bird or animal. My father had let it grow, of course, to see what kind of apple it would be. It might be a brand-new variety, or one that could be budded or grafted to make a new one. I had often gone to this tree for solitude and comfort. Now I went down to it, put on the tight shoes and laced them up, and decided that if I ran from the tree to the woods and back a certain number of times (ten, as I now remember), the shoes would be comfortable. So I did that, and after that the shoes and I were good friends. Naturally I didn't tell anybody or take any witnesses along for this disciplining project.

      🌰   🌰   🌰

In the supervisor's yard that October afternoon the grass was green and neatly mowed. The quince bush was gone. The two big glazed tiles in which every summer my mother planted red cannas and big-leafed elephant's ears were gone. Gone was the row of tall golden glows that came up every spring and grew taller than the clumsy, high, unpainted picket fence. My mother planted cosmos by the kitchen window in a grassless spot, nasturtiums and scarlet sage outside the "office" window, but nobody ever mowed the yard. The backyard was overgrown with long grass. There were bare spots and a cistern in the front yard, and near it the wonderful Lady-in-Gold peach tree.

The cut-leaf weeping birch my father planted and protected in winter by fastening burlap around its slim white-barked bole was still there in the supervisor's yard, larger now and able to shift for itself. Some small Carolina poplars were there, descendents, likely, from the row of them that shielded the bare old house from wind on the kitchen side.

There was still one evergreen that the orchardist had planted near the "cave" behind the house. The cave had been dug to hold the hundreds of quarts of fruits and vegetables we canned every summer. In rainy weather the water ran in and made mud on the earthen floor, and we put down boards to walk on. In storms, my mother was always afraid the old house would blow over and made us run to the cave. The cave was gone that afternoon. Gone also was the smokehouse that had been nearby and is memorialized forever in my mind as a place of prayer. Because once, when my little sister Joie was ill, she suddenly went into a spasm and we thought she was going to die. While my mother bathed her in warm water and rubbed her arms and legs, murmuring, I ran out behind the smokehouse and prayed with all the fervor of a person fighting fire. When I went back in, the spasm was

3 1

over. Joie recovered and grew up to become the editor of a Sunday newspaper magazine in Arizona. Whether my prayers helped as much as Mother's massage I never really decided. Many times since then, however, I have had occasion to test the usefulness of prayer in my personal affairs, and I am convinced that although the Lord does not always say yes, He always listens, which may be more than we really deserve, or at least as much as we need. Moreover, I believe the invitation "always to pray and not to faint" was one of the finest gifts Christ brought us, and it ought to be used earnestly and often, and in private. You don't have to have a smokehouse. Prayer is like an electric cord that carries energy into a receptive appliance.

I think my mother may have had a special tenderness for Joie, anyway, because on the cold February day the baby was born, in a stove-heated upstairs bedroom with a red rug on the floor, Mother suddenly discovered Joie had stopped breathing and she always said she restored life to her by holding her close and giving her the warmth of mother's love and body. When Joie was nine years old she had typhoid fever and came near dying. All her hair came out, and we were proud of her because it came back in, curly. She had wide, appealing blue eyes and thick, dark lashes, and always had a delicious-sounding laugh.

Once when she was five years old and my brother James and Nina and I had run off to the woods to play, we took Joie along. Crossing a creek, she slipped on the stone bed and fell, striking her head a severe blow that raised a frighteningly big welt. We put her bonnet on her head and told her not to take it off under any circumstances. At supper that evening my mother, who should have been accustomed to the eccentricities of her children, asked mildly, "Joie, why don't you take off your bonnet?"

Joie raised her appealing wide eyes to Mother and explained candidly, "Oh, I can't do that because then you'd see where I hurt my head and they told me not to tell you!"

      🦋   🦋   🦋

Gone by now, obliterated by brush and young trees closing in around it, is the path that led down the steep hill past a towering walnut tree to the Little Spring from which we carried all of our drinking water. The size of a dishpan, it was dug out of rock, and the water was cold even on the hottest days. On summer nights we bathed by throwing buckets of cold water on each other, convinced that this would enable us more easily to withstand the coming winter. The Little Spring water, tested by the State Board of Health, was reported to be pure and of exceptionally good quality. In these days of overmuch spraying, I doubt that it would be safe to drink from any spring.

From there we could go on down to the woods where in spring the hillsides were truly covered with wild flowers. It was a place we liked to explore. There was a big tree that had fallen across the deep creek bed, making an exciting bridge to cross on. From there we could go on up another hill and swing on the wide, outspread limbs of big walnut trees. At the top of that hill a deep gully had eroded under the fence. The fence was completely covered with wild grape vines that bore heavily every year. There was an apple tree at the rim of the gully, self-planted, that bore tasty, red-striped apples and helped hold the soil in place. When we went there to gather apples, we took time to slide down the clay bank of the gully as on a school slide. We called it the grape ditch and enjoyed it and gave no thought to the ominous significance. The soil of that hilly clay area was as subject to erosion as a school child is to measles. A field plowed and left without ground cover soon began to look like the relief maps in our geography books.

♣   ♣   ♣

In summer the huckster came up the Hacker Creek Road. He had a little grocery store at Mahalasville, five or six miles away. He drove two horses to a light wagon, and as soon as he reached the clearing beyond the woods, where the road ran between a peach orchard and a pasture, he began to blow on a horn he carried in the seat with him. By the time he reached the dusty road between the house and the lower barn we were all there eagerly waiting. Mother sold him eggs and chickens. She bought groceries, and he filled the coal-oil can and told the news he had collected along the way. When we got coal oil in town, the grocer had to stick a raw potato on the end of the spout to keep it from spilling on the way home, because, of course, the cap was always lost.

The charm of the huckster's coming was in the old-fashioned pure-sugar stick candy he sold. It was peppermint, lemon, vanilla, sassafras, clove, wintergreen in flavor, all meltingly delicious. Mother bought other kinds of candy when she went to town but it was only from the huckster that we could get that wonderful stick candy. Most of us ate our portions at once, but my sister Nina, who always "saved things," took her sticks out and hid them under a loose board in the broken floor of the lower barn and kept them awhile.

The huckster went on past the house and drove home by the Happy Hollow Road, which was the way we went to the mailbox or to town. It went down a steep hill between banks of woods. In winter the banks were covered with snow, and on top of the snow the tall, dark-green winter ferns lifted their splendid fronds above the snowy banks like a bouquet set on the cloth of a Thanksgiving dinner table.

♣   ♣   ♣

In every orchard the orchardist had some little experimental item, something flippant or poetic or just for curiosity's sake. In the Shipper's Late Red orchard it was the big mulberry tree at the far side. We went past it in good weather when we took the shortcut to school.

I wish the state could have got the Hubbard school in time to preserve it as an example of Indiana's early district schools. There is nothing left now of the one-room, unpainted building, not even the two long stone steps at the door. There were two windows on each side. It never had an enrollment of more than twenty when I knew it, and usually fewer. The teacher was usually a young woman, a beginner who had just finished a summer's term of preparation. There were a few veterans, though, who went from one school to another in the district, one of them a man who had taught several years there. That was before soft drinks were as common as they are now; "coke" was a word found in the geographies and referred only to a kind of fuel. A country pupil whose parents burned only wood might not know this. For that matter, the veteran man teacher might not, either. " 'Coke,' " he exclaimed jovially when asked; "don't you know what 'coke' is? Why, it's what women put on top of cakes. I've et a many a cake with coke piled high on top of it!"

When the teacher went to the door and shook a small hand bell, the pupils came in and sat in their double seats and "books took up." There was a fifteen-minute mid-morning recess, another in mid-afternoon, and an hour's recess at noon. If there were pupils in all eight grades, the teacher taught all the subjects of all eight grades. In my grade there were two others—a boy, and a girl my age who was my dearest schoolmate. Her name was Mary Shipman, and all her several brothers had genuine drawing talent. All classes, to recite, got up from their seats and went to the front of the room and sat on the long recitation bench. The teacher had a chair and small desk in front of the blackboard.

One of the coveted special privileges of the Hubbard school was to be sent for a bucket of drinking water "in time of books." Two of us went together. We removed the long-handled dipper from the blue-and-white-enameled water bucket sitting on the top of an unoccupied desk among dinner boxes in the back corner of the room. Coats and caps hung from nails driven into the wall in that corner, and overshoes clustered on the floor. The water-bringers left the room quietly, and until they were well beyond the playground clearing and out of sight of the schoolhouse and into the woods, spoke only in whispers. Then they laughed, talked aloud, feeling the luxury of it, and took their time. The water was dipped from a wet-weather spring at the foot of a hill in the woods, and I have always remembered with deep pleasure the smell of autumn leaves freshly fallen into it.

The school's one room was wide enough for three rows of double desks, but the half of the middle row nearest the teacher's desk was taken up by the flat-topped cast-iron stove that heated the schoolhouse. We parched corn and warmed our wet gloves on its flat top. One cold afternoon, having been fired too vigorously, the stove set the schoolhouse roof afire.

Our black-and-white Collie, Robert the beloved, having forbiddenly followed us to school that morning, saved the day by barking and warning us. We ran out, carried out our books, ran to the Hubbards' house, that was close enough for the teacher usually to room and board with the Hubbards, and we brought enough water to put the fire out before it did much damage. Within a couple of weeks we were back again reciting from the long bench.

You could, of course, hear every class recite, and by the time a pupil got from first grade through the eighth, he was almost certain to be able to pass the state examination required for receiving a grade-school diploma and entering high school. These county examinations were held after the close of the school year in the county-seat town for all county pupils. Town pupils did not have to take them. My sister Nina, having finished the sixth grade, went with an eighth-grade friend who was taking the examination. Nina took it too, to pass the time. She also passed the examination, as she discovered soon after when her grades came, and so went on into high school the following September.

Each grade had final examinations (held at the school) at the end of the "term." The state made and printed the questions for these and also provided the blue "manuscript books" for writing the answers in. We were required to write with ink in this book, and that was the only time we wrote with ink during the whole school year.

On the first day of school the room smelled of freshly

oiled bare wood floor, new chalk, new school clothes, new books, and children's lunches. At the end of the term the teacher made a written report giving the grades of each pupil, with recommendations, records of promotions or not-promotions, and statistics concerning the amount of time lost by absence or tardiness.

Equipment was meager—a box of long white sticks of chalk and a few erasers, some so worn they squeaked when used on the part of the blackboard that was only black-painted wall. The better section of blackboard was slate. There was a stove poker, a shovel, and an ash bucket. No teacher was ever known to use the two framed maps of the hemispheres hanging on the wall between the windows. There were no lamps. On the few occasions when we needed light at night, such as when we had box suppers to raise money for a school library, parents brought coal-oil lamps from home.

Most pupils were promoted every year. One second-grade girl almost got a double promotion one year, not because she was a good reader but because her father, when he drove the nine miles to town for the regular trading and took occasion to buy her reader, bought her one a grade too far advanced. The teacher let her try it, but gave up exasperated and de-moted her when the girl, reading a story, read "I was not meant to be 'children' (for 'hidden') always."

I loved the Hubbard school. And there, in the seventh grade, I had one of the best teachers I have ever had anyplace, even in high school or at Indiana University. It was her first school. She was eighteen years old and had taken the summer preparatory teaching course at Indiana University that summer. She was so good that when I took the final examination that year, one of the state's questions— "What do you think our schools need for improvement?"— reminded me how fortunate the Hubbard school had been that year, and unhesitatingly I wrote in my manuscript book: "Better teachers." My answer surprised and wounded the teacher, but fortunately she gave me an opportunity to explain, and it became a good joke between us.

It is my basic belief about elementary schools that consolidation is not the answer; the schools should be small, well equipped, and have superb teachers, highly paid. Expensive, certainly, but all good things are. Peace is expensive; freedom, the basis of peace, is even more expensive. Life itself is extremely expensive.

I did not always have this happy experience with country schoolteachers. There was one I remembered with anger for years. She taught me in an early grade. My sister Miriam, in an advanced grade, was a favorite with her and received the most flattering attention from her. For some reason (probably natural enough, for I may have been an unlikable child, simply odious to her) she disliked me intensely and habitually made excuses for making me stay in at recess. I was afraid of her and obeyed her. To a country child, the loss of recess is painful and humiliating, especially when there is the rare luxury of children to play with and exciting games going on outside . . . Andy Over, Barley Bright, Hide-and-Go-Seek, Run-Sheepie-Run . . . and in the woods there are grapevines to be cut and looped up into a foothold so one can swing far out across a valley and drop into a pile of dry leaves below. I suffered silently and learned to hate that teacher. I always planned that if I ever saw her again I would tell her, "I hated you then and I hate you now." Years after, I did see her. It was at a tea given in my honor after my first book was published, and I did not recognize the teacher when she stood before me. When she identified herself, I could hardly believe it. Now she looked so little, insipid, and harmless; I was taller than she was! Yet when I was little she had seemed so big, so cruel. She made some complimentary comment and I thought of what I had so long wanted to tell her, but all I said was, "I always thought you liked my sister Miriam, but I never felt you liked me." She said, quickly moving away, "Oh, I liked everyone."

I do not hate her now. But she had a lasting, damaging effect on me and because of her I do make the earnest suggestion that no one should be allowed to teach who does not know the difference between discipline and damage, and that teachers should be as devoted to teaching as ministers are to "the spreading of the Word" and farmers are to the preservation of their cherished topsoil.

♣ ♣ ♣

Three of the Eberhard children attended the Hubbard school and the two older boys worked for the orchardist, but our families never exchanged visits. The Eberhard house cowered back against a steep, bare hillside, and the road in front of it was called Mud Lane because in rainy weather the soft mud came up halfway to the buggy axle.

Carl Eberhard, the neighbors said, "worshipped the almighty dollar." He probably didn't make many dollars from his scrawny eighty-acre farm that was mostly steep hills and low wet fields. It was his ambition to get hold of a good bottom farm in the adjoining county and he almost did. That was before his oldest son was killed in a quarrel at a country dance and his second son went to war.

All of the Eberhard children were large for their ages. Of the three in school, the middle one was a girl, blond and not overly bright. She cried when someone pretended to be going to look into her desk, and the children teased her by doing this. The youngest child, a boy, was admittedly dull-witted.

Carl was large, sandy-haired, red-faced and rawboned, with a perpetual expression of grievance on his face. He worked hard, never went to church or to school box suppers, never visited any neighbor except on some unpleasant errand like demanding money for livestock damage to his crops.

His wife was a frail-looking woman with dark hair. She was pretty and pale; her timid manner always suggested a rabbit caught and trembling. She must have baked pumpkin pies every day during the school year. The Eberhard children brought big pieces of them in their lunches and ate them at recesses and noons—big triangles of brittle white crust with shallow, pale filling. The other children teased them, "Don't drop that on your foot; it'll mash it."

An Eberhard baby died one summer. It was eighteen months old. My mother and my Aunt Rosie (a loving, soft-voiced woman who had large brown eyes and many pretty, bright children) thought it their neighborly duty to go to the funeral. It was a sultry August day, and as they tied the horse to the fence to go into the Eberhard house my mother said, "It's going to storm, Rosie." They were both afraid of storms.

The undertaker was already in the house, restlessly waiting. Nobody spoke or greeted anyone else. The people sat around uneasily, while the heat increased and storm clouds gathered darkly in the horizon. Finally the undertaker asked Carl when the minister would be there. Carl said no minister was coming. The undertaker asked for a Bible so he could read a few verses, and Carl said they had no Bible. "Well then, what are we waiting for?" cried the undertaker. "There's a big storm coming up. We've got to get this over with!"

They hurried the little casket out to the wagon and started to the Miller cemetery a few miles farther on toward town. People got into their buggies and followed. They put the casket into the opened grave and the undertaker began to throw earth upon it.

"Oh, this is terrible," Aunt Rosie whispered to my mother. "Somebody ought at least make a prayer." There was a low mutter of thunder, sounding not far away. "I will make one myself," said tiny Aunt Rosie; and stepping suddenly forward, she touched the undertaker's arm. "Wait, I am going to pray." He stopped shoveling, waiting, but suddenly all she could remember was the bedtime prayer she had taught all her eight children. She said it, quickly: "Now I lay me down to sleep, I pray Thee, Lord, my soul to keep. If I should die before I wake, I pray Thee, Lord, my soul to take. Accept this child, O Lord. Amen."

"Amen. Thank you," said the undertaker, and resumed shoveling immediately. A flash of lightning and the first roll of earnest thunder came as the buggies began driving out through the iron gates, and by the time Mother and Aunt Rosie had reached the first lane, where the road went off past Aunt Lou Adkins' farm, the storm began wrathfully.

By the end of World War I, Carl Eberhard had enough money to make the down payment on the good bottom farm he wanted, and moved to it. But by that time the three older boys were gone, and his daughter was married. He had only his frail wife and the youngest boy and himself and it was not enough. He lost the good farm and had to retreat back to the one at Mud Lane.

♣   ♣   ♣

That October afternoon my sister Nina and I seemed to
have the whole forest reserve to ourselves. We saw nobody
working, but people had worked there, erecting buildings,
mowing weeds, clearing brush, planting evergreens, setting
up informational signs. The state has no lack of laborers.
The reserve had a well-kept, competent appearance, a look
of leisure and invitation that has inspired many people to
come there to relax and enjoy the occasional return to the
land which is essential to humankind, more so than ever in
this privileged and pressed-against generation.

In the orchardist's time there was always more work than
he could get done, even with the help of his children and
the hired men. At one time or another, most of the men
living around there worked for the orchardist. They walked
to the farm, arriving by six o'clock in the morning, hung their
dinner buckets and coats on pegs in the lower barn. They
quit at six in the evening and walked home, and the going
rate, considered adequate for this day, was a dollar. They
could keep their families on that. They had very little taxes
to pay; they had a house and most of their food from their
small farms and the woods surrounding them. Occasionally
they had the use of the orchardist's driving horses.

One of my father's favorite stories was about the time
one of the young hired men, of courting age, came early
one fine Sunday morning and asked to borrow the best

driving mare and buggy. He was dressed up, obviously intending to make a celebration of the kind he had a reputation for. Knowing Fred would not be trustworthy with a lively mare that day, my father made the excuse that he needed the "rig" himself.

The exasperated hired man cried, "Now, Frank, you know you cain't use that buggy and hit a-rainin' like hit air!"

In addition to the hired men that came by day, the orchardist usually had one or two of Aunt Rosie's big boys living with us. They were like brothers to us. One was bossy and domineering, the other loving and helpful. In those days farmers and hired men alike were always thin. They wore suspenders instead of belts; their clothes were baggy at the knees and elbows, their shirts always had long sleeves. The widow's young son always wore work gloves. I never saw a fat farmer until I lived on a livestock farm in a different county after Dick and I were married. Most of the hired men could chew tobacco, and one generously gave my sister Nina a good big chew one day when she was in the field where he was driving a team of horses to the roller. She chewed it and did not get sick, which may have been a disappointment to him. Indubitably the hired men suffered to some extent at the hands of the orchardist's children.

In his rather extensive travels, my father was always meeting men he considered interesting. If they owned land, he encouraged them to plant orchards (trees to be supplied by him, of course). Otherwise, he invited them to come and visit us or work for him. Many came. Many came often. The editor of a poultry magazine came often from Illinois; the manufacturer of a famous tonic came and discussed the decline in his sales that resulted when he was required to change its formula; a real estate man came from Ohio; the state entomologist came often and took photographs; a young Assyrian immigrant came bringing the English book he was studying in order to apply for U.S. citizenship. My sister Miriam undertook to teach him English, and as soon as he learned enough English words, he proposed to her.

Bill Pofall came to work and lived with us. He was a German, obviously had delusions of grandeur, but was harmless. His German military training was evident in the way he walked, sat, and saluted. He entertained us with splendid stories of his warm friendship with the Kaiser. He played German ballads on a good harmonica, which was about all he had of worldly possessions. Thriftily he wove long ropes out of short lengths of rope and pieces of binder twine. His favorite work horse was the blind sorrel Queen. At the barn he greeted her personally (to the gusty appreciation of the other hired men) with a cheerful "Eight o'clock, Queen!" and talked to her all the time as he guided her along at work. Once, driving Queen to the slip scraper to take away earth thrown out from where a cistern was being dug, he let her get too close to the edge and she fell into the excavation. Getting her out, somewhat skinned up but not crippled, required everybody, including the Beebe cousins visiting us that summer.

If we wanted time for playing on workdays, we had to sneak away without attracting the orchardist's notice. One of his favorite admonitions, learned from his Quaker mother, was "Satan finds work for idle hands to do." He reminded us that she had often said to him, "Thy time, thy precious time!" He himself believed "There is no excellence without great labor." Without ever telling us in so many words, he made us realize we were expected to carry in wood and water to the kitchen. When he wanted something done well, he encouraged us by telling us, "You can do it to a queen's taste."

Unwittingly, he probably fostered everybody's writing proclivities by a bit of wry advice he gave us when we complained: "If there's something that doesn't suit you, just write it down and burn it up." There were so many things that didn't suit us that we had abundant practice in writing.

♣   ♣   ♣

There is no doubt that the orchardist loved his children deeply, but he was stern, often autocratic. At the table he told us what his mother had told him, "Eat what is set before you, asking no questions." It was years, however, before I knew this was quoted from the Bible. No one was permitted to interrupt his conversation at the table, regardless of whether it was interesting. Often he began a long, detailed story, then stopped to eat awhile before resuming the story, but we had to wait until he finished it. He made absolute rules and we broke them absolutely, but we did so at our own risk and tried not to get caught. One place we were strictly forbidden to invade was his "office," so, of course, we were drawn into it as irresistibly as a moth to the chimney of a coal-oil lamp.

It was a downstairs room, blessed with its own outside door in addition to the door leading into the small front hall at the foot of the stairway. There was a big dining table there, always overloaded with stacks of papers—*The Indianapolis News*, *The Chicago Packer*, horticultural and poultry and farm magazines, nursery catalogs, seed catalogs, almanacs, calendars, and agricultural yearbooks. They slid off the table in an ever-flowing glacier. More were stacked inside the tin-door safe, in which also were the breathtaking nursery salesmen's books we coveted. These had hard covers, long and narrow pages, slick-paper pages printed in marvelous colors and showing fruits and flowers of such opulence as one sees only in dreams, and then only if the dreams have been well cultivated, pruned, sprayed, nourished, winter-mulched, and hand-thinned.

His typewriter table was a small kitchen table and above it was a kitchen-cabinet top with pigeonholes and doors and drawers begging to be explored. Every child in the family yearned to possess that room for his own, and every one of us stole in from time to time to try a couple of fingers on that old Monarch typewriter. I learned to type in those golden, stolen moments. I never learned to type accurately, but I learned to type fast, because if the orchardist found one of us there it would be a painful encounter. He sometimes sent us out to break off the peach switches with which we were to be punished. We could delay the moment then, but only temporarily. His worst punishment resulted, probably, from his Quaker upbringing. In a family of seven lively children, the embattled clashes can be noisy. Ours often were. The orchardist was always able to hear them. No matter how far away he seemed when the quarrel started, he heard us by the time it got satisfactorily under way. Invariably he stopped his work, called us to him, and gave us a long, boresome sermon on love. Then he required the fighters to kiss each other and dismissed them. We gritted our teeth and kissed, but as soon as we were out of his sight, the fight was resumed, even more bitterly, but this time quietly.

His Quaker upbringing was responsible also for silence instead of spoken grace at meals. The silence was not always reverent among his children because he did not instruct us in its meaning or bring us up as Quakers, which I for one sincerely regret. Years later, when I discovered the philosophy of the Inner Light, it spoke cogently to my condition. It may be that people inherit a tendency toward philosophical beliefs as truly as a tendency to write or to have brown hair and blue eyes, or to be left-handed.

My mother's family were devout Methodists, and before she moved to the country she had been active in church work, had taught a Sunday-school class, kept the Cradle Roll records, and played the organ. She must have missed this spiritual comfort when she came to the remote orchard farm, bringing three little girls and a somewhat frail little boy, and in the later years when three more little girls were born there.

Living in the country was new to her, to begin with, and hard. She had grown up in a small Ohio town and always got homesick when she went out to her grandmother's farm to spend a night. To her the evening song of the whip-poor-will from down near the Big Spring—a beautiful sound to the rest of us—was a lonely cry.

As a young girl she had always wanted to write, so perhaps it was some comfort to her that all her children grew up liking to read, and that most of them became writers. During her third pregnancy she wrote a book of alphabet verses for the baby. She always wrote letters, even in later years when her eyes had failed so badly that she could not read what she had written. When we were little, she drew pictures for us on sheets of school tablets. They were always the same: there was a house with smoke pouring out of its chimney, a wild rose, a ripe strawberry, a man pumping water from a long-handled pump, a woman holding a bucket, a cat, a dog.

When the older sisters had boy friends in the living rooms (we had three living rooms by that time), the young men brought polite boxes of chocolates and Mother took the younger children to the kitchen and made fudge or popcorn for us. She was an excellent cook, and my father often remarked, proudly, how she always had dinner, a noon meal, right on time. She simmered meat, or boiled beans, potatoes, corn-meal mush, or wild greens in the black iron kettle on the wood-burning range. When she wanted to hurry it up, she lifted out the round stove lid and set the kettle down into the blaze. She seldom baked pies or biscuits, but she made gingerbread, corn bread, and baked beans you could write poems about. Twice a week she baked eight loaves of crusty brown "light" bread in long black pans.

She made apple butter, peach butter, quince honey, strawberry preserves, pear preserves, plum butter, plum preserves; and spiced peaches (using the little brilliantly red Indian clings). She made mixed-pickle and Copley Plaza relish.

She baked apples. In winter, somebody took a pan and went out to the apple hill where Jonathans and Ben Davises were buried, frostproof under straw and earth. You scraped back the burlap curtain, earth, and straw and lifted back the board that closed the opening. The wonderful apple-hill smell came out as you reached back into the cool, straw-lined mound for the cold apples and filled the pan. All winter apples taken out of the apple hill were cold, sound, unwrinkled, and juicy and had a distinctive apple-hill flavor. The orchardist always put good apples into the hill, and enough so that there were always some left late into the spring.

By Thanksgiving, too, the Kieffer pears were ripe that had been properly picked when they were still hard, and had brown splotches like lichens on their green skins, before they developed woodiness. They were stored away until they turned yellow and then they were juicy, sweet, and sought-after. It is only the people who don't understand the proper care of Kieffer pears who underestimate them.

When she first came to the farm, Mother learned about the prevailing Hacker Creek religious order and went to one of their meetings. They were called Crabbites, believed in handling snakes, and in times of extreme devoutness sometimes "went into the unknown tongues." In summer, when the narrow roads were good, we went to little churches some miles away. It was a great pleasure to my parents when one day a young man stopped with Bible storybooks to sell and said he was going to represent the American Sunday School Union in the community and would organize Sunday schools in various places. The Reverend Mr. W. C. Chafin became that day a good friend of the orchardist's family and always remained one. He finally inspired the Hacker Creek people into building little "Valley Chapel" a few miles from the orchard farm. In his years of itinerant service the minister has traveled thousands of miles, worn out several horses and buggies and cars; performed hundreds of marriages (including finally that of Harve and the widow Hattie Bales), more hundreds of baptisms, and preached words of comfort at many funerals. He grew older, plumper, balder, and always more loved in the community. He said, "I wouldn't have time to be President if I were elected. This work is more important." He said, smiling, "People tell me their troubles and I listen; it gives them some comfort, and it doesn't hurt me to listen."

The orchardist's children never attended any of the Crabbite meetings, but my sister Nina and I once heard one of the believers "go into the unknown tongues" quite unexpectedly. It happened late in the strawberry season. Mrs. Adkins' granddaughter Flossie, about the age of Nina, had come to pick late strawberries for her grandmother. She was alone up in the long strawberry patch on the open ridge above the locust grove. It was mid-morning of a clear, bright day. Thinking to make a little diversion for Flossie and being also eager to make the most of any unexpected opportunity for companionship, Nina and I painted our faces and bare feet with the juice of early elderberries, swathed ourselves in sheets, which considerably hampered our walking, and walked the long distance from our house up to the strawberry patch. Like the father of the prodigal son, Flossie saw us while we were yet afar off. She stopped picking berries, straightened up, and watched our stilted approach. Then, to our complete amazement, she suddenly screamed, "I know you, Nina, but who's that with you?" and then she dropped the bucket and ran from the patch. As she ran she "went into the tongues," a high-voiced, incoherent wail of unrecognizable syllables. It took us some time to catch up with her and bring her back and help retrieve the scattered strawberries.

♣   ♣   ♣

One of the last landowners to give up his land to the state forest reserve was Charlie Talbott. His farm was not far from High Gap. When he bought it (from the Hubbards, who were friendly young people and sometimes visited the school or came to help when there was illness and Mrs. Hubbard felt she could help), it was badly eroded and run down.

Charlie had come from a city a great distance away and the first time we saw him was one morning soon after he moved to his farm. He came to the kitchen door, angrily asking for the orchardist against whom he already had some complaint. "If he wants trouble, I'm Johnny-on-the-spot," he told Mother, "I'm not afraid of man or devil!" No doubt the city had treated him harshly all his life. He was a man of violent temper to begin with, and having been mistreated, always expected to be and was prepared to return it. One of his hired men told about Charlie throwing a pitchfork at his mule. The prongs went into the mule's flank and Charlie let the mule run with the fork dangling out of its side. He built up his road into a good road and threatened to shoot people who used it without his permission. People were afraid of him and for the most part let him alone. He settled down to improve his farm. He planted raspberries and strawberries, and for an interim crop while they grew into bearing, he raised tomatoes, which he hauled nine miles into town on a wagon.

A woman had moved to the farm with him, and after a few years he took her to town and married her. They both worked as hard as he expected his mules to work, and the farm began to build up profitably. Later that fall he came back to our house, bringing Mona, to pay a neighborly social visit. My parents were trying to put up the stove in the dining room. "You just let old man Talbott do that," he said jovially. "I'm Johnny-on-the-spot when it comes to putting up stovepipes." He cut his hand on a jagged piece of stovepipe and it bled, but he said, "Takes more than that to stop old man Talbott." At that time he was not really an old man, probably about forty.

One early summer day my mother sent my sister Nina and me to his house to buy some tomatoes. He got them for us but would not accept any money. Mona was just taking fresh-baked bread out of the oven. She cut slices of it, spread them with apple butter, and we all sat down and talked. Charlie, affable and expansive, was being "Johnny-on-the-spot" as a good host. When we were about to leave, he went upstairs and brought down a doll's headless body and gave it to me. It was the biggest doll body we had ever seen and undoubtedly the most expensive. Even its fingers were jointed. It had belonged, Charlie said, to his daughter, but that was all he told us about her.

In later years when they had made some money, Charlie and Mona built themselves a new house—literally; they did the work themselves. It was an ugly house. By the time Mona died, Charlie had a tidy amount of savings in the bank, and although people questioned some of his methods of accumulating it, nobody put the questions to him. When the bank failed, the banker was suspected of embezzling, and escaped trial by going to a Southern state and staying there. Many people lost money in the bank. Charlie lost all his savings. He stayed on in his ugly house, and revenge became the sustaining motive of his life. "Just let him come back to Indiana once," he told my mother about the banker, "just once. I'll be Johnny-on-the-spot and I don't care what happens after that."

    ♣   ♣   ♣

As Nina and I drove through the forest reserve that October afternoon, we passed a raw, muddy place where timber had been cut and the earth torn up. It was designated as "Mason Ridge," but it was not in that place that the orchardist's family had had any of its happy adventures or even spent much time. We had hardships, illness, pain, bitter discomforts, and heartbreak sometimes, but the farm never seemed bleak or flavorless. The land was healing, beautiful, full of adventure, beckoning.

The life there must sometimes, though, have been a heartache to the woman who had the responsibility of feeding, doctoring, inspiring, and disciplining a family of nine plus the resident hired men, and all without any of the conveniences modern farm women simply take for granted.

My mother was not of a gay temperament by nature. She was deeply conscientious, hopeful, loyal. Her children considered her all but omnipotent. When we were ill, we began to feel better the minute Mother came into the room. In a time of our despair she always reminded us that "the darkest hour is always just before the dawn." She was seldom ill, but when she was ill, or on the rare times when we saw her cry, the end of the world came right then. There was one summer she had to walk for several weeks with the help of a kitchen chair. She had driven the spirited driving mare, Axie, to town. Axie ran away, upset the buggy, broke the shafts, and Mother suffered a broken ankle. My brother James, a little boy then, had watched a long time for her to come home, and it was he who hunted up the orchardist finally and said, "Papa, Axie came home, but Mama and the buggy didn't come."

She had named James for her father, whom she had loved and idealized as much as the orchardist had loved and idealized his mother. There was a bond of mutual protectiveness between James and Mother. It was probably a secret pleasure to her that a visitor once prophesied to her, "James will climb up Jacob's ladder; don't you grieve after him." It was no pleasure to him, however, because his sisters remembered it and repeated it and even sang it to him in songs for years afterward. But he had his revenge, because from time to time other people said other things about the rest of us. I, for example, would gladly have wrung the neck of the well-meaning friend who endowed me with the title "flower of the family." Anything like this was sure to be used against you forever after and the Fifth Amendment offered no refuge.

The nicest compliment came from Ben Douglass, who was for many years Indiana's state entomologist and was a fine photographer. He spent a good deal of time with us visiting and photographing and in intellectual discussion with my father, and once later told an editor friend of his we were "nice kids, but simply running wild when I knew them."

Mother had her own places of refuge and recreation. Sometimes she drove to town for a day's outing and occasionally in summer took one of us with her. She took us with her to pick wild blackberries, to gather hickory nuts, strawberries. Sometimes on Sunday afternoons in late summer she walked over the farm to find a wild flower she particularly liked. It was the rose gentian, a shallow-rooted, not very tall plant that springs up in sunny open fields, erratically growing where it wishes and no place else, and asking very little in the way of soil fertility. It will not bear transplanting. You come upon it with almost shocking unexpectedness. The five pale pink, clear petals of its flower are joined at the base and make a five-pointed star, outlined in white. A small, delicate flower, it has a small, delicate fragrance and a look of simple, sudden loveliness that exhilarates the human spirit. I think that perhaps Mother felt a sort of kinship with it because it gave so much and never tried to be a martyr.

♣   ♣   ♣

The state planted its evergreens with the intention, I think, of selling some for Christmas trees. There were already some evergreens, suitable for Christmas trees, growing there. We always cut one from the farm; buying a Christmas tree was unheard of.

It has always amazed me how, in a family of seven restless, inquiring, mystery-probing children, Mother managed to keep the Christmas-tree ornaments hidden all the rest of the year. We saw them only at Christmas. We decorated the farm-cut tree with strings of popcorn, gold and silver tinsel, and colored paper chains. Then from her secret place Mother brought out the wonderful Christmas balls, imported from Germany. They were frosty white. They glittered. From their concave sides glowed the mysterious, beautiful world of Christmas, deephearted, transient, forever beckoning, forever mysterious.

In those days Christmas came like a locomotive; you could hear it for weeks off, whisting, rushing, growing louder and more unbearably exciting all the time as it came nearer. It shook the earth when it finally arrived and stopped beside you; its smell was unlike any other; while Christmas paused beside you, you could feel its warmth and the heat of its powerful heart. It was a tremendous, panting, fire-driven event, and when it had gone you could still hear its whistle dying away far off in the distance. Nothing could hurry Christmas, but neither could anything hold it back.

We hung up our stockings in the dining room on Christmas Eve and went to bed. Santa Claus came during the night and filled the stockings. Nobody saw him, but we knew what he looked like because his picture had been on several of the colored, embossed postcards that had arrived, naked of envelope and borne by a penny stamp, in our mailbox during the week before Christmas. As with all greeting cards, there was a schedule by which each of us in turn received a card to put into his individual postcard album with the slatted pages.

You might hear Santa Claus if you listened. But it was doubtful; it was a long, cold way from downstairs, where the stockings hung, to the bedroom upstairs, where you lay under at least three cotton-lined "pieced comforts," grateful for the added coziness of the newspaper-wrapped hot iron at your feet.

We made most of our presents for each other and wrapped them in red, green, or white tissue paper and tied the packages with gold or silver cord in a small, economical bowknot. It was an exceptional event if one child bought a gift for another. One Christmas, my brother James gave our sister Grace a small, gold-colored, silk-lined jewel case he had selected himself. When she opened it he stood up and cried proudly, "And it cost ten cents!" Our parents bought some gifts for us, and Mother made many more. In each stocking there were, in addition to small gifts, a few English walnuts, some candy, and on top of all, the luxury that appeared only at Christmas—the orange. For years the smell of oranges, to me, belonged exclusively to Christmas.

Mother got up first on Christmas morning and cooked breakfast. When she opened the hall door and called upstairs "Mer-ry Chris-mas!" it was the signal we had been waiting for. We surged downstairs to meet the filled stockings, and they were ours. As the family got older and bigger, Christmas grew also until finally our last big family Christmases were wonderful mountains of gifts, glitter, laughter, music, affection, good smells of food and women's perfume, cold air coming in as people came in and out, and baked-bean feasts late at night after all the gifts were wrapped and placed. By that time there were in-laws and grandchildren.

We came into the living room on Christmas morning where the tree and piano were. My sister Grace, and later Joie, played the carols we always sang before Mother distributed the gifts. The beautiful, sad, rejoicing Christmas carols! The timeless, immortal Christmas carols! The singing always began with my father's favorite, "Oh come all ye faithful," which my mother called "The March." She said, "Grace, play 'The March.'" Always, that is, except the year my brother was going to be married the day after Christmas. That year, to tease him, the Christmas march was replaced with the Wedding March. He laughed, blushed, and took it in good spirit. No matter how many or marvelous the gifts, the best part of our family Christmases were the jokes by which we expressed our affection and honored each other.

♣   ♣   ♣

"Why, you couldn't even find the town road to walk to the mailbox now, let alone ride a horse over it!" exclaimed my sister Nina as the October afternoon pushed closer toward sunset. The mouth of the old road that used to go past the lower barn was by then completely closed in a screen of new trees and bushes.

It was a two-mile trip from the orchardist's house to the mailbox, but we had to get the mail every day because we got so many letters and newspapers that the small box would not hold two days' mail. When my brother James went, he usually rode one of the horses. He liked horses. He rode them, worked them in the fields, fed and petted them, curried and harnessed them. At school he drew pictures of them on his school tablets and lesson papers. He never cared as much for trees and fruits as the orchardist did, although he learned to bud trees and worked in the fields with the hired men. No doubt, the orchard business seemed to him like a hard, uncertain way of making a living, and, like farming, it certainly is, unless it is your choice. When my brother discovered his real talent, it was in pharmacy. He went to pharmacy college, where he was a brilliant student, passed the state examination with the highest grade in the state, and the whole family, including his wife Lois went proudly to his commencement.

One reason my sister Nina and I liked to walk to the mailbox was that we could stop at the first house at the bottom of the last steep hill in Happy Hollow and ask Katy to go with us. She was about the age of my brother and went to the Hubbard school. The Bales house was a little two-room one far back from the road, barely out of the way of a creek there, which in spring fullness swelled up like an angry setting hen. The inside of the house was always as clean as the inside of a milkweed pod, but Mrs. Bales nevertheless apologized because it was not cleaner. She was little, shy, quick-darting as a mole. She had been a widow several years. Her son Spencer, a tall, yellow-haired young man with nice manners, worked for the orchardist, and every morning when he came to work his clothes were immaculate. He went overseas with the army in the first World War, and when he came back he seemed much older and different.

Mrs. Bales's kitchen was small and had a linoleum on the floor, a late-acquired luxury given her by her son, who was a good son and kind to her, as she constantly told visitors. She was so proud of the linoleum that she scrubbed it every day. Once in a while during the school year to my delight, I was permitted to go home with Katy and stay all night. We came down an almost perpendicular hill back of the house. We all slept in the second, larger room and Mrs. Bales kept a coal-oil lamp burning there all night. The walls were papered with newspapers, including some pages of colored comics, and it was pleasant to lie in bed and read the activities of the Katzenjammer Kids by the mellow glow of the coal-oil lamp.

When Katy went with us to the mailbox it was easier to get past the cross dog at the next house, where her uncle Jake lived. His yellow collie was named Sheriff and always came out and barked fiercely except when Katy was along, and we believed he meant what he barked. Jake had been a soldier in the Civil War but never talked to anybody about his war experiences. His wife was shy like her sister Mrs. Bales, but she also was kind; and once when Nina fell into a creek, she took us in to her fire and let us get warm and partly dry Nina's coat. The only time I remember Jake ever coming to our house was when his work mare had strayed away and he was hunting her. His question, "Have you saw ary nag?" sounded to us like a foreign language and so delighted us that we repeated it to each other for days afterward.

    ♣   ♣   ♣

When we got as far as the road that turned off to go to Aunt Lou Adkins' house, we were not far from the mailbox. At this point the road was on level ground and the better open fields began to show. Aunt Lou was not really everybody's aunt, but everybody called her Aunt. Her house was not visible from the road. It was a pretty house, two-storied, neat, well kept, an Indiana version of Colonial. It had the traditional evergreens in the front yard. The beds were made up with beautifully pieced quilts. Aunt Lou churned in a keg churn she kept on the clean-swept back porch in summer.

She was a kindly, small woman with gray hair and gentle hands and a knowledge of nursing. She came when a family had more illness than it could handle by itself, or when there was a new baby. She came when our youngest sister Kathleen was born, and declared that was the prettiest baby she had ever seen. She would have been interested to know that the pretty baby she bathed and dressed for the first time was going to grow up to become a script writer for the Voice of America in Munich.

Aunt Lou was the symbol of neighborly kindness, of

comfort. The day our best-loved dog Robert died, my sister Miriam was too deeply grieved to stay for his funeral. She went down and spent the day with Aunt Lou. I took my childhood treasures out of a blue painted wooden box and gave it for a casket for Robert. Spencer, the young hired man, helped us. We put Robert into the box and loaded it into the buggy. Spencer drove; my sister Nina and I rode with him. My brother stood up behind the seat and we went to Hillacres, where Spencer dug the grave and we wept as we buried Robert. Of all our many childhood pets, Robert was the best loved.

From Aunt Lou's turn-off to the mailbox there was only one more creek to cross. The water ran steadily and clean over the pebbled bed that crossed the road. When we came home from town we often unreined the horses there and let them drink. You could stand at the edge of the creek, watching the clear, shallow water rippling past, and suddenly you felt that you were sliding along and the water was standing still. Sometimes Katy and I took time to fish in the deeper water beyond the road.

Our mailbox was two miles from the farm because the mail route ended there, right on the borderline between two counties. The mail came out from the county seat of an adjoining county. We paid our taxes in our own county, but did our "trading" and went to high school in the other county, and got our mail from its county seat because that town was much closer than our own county-seat town.

Just beyond the cluster of mailboxes was the Downey farm. A rich farm, good, flat bottom land, well tilled. John Downey raised hogs and corn. He had a windmill pump, acetlyne gas lights, a telephone, an elegant house on a small hill. He had two daughters—we considered them stylish, sophisticated young ladies. He had a sturdy, fun-loving son, Chauncey, who returned to the farm to work after he finished school. He married, built another house close beside his father's, and gradually took on the farm management.

The Downeys were friendly, sociable people, always hospitable and interested when we asked to use their telephone in emergencies (such as the time the orchardist fell out of a peach tree and split open his scalp and Dr. Sandy came out and sewed it up with the hair from a horse's mane). The morning our sister Kathleen was about to be born, my father went to call the doctor from the Downey telephone, and one of the Downey girls was getting ready for her wedding that day.

The Downey men were progressive farmers and made money from their land without off-the-farm income. They educated their children, went to church in town, lived well, had a good time, were kindly, paid their taxes. The son, who followed in his father's furrow, did even better. The state never even considered offering to buy their land for the forest reserve.

♣   ♣   ♣

Now the town road itself was gone. The childhood farm we remembered was gone utterly. Nina and I sat in the car a few minutes looking thoughtfully at the place where the road had formerly gone down the hill. I thought of the story in my high school German book, about the city of Germelshausen that sank beneath the sea and reappeared only one in every hundred years.

A hundred years from now who will own this land? It has known many owners, will have perhaps many more. For the land belongs to no man, however much he loves it.

Probably the change was inevitable. Ours was not a repeatable pattern. Times have changed, people's ways of living and thinking have changed. As a public forest reserve, the land serves many people who need it.

By the time Nina and I had driven back to the Precinct, sunset was a great orange-red finality poised above the blue dusk. We hurried, suddenly feeling a great urgency to get away. We were not comforted . . . it would be a long time before we would know comfort after fulfilling the assignment ahead of us . . . but we were strengthened for it.

And it seemed significant that in a time of acute distress, when we had to accept an unacceptable fact, it was to the land we turned for wisdom and strength, to the land we had known and loved in childhood; the land, man's eternal kinsman.

♣   ♣   ♣

The Starling's Voice

"H E A I N'T doing any good," Mrs. Bluett said in a harsh whisper. She was hard of hearing and her voice was habitually loud, as if she assumed all her listeners also were slightly deaf.

With quick, birdlike steps she crossed the room to where Dakin, long and bony, lay on the bed with his face turned to the wall. She bent over him briefly, peering with bright, dark eyes, then returned to her visitor "I can't tell whether he's really asleep or not, Delithy," she said. "Let's go down to the kitchen where we can talk. You can come back up before you leave if you want to."

She led the way down the narrow stairway to Dakin's kitchen, where a fire was dying out in the cavernous smoke-blackened fireplace. The kitchen had the smell of a room in which one man has lived alone for a long time. A table with leaves dropped under a worn oilcloth occupied one corner. A milk bucket and strainer were turned upside down on it. Near it was a cream separator. In another corner was an old kerosene stove, encrusted with the accumulation of rust and grease splatters from years of use.

Mrs. Bluett pulled two kitchen chairs forward and laid a stick of wood on the remnant of coals. "Sit down, Delithy," she urged; "I can't stay long, either. I must go home and get supper, but I'm always juberous about leaving Dakin here alone. I'll send John or Harold back with a bite for him; he don't each much. Seems like he don't like anybody around doin' for him, either."

The visitor nodded and sat down. The coals caught the dry bark and broke into a little blaze.

♣   ♣   ♣

It was early April when Dakin first heard the starlings. He had gone up to his bedroom to mend harness because the ground was still too wet to plow. Spring was late that year; April was cold and rainy. Dakin had planned to break the southwest pasture that had been in sod since the spring of his mother's death eleven years earlier. He looked forward to it. Of all the farm work, the breaking of sod was most satisfying to him, and without realizing it, he had developed it into a kind of ritual. Rain, delaying the fulfillment of the ritual, frustrated him.

In the bedroom he pulled the harness stitcher close to the window and sat down on the narrow seat. It was an obsolete tool; even his father had discarded it years earlier. It had a foot-operated lever something like the pedal of a bicycle by which a pair of wide, wooden jaws above the seat were opened to hold strips of leather for stitching together. The stitching was handwork, done with long needles and linen thread which Dakin waxed by pulling it across a lump of beeswax. Dakin used the harness stitcher because he never threw away anything. He kept it in the bedroom because the light was better there from a south window than in the kitchen where there were only north windows. These two rooms formed a small wing to his big brick house. There were eight other rooms in it, but Dakin seldom even went into any of them.

He broke off a length of thread, and as he drew it across the beeswax, he became aware of the low murmur of young starlings. The sound came from the attic just above his bed, and it did not then sound particularly harsh, nor even unpleasant. Dakin remembered he had noticed a broken board just below the eave earlier that spring. "I reckon that's how she got into the attic," he said.

In the bedroom was a rocking chair his mother had always liked, and near it an ugly square table with legs splayed out at sharp angles and clutching glass balls in their clawfeet. A tall chest, with varnish roughened and checked from too many winters in a cold room, stood near the unused chimney. There was a flue hole in the chimney, but Dakin had never put up a stove in the room. He used this room for many uses. He had stretched a piece of heavy wire across one corner, and from the wire hung a few joints of smoked meat and some ears of sweet corn saved for seed and fastened together by the pulled-back husks.

In this chilly bedroom Dakin mended harness he did not need and probably never would use on his one team of horses.

By noon, when he went downstairs to prepare some dinner, he was glad to get away from the repetitious harsh murmur of the young birds.

In the kitchen he lighted a tall smoked burner on the oil stove and set the teakettle over it. From a wide cupboard built into the wall beside the fireplace he took out a kettle of cooked vegetables left from supper of the evening before and part of a loaf of bread, still in its wrapper. Dakin used very few of the pans and spoons and housekeeping tools left by his mother in the deep cupboards. He scarcely knew, in fact, what was on the shelves.

He had lived in that house all of his life. His grandfather had built it, baking the bricks from clay dug out of the fields. It was stately and elegant, a two-story brick house. There were four square rooms downstairs, separated by a wide hall that ran the full length of the house, and four more rooms exactly like them upstairs. There had been a fireplace in each one, but Dakin's father, who liked comfort, had closed up some and set up stoves. All the cupboards and the mitered woodwork around doors and windows were made of yellow poplar cut on the farm. The rail of the long stairway that went in spacious leisure to the upstairs hall was made of walnut cut on the farm.

Dakin was forty-six years old. He had been a young man when his father died. He understood the farm work well enough to go on with it. He and his mother had lived frugally from its small income. After her death Dakin had withdrawn into the back wing, which contained only the kitchen and bedroom and a sharp-turned back stairway and small cellar. Now the main part of the house was given over to dust and spiders and an occasional mud dauber that came in and built a long-celled house against the high ceilings. Wind rattled the loosening panes, rain ran down on the stone window ledges, and the house went on growing older.

Dakin had few visitors and seldom visited his neighbors. Mrs. Bluett would have been a frequent visitor if he had let her. The Bluetts lived in a comfortable little farmhouse a quarter of a mile east along the road. They had modernized their kitchen with a pitcher pump and kitchen sink. They were progressive; they had a kerosene lamp that burned brilliantly with a long mantle and gave a light almost like a gaslight. Mrs. Bluett ironed with a gasoline iron, and John Bluett was the first farmer in the community to buy a tractor. It had high steel tires with lugs, and he was not allowed to drive it on the road. Their boy Harold was in high school.

Mrs. Bluett liked to talk and cook. Sometimes she brought

Dakin a loaf of fresh bread or a bowl of doughnuts and left it on the kitchen table. She offered him news if she found him in the kitchen, and sometimes invited him to supper. Dakin never gave her much news in return; the intimacy of discussing one neighbor with another embarrassed him; besides, he didn't have much news.

Mrs. Bluett, speaking loudly, gave him unsought advice. She told him he ought to rent the part of his house he did not use. "Then if anything was to happen to you, Dakin, they'd be somebody here to know it."

Now, as he sat at the table eating the warmed vegetables, he looked out of the window and saw how the green was a deepening stain across the fields; buds were swelling in the neglected apple trees behind the house. There would be mushrooms there soon if the rain ever stopped and let the ground warm up good, he thought. Dakin's mother had always enjoyed gathering mushrooms.

All that afternoon, rain seemed always on the verge of stopping and drawing back to let the sun out, but never quite did. And the starlings continued their murmurous sound.

"They're only birds," Dakin told himself. "It ought not put me out so much."

In the evening he went out and opened the barn doors to let the cattle come in. Their hair was wet against their sides, their horns shining with rain. Dakin gave them some hay, milked two of them, and hung the bucket from a wooden peg in the feed room. The bucket was barely half filled.

John Bluett had advised Dakin to sell the six cows and put the money into hogs. "What good is it," he reasoned, "to milk just enough that you have cream to get rid of and not enough to have whole milk to sell?" But Dakin went ahead in his own way, separating the cream, keeping it cool in the cellar, and getting it into town about once every two weeks. Sometimes John Bluett hauled it in for him.

He left the milk bucket hanging while he went to close the door of the sheep shed at the far end of the lot. The path to the sheep shed went past the loom room that had been a busy place when Dakin's grandmother was mistress of the farm. The carding reel and spinning wheel she had used were there now, dust-covered. Dakin's mother had never used them. She had helped Dakin's father, and Dakin afterward, at the smokehouse. There was a long wooden trough in the smokehouse for brine-curing meat, and a big iron kettle in which they rendered lard. In a small dark section of the smokehouse, the hams and shoulders and wide, thin slabs of bacon had been suspended from hooks in the rafters and smoked slowly over a fire that was never allowed to blaze. Dakin still butchered a hog every year and smoked the meat there, but the butchering was done at the Bluett farm, when John Bluett butchered. One man can hardly handle it alone.

The sheep had gathered in the sheltered part of the shed. The spring lambs, frisky and strong-legged, leaped and played, and their voices sounded like children's voices. Dakin drove them into a compartment that had a door he could close and fasten tightly. Angrily, John Bluett had sold his sheep because every year, once or twice, stray dogs got into the flock and killed and maimed some, and caused some of the ewes to lose their lambs. It was a dirty shame, he told Dakin, because in that hilly country sheep-raising would have been more profitable than crop-farming, except for the dogs. Dakin kept only twelve ewes. He liked a small flock; they ate a good many kinds of weed cows wouldn't eat, and he liked seeing them docilely grazing in the fields or getting up in the evening after a hot day and going slowly out to the pasture.

The rain-dimmed late afternoon had sent the chickens to roost early. Dakin went into the henhouse and gathered the few eggs. Some of the hens, in a fervor of spring plans, had stolen out nests and were hiddenly sitting on the eggs they had laid in them. Dakin put five fresh eggs into his jacket pocket, stopped at the barn to get the milk bucket, and returned to the house.

Rain was still dripping, like spent tears that cannot stop, when he went to bed. Once, when the starlings began their clamor above his bed, it bothered him. "I'll have to learn to like it or it'll drive me crazy," he admitted finally. But he could not learn to like it.

It began softly, a sound shaken back and forth rapidly, increasing in loudness as it continued, and always subsided after an almost intolerable length of time, but it always began again. Day after day that week as Dakin sat in his chilly bedroom, the voice of the young starlings became more difficult to endure.

Once he went downstairs and got the broom and used it to beat against the ceiling.

Finally a morning came when the rain had stopped, the sun came out, and the ground was dry enough to break. Dakin curried the horses as if for a ceremony, harnessed them, and went out to the field. As he drove in between the sawed stone posts at the gateway he could hear John Bluett's tractor already plowing the field across the road. Although he knew John Bluett would be done with his hundred and fifty acres before he could get twenty-five plowed with a team and walking plow, Dakin was jubilant as he prepared to lay off the first land. He could not have expressed this exultation in words, nor explained why, with the plow point in place and the team waiting for his "Git up," he had to pause, take a deep breath, and look across the thick, greening sod of this field. This was his best field. It lays well, Dakin thought with satisfaction. Green and fertile, it was enclosed by a stone fence that followed the natural contour of the land. His grandfather had laid out the fields and hired expert stone masons to fence them with flat stones brought in on oxcarts from back on the farm. Their deep underground foundations made them secure against burrowing animals or frost-heaving. The top of the fence was a line of stones laid on edge. The fences were old and weathered and solid and the sight of them gave Dakin deep pleasure.

He looked down the long line of green sod into which his plow would soon cut, and noted the sunlight falling goldenly upon it. At the far edge, redbud seeped pinkly out of the softly greening woods. Dakin knew that before he had this cornfield finished the redbud would be fully open, paled to the pink of raspberry juice blended with cream on a dish of cobbler. Sassafras already was a golden haze on the green bushes, and in the big gray beech tree the bronze-green sharp points tilted upward, ready to open into new leaves. A red-winged blackbird suddenly cried, "Walkee, walkee, walkeree!"

Dakin had tied the lines together so he could have both hands free for the plow handles. Now he settled the loop of line around his neck and started the team. The plow cut into the moist, green sod, folded it over in a shining brown line, leaving a clean brown trough.

"It's scouring good," said Dakin with deep satisfaction. The fragrance of freshly turned earth was pleasant to him, and when he had reached the far end and looked back, he saw that it had attracted birds, too; they were looking for earthworms turned over in the furrow. For a short time Dakin was supremely happy.

But it was brief. The sun withdrew, the sky seemed to contract, and rain was certain. Stubbornly Dakin went on until the backs of the horses were wet. Then he took them to the barn but left the harness on, as if by stubborn unwillingness to accept rain he could stop it.

When he went upstairs to get a piece of smoked meat to cook some dinner, the starlings set up a long, shattering cry and suddenly Dakin could not endure it any longer. He left the meat on the table and went to the barn for the long ladder which he set up against the house wall, directly under the broken board by which the starling had gone into her nest in the attic. The ladder was too short; he could barely reach his hand into the opening. He got down and found a long stick with which to poke into the nest. It was not quite long enough.

The starlings shrieked; the frightened mother bird flew out and passed close to his face. Dakin ducked aside, throwing his weight to one side of the ladder. Under the uneven pressure the ladder sank suddenly into the rain-softened ground and tilted out of balance. Dakin clutched for the eave, missed it, and felt himself falling helplessly outward, plunging into pain and then darkness.

When he awakened later he was in bed in his own room. A lamp was burning on the square table, and Mrs. Bluett was sitting in the rocking chair. Seeing that he had opened his eyes, she came toward him bringing a glass of water and urging him in a harsh murmur, "Rest, Dakin, don't try to git up. Rest."

It was difficult to get out words asking her whether it had

stopped raining. She said the rain had stopped, and Dakin attempted no further words.

Time passed for him in a blend of pain and confusion. He seldom knew whether it was day or night. He did not know how long he had lain there. He swallowed what Mrs. Bluett brought him and told him to swallow. Sometimes she was there, sometimes John Bluett was there, and sometimes the boy Harold was there. Once in a while, when Dakin opened his eyes and saw no one, he thought that perhaps he had died. He kept waiting with an acute dread for something he could not quite identify, until suddenly he realized it had been a long time since he had heard the starlings.

♣   ♣   ♣

"You know, Delithy, he never was a hand to talk much," said Mrs. Bluett. She spoke loudly now that they were in the kitchen and she did not feel required to whisper. "It plum surprised me how much he talked when he didn't know it. And what he said. He kep' goin' on about some birds . . . they was a nest of young starlings in the attic. I had Harold go up there and tear it out."

She leaned back to look out through the window, then turned again to her visitor.

"And he talked about that field that he was aimin' to break this spring. Seems like it worried him terrible." She

84

bent toward the visitor with a kind of awed, almost frightened bewilderment on her face. "So as soon as John got his own cornfield broke nice with the tractor . . ."

♣   ♣   ♣

Dakin had heard Mrs. Bluett coming up the stairway. Sunlight was pouring in through the south window and he knew the rain was over. He raised himself up on one elbow to look through the window and see whether the field appeared dry enough to plow, but the pain that followed this small exertion brought him back to his shoulders again.

At this moment Mrs. Bluett stepped briskly into the room, happy with good news. "You don't need to fret any more about that field now, Dakin. John's got his own corn ground broke now, and just as soon as he finishes his bite of dinner, he'll bring the tractor . . ." Dakin interrupted her with a cry that Harold Bluett heard even downstairs in the kitchen. Mrs. Bluett stepped back and screamed as Dakin struggled out of bed, fighting his own protesting body, and reached the stairway where he collapsed in pain on the floor. Harold, running up the stairway, caught him before his head struck the floor. Together Harold and Mrs. Bluett got Dakin back upon the bed.

♣   ♣   ♣

"I tell you, Delithy," continued Mrs. Bluett in the kitchen, "I wish you could have seen the look on his face! It was like something back from the grave. The way he jumped out of that bed, and him so crippled up he hadn't even been able to hold a spoon and feed himself. He kep' a-screaming 'No! No!,' and I thought we was hurting him, getting him back into bed. But come to find out, it was the field he was talking about. He didn't want John to plow it with the tractor! I told him, I says, 'Dakin, you'll never get that field broke and it as late it is, with the horses.' But he just kep' hollerin' and moanin' until John come in and promised he wouldn't touch it. Then he got quiet. He's been mighty quiet ever since."

She was silent, looking out of the window at the spring-swept land. "Do you want to go up and see him for a minute, Delithy?" The visitor shook her head, no, and Mrs. Bluett went with her to the back door. "Looks like it's really spring now, don't it?" she said cheerfully, harshly. "Well, come back, Delithy."

♣   ♣   ♣

Upstairs, Dakin lay still. His whole body ached, but he was grateful to Mrs. Bluett that she had not let him die. He felt a deep sense of sorrow, of loss, but also of peace. It was almost the way he had felt at the death of his father. He knew now for a certainty that he could not break his field that spring, but also he knew no one else would break it. This was his portion of earth. He thought now of the clean, brown, yielding furrows, the fragrance of freshly turned sod. Thinking, he surrendered himself to a profound peace. He was kindred of the earth, and like it, durable. He, too, could wait.

Wide and
Starry Sky

THE PEOPLE, chiefly, and their times:

Walter Beem Peden (1867–1961), Owen County farmer

His father, Thomas Alexander Peden (1830–1912)

His mother, Sarah Beem (1843–1919)

His paternal grandfather, Jesse Peden (1800–78)

His maternal grandmother, Levi Beem (1803–95)

His maternal great-grandfather, John McCormick
(land by pre-emption, 1816)

His paternal great-grandfather, Daniel Beem
(land by pre-emption, 1816)

Walter Peden's wife, Clara Ellen Ness (1875–1961)

Walter Peden's sons, Richard, Paris, Mark, Thomas Milton

Walter Peden's grandchildren, Joe and Carol (Children of
Richard), Mark (son of Thomas Milton)

WALTER PEDEN always said he had lived in Spencer longer than anybody else had; always, that is, after he had become old enough to boast about his age and had begun signing his family letters "Grand Pa at 90+."

He lived to be ninety-five years old, and in his last years when he had finally delegated the care of his Owen County creek bottom farm to his third son, Mark, he spent much of his time reading, keeping farm records, and writing letters to the families of his sons Tom and Dick and to people whose public records particularly engaged his interest.

He had always read extensively, newspapers and histories, especially Civil War history, even in the busy days when he and his brother Howard drove a horse and buggy out to their partnership farm near Rattlesnake Creek every morning. In the later years, when they drove a partnership car, Walter still got up in time to build a fire in the coal-burning water heater in the kitchen, make coffee and eat breakfast, and have an hour for reading before going to the farm.

For although he was insatiably a farmer and his father and grandfathers and great-grandfathers had been Owen County farmers, he did not live on his farm. He had lived in town from the time he was seven years old, when his father, growing wealthy and successful from farming, moved into the little county-seat town. When Walter and Clara were married in 1903, they began housekeeping in the town and never moved to the farm. "Grand Pa+" lived in a big white house on Washington Street. It had three living rooms connected by sliding doors and a wide hall with a stairway in it. There was a round window of imported red glass in the south wall above the stairway landing. When the sunlight came in through that window it turned everything red that passed it, and whatever was already red, a woman's dress or somebody's lips, seemed to lose its redness. Clara Nees had always wanted to live in that house, but it was not until after her fourth son was born that she attained it. She had grown up on a farm near "Jerden" village on which her widowed mother and two brothers made a comfortable living for six people. After she graduated from high school she went to Teachers Normal school one summer, and by the time she was eighteen, was teaching a country school. She had been teaching in the Spencer school system four years when she married Walter Peden, choosing him from her several beaux.

That was before rural electricity, furnaces, power mowers, good roads, or the daily mail delivery came to the farms.

Land and livestock were wealth, but town living was considered more elegant. Clara liked elegance. She liked things decorated, nothing really plain: embroidered dresses, carved furniture, Haviland china with delicate floral patterns, dinner knives with mother-of-pearl handles, sterling silver forks heavily embossed. She was a pretty woman with shining light brown hair too silken to hold a wave. She had a pink-and-white, petal-soft complexion as all the Nees women did. She had a slim waist and full, red lips that never needed lipstick. She liked to sing. She liked to talk about the beauty of farm sunsets, and to admire good, purebred cattle, and she enjoyed a drive to the country where in autumn she could gather bouquets of small lavender field asters from the roadsides, or bring home wild grapes to make into dark jelly, but she did not want to live on a farm. She liked being a part of town society, the wife of a wealthy farmer's son. She was interested in art and music, pretty clothes, a nice house, and the pleasant things of town living.

At the time of her marriage the Peden brothers and their father, Thomas, owned four large farms in Owen County and most of the Beem-Peden bank besides. It was easy for Clara to persuade herself that her farm-managing husband needed to live in town so he could go downtown every day to get shaved at Stimson's barbershop where he kept his shaving mug with his name on it, or to keep up with the livestock market or town affairs or whatever there was to keep up with, and talk to traders who might want to buy or sell hogs, cattle, mules or hay, or townspeople who needed hay for their town-kept driving horses.

It may have been hard for Walter to adapt his pattern of fiery, impatient haste to the tempo of a wife who genuinely preferred to be a few minutes late to church, and was always fifteen to twenty minutes late getting meals on the table, and detested getting up early to get a farmer's breakfast or pack lunches to take to the farm, and sometimes was in tears while she did it. But as long as he was free to devote the major part of his time to his farming, living in town suited him. All his life the farm came ahead of his other interests.

He had a gift for remembering what he read and heard, and for getting answers to what he asked, and for quoting it in his conversations. By the time he was in his eighties he had accumulated such a voluminous mental file of Owen County history and biography that reporters were calling him the county's philosopher-historian, and he was always a fertile source for a reporter who needed a nostalgic local-history story.

He was small, witty, wiry, perpetually restless, and loved to talk. Even when he was eating he liked talking better. He didn't care too much about what he ate, though he liked a piece of bread to eat with everything, even pie or candy. He liked sandwiches of sliced radishes between slices of buttered bread. He liked a special corn casserole I baked for him. But he liked talking so much more that I sometimes suspected he enjoyed mealtime chiefly because it was a way to get people together and keep them quiet while he talked.

During the two depression years, when Dick and I lived on the Rattlesnake Creek farm, Walter and Howard brought their lunches from home and ate in the kitchen, by the warmth of the big coal-burning base burner, while I cooked dinner for Dick, who worked in town and came home later. Howard's wife packed him a careful lunch, including a thermos bottle of hot coffee. The thermos bottle was his special pride, and he showed me its temperature-holding glass lining, explaining it. One day in particular I watched the two men at dinner, Walter sitting cross-legged on the floor in front of the stove, eating buttered white bread and talking. He was enjoying himself so much, I secretly buttered a slice of bread and ate it to see if it could taste that good. It didn't, of course, but then I was not sitting on the floor, cross-legged and talking like a motor at a drag strip. Howard was sitting on a chair in the corner behind the stove, quietly enjoying his sandwiches and little dishes of apple sauce and baked beans. He finished the last drop of coffee, replaced the thermos cork, and gave it a loving tap— too firmly. The glass lining shattered, and Howard looked across the room at me with an expression of positive bereavement on his face. Walter went right on talking.

Walter's birthday was on May 25th, and traditionally Clara baked strawberry shortcake for him that day. Somebody usually gave him a box of cherry cocktails, his favorite candy. Clara was an excellent cook and enjoyed holiday dinners and family homecoming meals which she prepared in the inconvenient, too-small kitchen of the big house and served in the dining room that looked out upon a side street. In this room she had three glass-doored cabinets filled with pretty, fancy, and old dishes. But by the time Walter had become Grand Pa 90+ she was not able to do much cooking; they went to their sons' houses for Christmas and Thanksgiving and birthday dinners.

They had four sons: Richard, Paris, Mark, and Thomas Milton. As soon as the boys were old enough to know the farm and occasionally go there and to work on it in summer, they wanted to move to it. But Walter and Clara never seriously considered moving to the farm; they hadn't even considered it earlier when the bank failed and Thomas Peden sold all the farms and the livestock, and living on the farm might have been thrifty. Rattlesnake Creek farm, which Walter and Howard had bought back, at that time had a small, charming, two-story poplar house built in 1849. It had a fireplace and a hand-carved mantel in each of its five rooms, Colonial windows with small panes, wide random-width boards in its floors and inside walls. But Clara had no desire to live in it. They lived, instead, in other houses with far less personality. One, for a few hard years, was what Dick later described as "a little shotgun house; you could stand in the front door and look right through all three of its rooms." It was so close to the tracks of the noisy, cinder-spouting train that no grass or flowers would grow in its yard and the boys could not walk there barefooted. They lived in another house called "the goat house" because it was during that time the boys had a goat called Mabel, and harness and a little wagon to hitch her to. They moved later to

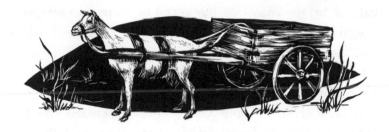

a small, quaint, and much-wanted house on Hillside Avenue. Their youngest son was born while they lived there, and from that house, despite the pleas of the older sons, they bought the Washington Street house and moved into it.

The first of the Peden family ever to live in the Rattlesnake Creek farmhouse was Richard, after he was married. We repaired the warped floors and broken stairway, replaced the broken windowpanes, roofed the house and put back the small portico, painted and papered the inside, opened up the fireplaces and repaired them, and built a cistern. But it was not a successful arrangement. After a couple of years Dick transferred Howard's half of the farm to Walter and we moved to a farm in another county.

It seems strange that a man who said, "I had to farm;

it's in my blood," would not have realized that farming was likely to be also in the blood of his sons, and would not make a place for them on his farm. But Walter had reasons for never taking his sons into actual partnership. He always said the farm would not support another partner. He and Howard went through the difficult depression years and years of being always on the verge of financial emergency, as well as through good years. Howard kept the bank deposit book, but Walter wrote the checks and kept the meticulous, detailed farm records. Actually, I think he could never bear to share the authority of his farm with anybody until he had to. He and Clara never discussed the farm problems or made farm decisions together, and that was probably because the farm was a business, not their home.

Creek bottom farmers did not use commercial fertilizer; they counted on the fertility washing down upon their fields from the hill farms. (They discounted the burrs and weeds that washed down with it.) The sandy loam fields of the Rattlesnake Creek farm produced lavishly without commercial fertilizer, but there was always the menace of spring floods. The farm was threatened by the flood waters of White River which also invaded the town, and of Rattlesnake Creek which was nearer. One year, when Dick and I lived there, the flood came up into and around the lower barn and stood there so long it filled the air with the odor of fish, even up to the house on its high sandy knoll.

Several years later, one May, when we were living in a

different county, Walter wrote me in quiet sorrow, "We are having a flood here. More than a hundred acres of fine corn under four or five feet of water." It happened many times. The farm he loved was treacherous. Like a jealous woman it could be beautiful, lavish, or cruel. But he never stopped loving it.

♣   ♣   ♣

He was innately unable to be idle, and he was not a complainer; so when he was no longer able to go to the farm every day, he turned to reading and letter writing as if from a thirst to be quenched. He wrote me many letters. His style was formal in an old-fashioned way, simple, dignified and brief, with an undercurrent of humor.

He mentioned the same topics many times: Sir Francis Drake's drum, Abraham Lincoln's Second Inaugural address; Captain Slocum's trip around the world in a fishing boat; the cowboy's epitaph; the Laplander people; his own Beem, Peden and McCormick ancestors, all farmers; Harold Macmillan's American-born mother whom Walter knew in Spencer; the monument erected in Scotland to the memory of martyred Alexander Peden, years after the martyr's death. He wrote of his farming theories. He liked his Shorthorn cattle, but I think he liked his Berkshire hogs better. He estimated that in his seventy years of hog raising he had devised registration names for more than a thousand purebred Berkshires and this he said was the hardest part of the hog business. He kept books of hog records and accounts and worked at them without diminishing interest. He laughed when I wrote him, "Give our love to the hogs."

In conversation he often told the same stories he had mentioned in his letters. His longer stories, of course, he preferred to tell rather than to write. When he asked, "Did I ever tell you about Berry, the insane horse we had?," I always said, "No," so he would tell it again. He told of the East boys, traders; of Boone's cave in Spencer; of homesick old Peter Abernathy; of the time little Tom Thumb came to Spencer with the circus; of five hundred Indians passing through Spencer one Christmas Day, sadly leaving their homeland; of the time Morgan the raider came almost to nearby Bloomington.

He told about his farming ancestors and how they came to Owen County in the pioneer conditions of 1816. He was proud of them. By the time he had become Grand Pa+ and I was writing a farm column for two city newspapers he was proud of me, too, and affectionately considered me one of his relatives. He often addressed his envelopes to me by my column name, Mrs. R.F.D., and usually began the letter in his lovely, old-fashioned, formal courtesy: "I wish to congratulate you on your column of . . ." or "Thinking it may have escaped your notice, I hand you . . ." and often ended the letter with what he believed to be an Irish greeting, "More power to your pen."

His compliments were appropriate to the season: in March he wrote, "Getting a letter from you is like a breeze from Florida in winter," and in June, "A letter from you is like a bottle of whisky to a Kentucky colonel." One compliment he repeated many times, in different seasons: "I still think of you as the modern Harriet Beecher Stowe. I know of no greater compliment than that." The reason he considered this the greatest possible compliment was that in his intense interest in the Civil War and everything concerned with it (including his relatives who had served in it), he regarded Mrs. Stowe as the only woman writer worth noting. In his middle-aged, busy farming years, however, he had read and greatly admired a column written by "The Country Contributor," Mrs. Juliet V. Strauss of Rockville, Indiana, for *The Indianapolis News.*

In a gently teasing way he explained his choice of nom de plume. "These literary people seem to need a name to write under to be in style. I have chosen Grand Pa+, as you may have noticed. I feel some distinction in this as there are but few writers nincty years of age."

Writing a letter to a person he did not know but admired, or for whom he had some pertinent message, was a kind of adventure for him. He said in one letter, "I have always measured my ability to write an interesting letter by whether or not I received a reply. I have received agreeable replies from such people as Bruce Catton" (to whom he had offered a slight correction in description of a church which Mr.

Catton appreciatively conceded) "and Alan T. Nolen, Sam Guard, Prime Minister Harold Macmillan, Governor Harold Handley, David L. Chambers, Jr., president of the Indianapolis stockyards. And last, but not least, Mrs. R.F.D."

We carried on a gaiety in our correspondence. Once he wrote, "Reflecting on my ninety-one years I feel I have not lived in vain; I claim to be the only man who ever received a dishcloth as a Christmas present. And second, I believe I am your oldest fan correspondent."

I often quoted him in my column and he loved it.

On his ninety-first birthday we had flowers delivered to him and the Spencer florist enthusiastically added bluebirds, bumblebees, and such touches. Walter wrote at once: "To the Richard Peden family, including the dog, Rose: I wish to express my appreciation of the birthday flowers. The first flowers I ever received. It took ninety-one years of living to attain to that. I thought of Napoleon addressing his army encamped in the shadows of the pyramids in Egypt. He said, 'Soldiers of France, six thousand years of history look down upon you, etc.' With an affectionate greeting to you all, Sincerely, Grand Pa at 91 +."

♣　　♣　　♣

Walter's farming roots went back a long way.

In 1816, two years before Owen was organized as a county, its 251,520 acres of land were offered for sale at the land grant office in Vincennes. Among the men filing land claims in September of that year were the two men destined to become the great-grandfathers of Walter Peden, fifty-one years later.

They were Daniel Beem, whose claim was filed for him by his son Richard because ailing Daniel was unable to go in person, and John McCormick.

Richard Beem chose land in the flat area near White River, but John McCormick went across the river and selected a high spot with a creek on it.

Two years later the newly organized county was named Owen, in honor of Abraham Owen, an officer in the battle of Tippecanoe. Many years later, due chiefly to the effort of Spencer newspaper editor Carl Anderson, the county began to be known as "Sweet Owen." "Sweet Owen" is twenty-three miles wide east to west, twenty-one north by south. It contains 329 sections of land, if one chooses to count the space taken up by its hills and ravines and undisciplined creeks. It has always been considered beautiful landscape.

Its two rivers, Eel and White, are fed principally by McCormick's, Wyatt's, Big and Little Raccoons, Fall, Mill, Rattlesnake, Fish, Sandlick, Six Mile and Jordan creeks, the last locally known as "Jerden."

Geographers like to say the white settlers were the third people to live there; that the land was probably first inhabited by prehistoric people who have left mounds and burying grounds as evidence of their use of the land. Indians of the Delaware, Eel River, Miami, and Pottawatomie tribes next claimed the territory and gave way reluctantly before the relentlessly incoming white settlers.

Captain David Beem, writing years later about the hard times the early settlers had in conflict with Indians, wrote that the Delawares, Miami, and Eel River Indians, when they attacked, were mostly satisfied to plunder, but the Pottawatomies were "more murderous and bloodthirsty." One fact seldom mentioned is that the Indians, like all land-owners, loved their land, needed it, and wanted to keep it. The white settlers were invaders, whether they bought the land or took it by force. Their use of the land and the Indians' use of it were inimical. As any farmer knows, land is a basic need of mankind and many wars have been fought to get or to hold it. Whether the invaders are white settlers from a far-off country, or new and dangerous influences and social demands of an increasing society within his own country, if it requires his land, the owner will fight for it in whatever way he can fight.

In one letter Walter wrote sympathetically, "By the terms of a so-called treaty in 1810 the Indians had ceded all the land east of the Wabash River to the white settlers.

"The Indians, loath to leave their native land, lingered on until the late autumn of 1817. In the summer of 1816 the Indiana territory contracted with the militia and or-ganized frontiersmen to 'drive the Indians beyond the Wabash.' Of course, 'driving the Indians' consisted in killing any Indians found east of the Wabash. Sad to relate, three of my grandfather's brothers were in this drive.

"The Indians had planted a small plot of ground to corn in the spring of 1816. Right where Dr. Belles, father of Nellie Belles Macmillan, is buried in Riverside Cemetery. My grandfather Beem's family, having entered a claim for this land in September 1816, fell heir to the Indians' abandoned corn. The Beem family harvested it, made corn meal of the grain. Grandmother Mary Neely Beem boiled the cobs in a pot hung over the fireplace and wintered the cow on boiled corncobs."

It would have been a hard winter for the Beems without the Indians' little corn patch.

Years later the site of the Beems' first cabin had become a part of the Riverside cemetery. The stones of the fireplace over which Grandmother Beem boiled the cobs were still visible in the cemetery. Walter liked to add, as in that letter, "So, although Purdue University did not learn of the value of corn cobs in a cattle ration until 1946, Grandmother Beem knew it 130 years earlier. My grandfather once pointed out to me the very spot where, the next spring, 1817, he and his brother planted the first grains of hard, flint corn ever planted by white men in Owen County. On May 14 and 15."

The county developed, the Beems survived the hard winter, prospered and increased. Daniel Beem's funeral in 1819 was the first in the county. He was buried on a part of his own land, which he had given for a cemetery. It was low-lying and subject to spring flood. About a hundred years later the bodies of Daniel and Mary Neely Beem were removed from that part of the cemetery to higher ground. Walter Peden, who was present at the disinterment, was surprised to note that although the wood of the old tapering-shaped caskets had disintegrated, so that the casket outline was marked only by a row of rusty nails, the ground had not healed where it had been dug into.

In February 1820, a site for a county seat town was selected, part of it being the seventy acres donated by Daniel Beem. The new town was named Spencer, in honor of another brave Tippecanoe officer, Captain Spicer Spencer. It was still fifty-four years before Walter Peden would become a citizen of the town.

"Historically I started out all right," he wrote me in 1958. "My mother always told me I was named for Sir Walter Raleigh, of English history." She couldn't have known how appropriate the name would be, in view of the old-fashioned courtesy he displayed when he grew up. His middle name was Beem, given him by his mother, Sarah Beem, because of her pride in the family name and admiration for her father, Levi. Levi Beem was fifteen years old when Richard Beem filed the land claim for their father in 1816.

In 1817 Levi and Richard came to the newly acquired land and built a half-faced cabin, and when the family arrived later they built a log house.

106

There were no schools. When Levi went to vote in 1821, he was eighteen years old and could neither read nor write, and knew nothing of national affairs. Even at that time the country was seething in the effort to keep the balance between slave and free states. Missouri entered the union that year as a free state, making the balance equal, twelve free, twelve slave. Thomas Jefferson had said that the suddenness with which the slavery question arose terrified him "like a firebell in the night." President James Monroe was running for a second term on the Republican (then also called the Democratic) ticket. At the polls, Levi asked the issues and was told, "The Republicans believe in manufacturing goods in this country; the Federalists believe in buying it from Europe." Levi, shrewd and resourceful, believed in doing everything for yourself if you can, and angrily recalling stories he had heard about the American Revolution he immediately became a Republican, voted for Monroe, and remained a Republican the rest of his life.

In 1825 he married Sarah Johnson, the daughter of an itinerant Methodist minister, and she taught Levi to read and write. This skill was a great comfort to him in later years when, having been stricken with asthma at thirty years of age, he was unable to work in his fields. "For fifty years," Walter liked to tell us, "Grandfather never did a lick of work." He read a great deal, was one of the few local people who subscribed regularly to a newspaper, the Indianapolis *Journal*.

But, even though he could not work in the fields, he was a good farmer. He hired men to work for him for fifty cents a day. His sons worked for him, but he never allowed his daughters to do any farm work. He had ten children of his own and adopted four more. He raised corn, wheat, and rye, "and," Walter would say, pointing an emphasizing finger at his audience, "never harvested a crop. He let the hogs and cattle do it for him. They could do it more profitably, he claimed, and they improved the soil more than the harvesting machinery would. In sixty-five years he never had a grain cradle, sickle, or reaper in the fields of his eighty-acre farm. He just turned the hogs and cattle in on the field."

The yellow-poplar, story-and-a-half farmhouse was hardly more than a mile outside of Spencer, but Levi went to town only twice a year—in spring to sell the wool and pay the taxes, in the fall to buy a barrel of salt for curing the winter meat. He never allowed Sarah to sell butter. "He didn't believe in it," explained his grandson; "he claimed he could make five pounds of beef on the same amount of feed required to produce a pound of butter, and beef sold higher. He took bacon down to the flatboat on White River and sent it to Louisville and sold it for a cent and a half a pound. In his day you could buy a good cow for $14, and horse for $30."

Horses and mules, raised on the farms, provided work power. They provided power for raising their own fuel— corn and hay—instead of requiring off-the-farm purchases of transportation and power fuel as today's machinery requires. And if a farmer needed extra cash, the same mare that produced work power could also produce a colt to sell.

The family raised most of its own food and their taxes were low.

Levi was a trader, and progressive. In 1856 he put the saddlebags on his horse and rode to Lexington where he bought a purebred Shorthorn bull, a white heifer, and two cows. They were the first pedigreed Shorthorns in Owen County. Levi, on horseback, drove them back to Indiana.

"He had rail fences," said Walter. "I never knew him to have a tool on the place, except an ax." Logs were split into fence rails with the aid of an ax and wooden "gluts," long tapering wooden wedges driven into a split started with the ax. The gluts were usually made of dogwood, because it was considered the hardest of woods.

Levi's farm practices were profitable for him. From his moderately fertile, cold, white creek bottom farm of eighty acres he made enough money so that he was able, as each child married, to give the child $500 in cash; at his death in 1895 he left an estate valued at $27,000.

In 1875 when Levi and Sarah celebrated their golden wedding anniversary it was a large social affair with much ado, food, gaiety, and many descendents, some of them already notable in Spencer history. There was Captain David E. Beem who had served in the Civil War. Returning safely from it, he had built a brick house of great splendor high on the hill on fashionable Hillside Avenue. He had attended Purdue University, later was for several years a trustee of Purdue, and in 1905 vice-president of its board of directors. Captain Beem wrote an account of the golden wedding celebration, which was reprinted in a little booklet enclosed within limp black covers imprinted with gold lettering. In this account he wrote, "The children presented Levi and Sarah each an elegant pair of gold spectacles worth $15 a pair." Surrounded by success and happy relatives and proof of the excellence of his farm policy, Levi became a part of Owen County's history.

His daughter Sarah, grand-daughter of Daniel Beem, received her $500 wedding endowment from Levi when she married the grandson of John McCormick and moved to the McCormick farm as the wife of Thomas Peden. Thomas was the son of John McCormick's daughter Nancy and Jesse Peden.

Selecting his land in 1816, John McCormick, a West Virginian, had by-passed the flat bottom land preferred by his contemporaries the Beems. He went across the river and up to the wooded heights because he liked the hills and the fast bright creek that ran between them, with its falls and, he thought, the possibility of a grist mill site, and the deep canyon. He had no way of foreseeing that from the ledge of good limestone on his farm, years later, the state of Indiana would choose stone for the new statehouse in its capital city. Nor that, nearly a hundred years later, thanks to the unremitting effort of Colonel Richard Lieber, Indiana's first director of its Department of Conservation, and to the generosity of Owen County people, the McCormick farm would become a part of the first of Indiana's excellent state parks.

John McCormick built a one-room log cabin and log barn, cleared and fenced land. His widowed daughter, Nancy Ragsdale, and her children lived with him and continued living with him even after she married Jesse Peden, who was a few years younger than Nancy.

Jesse Peden was a Quaker. He was twenty-two years old when he came to Indiana from Washington County, Pennsylvania, in 1822. He had been dismissed from the meeting there because, among other infractions of Quaker belief, he had secretly drilled with the militia. Whether this was because of his inherent military convictions, or because of the government's generous policy regarding land grants for men with military records, Walter always defended his grandfather's illicit military activity. In his letters and in conversation he frequently asked, "To whom does this country owe most, the military or the clergy?"

To the military, he believed; and in one letter he wrote, "I note your reference to war and the noble belief of the Quakers regarding war. My grandfather Jesse Peden was born and reared in an old Quaker family in Pennsylvania and always spoke the Quaker dialect of 'thee' and 'thou,' etc., when he lived up there on the McCormick's Creek farm. I often think any good in my character must have come from that long line of Quaker ancestors in Pennsylvania dating from 1754.

"The Scripture reads, 'There will always be wars and rumors of wars.' Since there will always be war, somebody has to do the killing, and only soldiers can do that. It was not the prayers of the righteous that defeated Lee at Gettysburg. It was the powder and lead and blood of thirty thousand Union soldiers that did that."

Nancy and Jesse's two children were Margaret Amanda and Thomas, the future father of Walter. Jesse built a three-room house with a stone basement and stone entryway thereto. He helped his father-in-law fence more land until they had around six hundred acres enclosed by rail fences. "Grandfather often spoke of 'the gloom of the forest,' " Walter said, years later. In 1830, the year his son Thomas was born, Jesse planted an orchard of plum, apple, and Kieffer pear trees. The orchardist's adage that "he who plants pears plants for his heirs" was there attested. When the pear trees were nearly 130 years old and Jesse Peden's lively little grandson Walter had become an old man calling himself Grand Pa 90+, a reporter came down to Spencer from *The Indianapolis Star* and took Walter out to the old farm, which had become a park by that time. The reporter took a photograph of ninety-two-year old Walter pointing to one of his grandfather's Kieffer pear trees which that April morning was blooming abundantly and preparing to bear a good harvest in September.

At the McCormick's Creek farm, Nancy Peden made butter and gathered eggs and took them down to sell in the little town three miles east of the farm. She got three cents a dozen for eggs, ten cents a pound for butter. She did not go to town often, but when she was there she made some purchases at the Parks and Moore General Store. Her purchases in the store's daybook for one October day in 1839 included "pare of spectacles 50¢, and 2 ozs indigo and madder 37½¢."

Walter told me, "In April, when White River was swollen and high enough to float boats, there were hucksters' flatboats that came to a river bend near Spencer and tied up there. They chose this place because it was near a flowing spring, and of course the boatmen didn't want to drink the muddy White River water. Farm women like my grandmother, Nancy Peden, saved their eggs through the late winter and brought them down to the flatboats to sell. After a few days the boats went on to other places, Worthington, Freedom, and made their way on down to the mouth of the Ohio and finally to the Mississippi, buying three-cent eggs as they went along. No wonder that by June, when they got to New Orleans, some of the eggs had hatched!"

In winter, sometimes, as Nancy came home on the horse-drawn sled, on the cold uphill drive and along the wooded level stretches (where now the state park's Canyon Inn and the saddle barn and shelter houses are) gray timber wolves came out and chased the sled. Trail 5 of the park now leads past "Wolf Cave" close to where Nancy's log house was, and where the old rock-walled springhouse still is, and near the remarkable big barn built by Jesse's progressive son Thomas in 1857.

There are no wolves there now and Nancy Peden has been gone a long time, too. She died in 1854 when the community was scourged by smallpox. All the Peden family became ill with it. Neighbors were brave and kind. In that dangerous pre-vaccination era they brought food and set it down at a safe distance from the house and "hollered" to ask about the family's health and what they needed. Nancy and Margaret Amanda died and were buried, by courtesy of kindly neighbors, in the Litten family's private burying ground on the Litten farm near the McCormick farm.

Nine years after Nancy Peden's death, her son Thomas married Levi Beem's daughter Sarah and brought her from her father's flat, bottom farm a mile from town to Jesse Peden's farm at McCormick's Creek.

Thomas was the empire builder. It was a highly appropriate coincidence that his middle name was Alexander. His talents were varied, his energy boundless, his judgment was good, and he had imagination. At the height of his career he owned Rosebud farm of one hundred acres, a mile south of Spencer; Rattlesnake Creek farm of 268 acres including 150 acres of fertile creek bottom fields three miles west of town; Pottersville farm of 350 acres of White River bottom land; and the McCormick's Creek farm of around a thousand acres. He was the Peden in the Beem-Peden bank in Spencer. (The Beem was Captain David Beem.) Thomas had a meat-packing business on Porkhouse Hill. In his lifetime he made $150,000 buying and selling sheep and cattle. On a stock-buying trip, he rode horseback so that he could drive the stock home with him right then.

In the autumn of 1848, when he was eighteen years old, he enrolled at Indiana University in Bloomington, sixteen miles southeast of his father's McCormick's Creek farm home. There were twenty freshmen attending IU that year. He could not afford to pay room and board away from home all week, so he came home on Friday evening and returned to Bloomington on Monday morning. Every Friday after-noon during that college year Jesse saddled two horses and rode out toward Bloomington to meet his student son who had started walking home. And on Monday morning, when they had ridden halfway to Bloomington, Jesse brought the two horses back to the farm.

After one year in college Thomas began his real career, farming. In 1857 he built a large new barn, which is still standing. In 1861, at the seventh Owen County Fair, his exhibit of Jesse's apples won, as first prize, an engraved silver cup which Walter's little boys many years later played with until they broke off the handle.

Thomas plowed the fields and tended and increased the livestock, bought more land, and planted corn. By that time farmers had improved the seed corn considerably over the hard, flinty maize the Indians had originally planted. The Peden farm was joined by the Cline farm, and there was a friendly rivalry between Thomas Peden on one side of the line fence and Rufus Cline, on the other side, to see which man could plow more in a day.

"Of course all they had was a walking plow and a horse," Walter said, telling this story, which he particularly liked to tell; "on every row they had to walk down all the way across the field on one side of a row and come back on the other side of the row. Just one row at a time. They both got up early and stayed late in the fields. And of course the last thing each man did when he left his field, was to look and see how far the other had got that day."

Walter liked this story because it was flavored with Civil War history of which he seemed never to tire.

Both Jesse Peden and Thomas were ardent supporters of "Old Abe," he explained, but neighbor Cline was a Southern sympathizer and secretly belonged to the Knights of the Golden Circle. "But they were good neighbors and the plowing rivalry was friendly."

In corn-planting time in 1863, word reached the neighborhood that "Morgan the raider" (John Hunt Morgan) was getting through the Midwestern states, including Indiana, and had already raided the southern counties. He had come as far as Salem, the report said, and there the frightened people gave way and let him come on through. Word received by Owen County farmers was that Morgan was coming on into Bloomington in the county adjoining Owen.

This word delighted Rufus Cline, who decided secretly to go to Bloomington and offer what help he could. Unfortunately for Rufus's plans, the word got around to Governor Morton as well as to the sympathetic Knights and the farmers of Owen County, and Governor Morton sent down a trainload of soldiers to Bloomington to deal with Morgan and his "terrible men." Morgan, also a smart listener, with his ear to the grapevine, learned of the governor's coup and pulled one himself by changing his route and by-passing Bloomington. Rufus did not learn of this change in time. He got on his horse at night and rode on to Bloomington, and when he saw the trainload of soldiers get off at Bloomington, he decided to go home. It was late then, Walter explained, and Rufus was afraid that anybody meeting him on horseback along the road at that late hour might ask embarrassing questions. So when he got back as far as his farm he just hitched his horse to the plow and finished plowing his cornfield. When Thomas came the next morning to start plowing, he saw that Rufus's field was done and he asked his neighbor what time he had finished it. Rufus hedged and hummed and said he did start pretty early, but he wouldn't tell exactly when. It was years before he admitted the whole story.

In 1874 the town was fifty-four years old. Thomas was accumulating land, livestock, and prestige. An era was beginning in which successful farmers liked to move into town where they could live more fashionably and luxuriously, they thought. Thomas and his wife, Sarah, had three sons; Jesse Powatan, of school age; Walter Beem, seven and ready for school; and Howard Levi, four. The family moved into Spencer, first to a two-story brick house at the west edge of town. Later they built and occupied a large, somewhat pretentious house on fashionable Hillside Avenue. The Hillside house had the distinction of having a south window in every one of its many rooms, including those in the deep, usable basement and those in the attic, and all of them on the two stories. The house also had one of the first bathrooms in the town. The tub was small, deep, and stood on tall, narrow legs shaped somewhat like the legs of a low-slung dog. It was high fashion, it was luxury. But penny-wise, thrifty Sarah Peden, a Beem to her innermost forthright core, was still as frugal as a pioneer. She still used bacon fryings in her pie crust (which her small grandsons considered particularly appetizing), and when she dressed a chicken to stew, she cleaned the feet and cooked them in with the gravy. "This chicken tasted delicious," said one of the grandsons years later, "until you dipped in the spoon and brought up that awful claw foot . . ."

Living in town, where he was a staunch supporter of the Farmers' Institute, Thomas dressed just as he had when he lived on the farm. He walked along Hillside Avenue wearing an old slouch hat and work clothes, and he had many friends.

People respected and trusted him. His expression of profanity was "By Gordon."

"He was a success," said Walter once, "because he studied the business with great care and was able to give a logical reason for everything he did. It was his profound belief that every farmer should improve his land and leave it in better condition than when he found it." It would be hard for a son to follow in the footsteps of such a father, lengthening them. It may be that Walter's somewhat dominating attitude toward his brother and sons, in the farming, was his way of trying to live up to his evaluation of Thomas.

When the bank failed in 1909, it took a day and a half just to get the good livestock driven in from the Pottersville farm and through town down to the loading place on the railroad. The farms were all sold, and the livestock also from all of them. From her portion, as the wife, Sarah Peden kept the Hillside house for her son Jesse, and invested what money she had in the Rattlesnake Creek farm for Walter and Howard jointly. Thomas Peden died three years later.

In the light of its record, it seems the bank actually was solvent. It paid 85 per cent to the depositors, besides 20 per cent to the receiver, and all the costs attending the debacle. There was wide disagreement over the real cause of its being thrown into receivership.

♣   ♣   ♣

Those first seven years of his life, spent on his grandfather's farm, served to germinate the seed of Walter's inherent love of farming and livestock management. Through ensuing years, this grew greater, as a sapling sprouting from a small seed reaches toward the sky and finally the tree towers above all else.

Wise Thomas Peden started his sons early in their livestock careers. When Jesse was seven and Walter was five, he gave each boy a pig. Jesse was in school, but Walter was too young to go, and it was in the care of this pig that he learned the first law of hog-raising; that a hog does not stand back from the trough out of brotherly love or shyness. After Jesse had gone to school in the morning, he took a stick and kept Jesse's pig back from the trough until his own had eaten all it could. Naturally his pig gained faster than Jesse's pig.

In his later years, however, when he had bought and sold so many hogs that he was able to guess their weight pretty accurately by the pitch of their voices, it was not by deceit but by study and progressive methods that he was able to do well with hogs. He was one of the first farmers to realize the value of adding mineral supplement to a hog ration. By doing this, he was able to buy underfed hogs from all over the county, paying the going market price, and take them to his farm and fatten them faster and better and show a profit.

In our correspondence I often sent "regards from our

hogs to your hogs." Walter appreciated this kind of gaiety and answered in kind. In 1954 he wrote, "When a person reaches the eighty-eighth year, some days they wonder whether life is worth living any longer. However, I got a big boost this week when I got that message from you and took it out to the hog lot. I took it out to where approximately a hundred hogs were eating their breakfast of corn and supplement. When I read the message the whole hundred head paused from their breakfast long enough to respond with loud and unanimous grunts of apppreciation. Although sixteen miles intervene between the two lots of hogs, if the wind had been blowing in the right direction I am sure your hogs would have heard those grunts of appreciation, feed-lot odors and all. Affectionately, especially to my grand-daughter Carol, Grand Pa."

One year he wrote happily, "No joking, the hogs have done pretty well this year, returning a net profit of more than a thousand dollars so far this year. I got a call from Indianapolis and the letter I had written Mr. Chambers and the stockyards people was read to me with flowery comment. I have just finished washing the dishes. I have learned how to boil beef and potatoes, or beef and cabbage. But my first love is still with Mr. Hog. I got a big write-up by the farm editor of *The Indianapolis News*, 'Hogs.' They are sending me several copies. I will save one for Richard. Grand Pa at 89."

He liked hogs and cattle for interest and profit. For pets

he liked cats. He petted them and teased them, fed them, patiently let them into and out of the house through the tall front door. In the furnace room, for their sleeping comfort, he had built a door in the basement window that would swing in or out as the cat wished, and the cats could come and go at any time.

In his farming, by the time I knew him, he never paid any attention to chickens. But on the McCormick's Creek farm, when he was five years old, he had a pet hen, Old Blackie, and remembered her afterward with enough affection to make him tolerant of the wives of his farm tenants who insisted on keeping a few chickens. On March 4, 1872, which was, as he always told us, the day of General Grant's inauguration for his second term, a hen came out from under the porch with six newly hatched chicks.

It requires persistence, long-range planning, and a passion for motherhood to enable a hen to hatch eggs outside by this time in March. She has had to sit on the eggs twenty-one days, incubating them, and before that she has had to lay them one a day in a hidden nest someplace. Walter's mother, Sarah Peden, knew the hen had started her motherhood project some cold day in January and was so impressed by this henly achievement that she always afterward referred to General Grant's inauguration day as "the day the old hen hatched under the porch."

The little boy admired the fluffy, many-colored chicks and wanted one for his own. His mother gave him his choice and he chose the black one which he, of course, at once named "Old Blackie." He lavished attention on Old Blackie and the hen lived to be really old, seven years, and died a natural death peacefully at the last. But there was a long time when the little boy suffered painful suspense over the life of Old Blackie.

Mag, the hired girl, had decided to marry, and Sarah promised her a chicken dinner as a wedding present. Mag, who always like to tease, told Walter she was going to stew Blackie for the wedding feast and he believed her. Early on the wedding morning he got out of bed and caught his pet and hid with her in the hog lot until mid-morning, when Mag came out to get her wedding chicken. She discovered him hiding, decided the joke had gone far enough and told him the truth. It seemed noteworthy that, even then, the hog lot would be a place he would turn to for refuge in time of distress.

To a small boy, the big barn Thomas Peden had built on his father's farm in 1857 looked "bigger than the State-house." Its hand-hewn beams, sixty feet long, twelve by fourteen inches thick, were made from poplars cut on the farm. Thomas wanted a big threshing floor with no center supports to be in the way as he drove the ring of horses around and around, treading out the wheat. The hayloft was supported on a truss set on heavy oaken beams that rested on stone masonry. The stone shafts were four feet square, also taken from the farm. On one of the posts the date "1857" was carved. The threshing floor was double so that it could never sag, although in its hundred years of use it carried the weight of thousands of tons of hay. The threshing floor was on a level with the ground at the front, so the wagons could haul the sheaves of wheat to the floor without any lifting. But under the threshing floor, open at the back and sides, was an earth-floored shelter for sheep.

The barn was so big and the log house so little, Walter said, that one time when the house was overflowing with Ragsdales and Pedens, and Walter was a little boy, the men and boys slept in the barn, and the women in the house. One of the visiting Ragsdale cousins, who later became ambassador to China and lived there thirty years, remembered the barn-sleeping with so much pleasure that he came back to visit the barn again when he was an old man.

Walter had an even better reason to remember the barn; when he was five years old he had an adventure in it. He and his seven-year-old brother Jesse had gone out to the barn to watch the threshing. Grandfather Jesse stood in the middle of the great floor holding a long whip and driving a ring of horses around and around, threshing out the grain. It was a big wheat harvest that year and Grandfather had brought in all his own horses including a pair of unbroken yearlings and all the horses he could borrow from the neighbors. Their running made a great clamor of dust and noise.

The two boys stood in the doorway fascinated and watching as Grandfather, in the center of the ring, cracked his whip and kept the horses going.

"After a while," Walter told me, "we decided it would be more exciting to be where Grandfather was than where we were." All his life Walter wanted to be on the inside of any farming excitement that was going on.

Behind the last team of horses there was always an interval of about two and a half minutes when there was a cleared space through the straw to the center of the floor. The boys watched their chance and started, of course without consulting Grandfather Jesse. The older brother got safely across, to the center, but the five-year-old slipped in the deep, tangled straw and fell face down, small arms spread out wide. It was impossible to stop the horses. On they came, running, although Grandfather Jesse immediately dropped the whip and started for the boy.

"You know," Walter said, telling the story, "a horse's hind legs are not straight. The horses jumped over me with their front feet—a horse will always try not to step on a person—but their crooked hind legs gave me, every time, a little roll toward the center of the circle." By the time he was thus pushed into the safe center he was unconscious, but "I didn't have a scratch on me." His legs and arms dangled limply as Jesse picked him up and carried him to the house to Nancy.

If the adventure taught Walter anything, it was only

that the Lord looks after farmers and children, and a farmer has to depend on his ingenuity in dealing with horses.

The town house to which Thomas first took his family was a brick house with a tall stairway and a hard, paved tile floor in the hall. Walter always remembered it for an experience he had soon after they moved into it. He was sitting on a step about halfway up the stairway one day, playing with a pet rabbit he had taken in from the farm. The rabbit leaped out of his arms suddenly, passed between the rungs of the railing and fell to the floor, breaking its neck. But it was from that house he started to school, which was a pleasant memory. His first school was an old one on East Franklin Street, but later a new building was erected at the end of Washington Street and he had to walk all the way across town to get to it. In rainy weather the unpaved streets were often deep in mud, and the boys all wore boots. "I always liked a rainy day, though," admitted Grand Pa 90+, "because on those days many of the children didn't come to school and I got to recite more often."

People sometimes dumped sawdust into the larger mud-holes out in front of their houses in the unpaved walkways. And since there were many people who kept a driving mare or milk cow in a barn or pen behind their houses, there was frequently some livestock in the streets.

Walter soon discovered one advantage about living in town; if anything exciting happened, a small boy would know it in time to get out and watch it happen. He had the faculty for getting to the right spot, at the right time. This is an hereditary trait a person either is born with or isn't, and all he can do about it is to indulge it if he has it, or wish for it if he hasn't.

"There was that time the circus came to town," eighty-six-year-old Walter told us. "It was Barnum and Bailey and they came into Spencer with two carloads of circus animals and people to perform. I was about ten years old then and I ran all the way down to the railroad tracks to watch the circus train come in. It stopped at the freight station, a few blocks short of the passenger station up on the square.

"The town was just full of people who had come down to see the circus pull in and the people get off the train."

The little boy watched awhile and then decided he could see more excitement if he were on the other side. "Grass and spectators are always greener on the other side, anyway," he said. It was a long way around the train and he was afraid he might miss something if he took time to go down to the last car and up on the other side, so he decided to climb between the cars. He took hold of a big iron bar he saw there and pulled himself up into the space between the cars, and then discovered the bar was in reality the handle of the lion's cage. The lion was lying there and not particularly hospitable.

"Did he get up?" I asked.

"No, but he growled at me," replied Walter, who all his life had a faculty for getting into danger and finding an ingenious, unexpected way to get out.

The little boy lost no time getting down on the other side, and was rewarded by getting to see dinner being served to the "common crew. They got coffee and sandwiches handed out from the car window," he said. "The big shots and star performers were to have dinner at the hotel uptown, a fact already well publicized by the hotel.

"These guests started walking uptown from the train. There were about forty of them, and among them was Barnum's famous midget, Tom Thumb. Already Tom had been the guest of kings and queens and Presidents. On his wedding trip Tom Thumb and his wife Lavinia had been entertained by President and Mary Todd Lincoln."

The circus people walked at their normal speed, and although Tom Thumb's midget legs moved fast he was not able to keep up, and presently he was walking alone. Close behind and closing in around him from all sides came a crowd of delighted, curious women, murmuring. Close to them was the equally fascinated little farm boy.

"The women kept talkin' about him," Walter said, "as if he couldn't hear them, or wasn't there. Things like 'Haint 'e little? Oh, haint 'e cute!' "

This walking-talking went on for some distance with Tom Thumb paying no attention and only trying to outwalk the women, and the women following faster.

"And then," said Walter, with deep delight at the memory, "suddenly Tom Thumb turned around and gave those women the awfulest string of cussin' I ever heard in my life." It was a performance not billed on the big flashy posters that were posted up all around the town, and Walter remembered it with greater pleasure than anything he saw at the circus performance inside the big tent.

♣   ♣   ♣

It was Thomas's wife, Sarah Beem, out at the McCormick's Creek farm, of course, who tore off the corner of an old letter and rolled it up around the pencil-thick swatch of Walter Peden's taffy-yellow, straight, thick baby hair. But years later it was pretty, romantic, family-conscious Clara who wrote the notation on it in blue ink on the outside, "Walter Peden's hair, two years old," and stowed it away in the lower part of the cupboard built into a corner of the dining room. This was in the Washington Street house where she lived for the last forty years of her life. In that cupboard she kept many other things: family photographs, old post-cards in a ragged album, a small autograph book with fan-shaped, faded blue velvet covers. There she had kept her first maternity dress, a rosebud-sprigged challis kimono-like garment which she gave me to make into a dress for her only granddaughter. There also she kept the luxurious velvet small blanket with which she comforted her babies when she wheeled them proudly in the fancy reed baby carriage along the street of the little town in which she then led a busy, happy social life. But the long embroidered muslin dresses and the fancy lace-trimmed petticoats the babies wore under them she kept in a flat shirtwaist box at the foot of her cherry four-poster bed. When the youngest baby was born, in the house that was later called the Beach house because Duane Beach bought it and made it into one of the showplaces of Spencer, Clara called all three of her older sons into her bedroom. Richard, the oldest boy, was about twelve years old. She had them sit solemnly on the shirtwaist box while she poetically told them "the story of life."

"By that time," wryly commented Richard some years later, "we could have told her more than she told us."

By the time I knew Clara's dining-room corner cupboard, it had become so filled with sentimental treasure that when you opened the doors, treasure came rolling out into your hands. And that was how, when we were emptying their house to sell, after their deaths two weeks apart one October, I came into possession of the swatch of ninety-three-year-old hair. The old handwriting on Sarah's scrap of letter was faded to the dim brown characteristic of old letters, but Clara Peden's rounded, smooth-flowing writing was still bright blue and legible. It was almost like receiving a loving communication from her that October day because, somehow, I had never seen the little packet before. The hair was still bright, though not as bright as the baby curls of Clara's own youngest son, Thomas Milton, nor those of her first grandson, Joe Richard.

In his college days and courting years and through his farming career, Walter parted his hair in the middle. It was thick and straight. By the time he had become Grand Pa 90+ it was gray but still comb-resistant. It fell down unparted, slightly like bangs, over his straight, high forehead, giving him the boyish, almost mischievous look his interviewers called "pixielike."

This pixielike look, together with a certain gleam in his luminous blue eyes behind their strongly magnifying glasses, was a clue to the fact that he had a story he wanted to tell right then.

"I'm in a reminiscent mood," he told Clara one Sunday afternoon when we were all sitting in the living room where the narrow tall windows reached almost to the floor, curtained with long lace curtains. Clara's favorite pictures—"The Song of the Lark," "Home of the Heron," "The Blue Boy," "Feeding Her Birds," and an English tapestry—hung over the horsehair-covered loveseat and chairs and the small marble-top table. On the table, beside the small white figurines she liked and a child's-size glass lamp which she kept filled with kerosene, were photographs of her three grandchildren, and an old (electrified) lamp with a round, brass bowl and brass feet and a round china globe.

"This happened," said Walter crossing his legs, "after

my father had moved to town. I was just a young man then and my father was, I guess, about middle-aged. Old Peter Abernathy was about ninety-eight years old then. He had been a country preacher in South Carolina and came to Indiana when he was around eighteen and lived here ever after. He never made much money, of course, traveling around preaching here and there. Nobody paid a preacher much in those days. By the time he was an old man, too old either to farm or preach, he didn't have many relatives left. He was then living with a niece and her husband on a farm about five miles out of Spencer. They didn't much enjoy having the old man around and they weren't very good to him.

"As a man grows older the memories from his childhood take on a peculiar, intensified charm, and old Peter Abernathy yearned to go back to South Carolina for a visit.

"His niece would say unsympathetically, 'What do you want to go back there for? There wouldn't be anybody you'd remember. Everything would be changed now.' And Peter would tell her, 'The old stone springhouse'd still be there.'

"He stayed with his niece and her husband only because he had no place else to go. The niece's husband was a penurious, vicious, hard drinker. He didn't like having Peter around, and when he was drunk he was really abusive to the old man."

One dark night about midnight, Walter said, there came a sudden violent knocking on Thomas Peden's front door.

Walter opened it and there stood old Peter Abernathy. Old and feeble as he was, he had walked five miles through the dark night, down a winding hill and into town, alone.

"I knowed your father when he was a nursin' babe," he told Walter, "and I want to see him now." Thomas Peden got out of bed and came downstairs. Peter explained that he had come because his drunken nephew had got a gun and was determined, finally, to kill him.

"Now I didn't come here because I was afraid to die," explained the old preacher gently. "I'm old and it's probably the best thing that could happen to me. But I didn't want Louie to have murder on his soul."

("A few years later," Walter explained wryly, "Louie did have three murders on his soul, anyway.")

"Now Thomas," said the old preacher, "you know I never wanted to be buried by the county. I've saved a little money and I want you to keep it for me and make sure I won't be buried by the county." He handed Thomas a little roll of money. It was $75 collected through goodness knows what sacrifices through his years of country preaching and farming and saved at goodness knows what effort by a homeless old man.

"But the story had a happy ending," Walter said. It was one of those coincidences that happen only in real life. On a small street not far from Hillside lived an elderly woman who had been married twice, the first time to one of Peter Abernathy's sons. "That husband and also the second one by whom she had three not-much-good sons had been dead for a long time, and she supported herself by taking in washing. She said she would gladly give the old man a good home and she did. Peter's last days were attended with tenderness from his one-time daughter-in-law and her son, no relation to Peter."

"Did he ever get back to see the springhouse in South Carolina?" I asked.

"No," said Walter, "there never was enough money for that. And anyway, he didn't live much longer. He didn't get to finish out his hundred years. But he had a good home and he was not buried by the county. My father saw to that."

♣   ♣   ♣

It was Walter's mother, Sarah Beem Peden, too, who gave him the big Bible he read from and frequently quoted, sometimes inaccurately, and in which, in his ninety-fifth year, he left the outline for his own funeral service. For this he asked that somebody read a poem he liked because he knew it was Abraham Lincoln's favorite, "Oh, why should the spirit of mortal be proud?" It fitted Walter in much the same way it fitted Lincoln. He was modest, but secretly he was proud, too, because he wanted to be worthy.

Lincoln was always one of Walter's sources of inspiration, in the good or in the hard times. Once he wrote me, "The time is 1 A.M., February 12. I could not sleep tonight, so thought to improve the time by writing you and getting an early start on celebrating the birth of Abraham Lincoln. The *Encyclopaedia Britannica*, thirty years after his death, described his Second Inaugural as being the greatest address ever uttered by mortal man and says it will live as long as the English language is spoken. Can you imagine how long that will be?

"The chief of the Census Bureau says it is not how long a person lives that counts, but how well he lives that marks his age; and that Abraham Lincoln lived more in his 56 years than Methuselah in his 969 tending his flocks in Judea.

"If I have written anything of interest to you I would wish I could lay it on your plate at breakfast this morning. Lovingly, Grand Pa at 90+."

A Methodist, though not fanatically religious, he never smoked and was not given to use of profanity. (That was reserved for times when ordinary speech had not enough horsepower.) He wrote, "Many and many a time I have attended church, listened to the sermon, come home and while Clara got dinner, read Lincoln's Second Inaugural and got more out of it than I had out of the sermon. So if you don't feel like going to church, read it. Your soul will be uplifted."

When he was graduated from Spencer High School, with an average grade of 90 and therefore listed with honor students in the Owen County newspaper of April, 1886, he

gave a commencement oration on John Brown. Proud of
him, his mother bought him a book then in high favor as
a gift from loving parents to children. It cost three dollars.
It was a large book with hard, brown covers and its title,
printed in gold lettering was *Mother, Home, and Heaven.*
It was a dull book of poems, essays, and short moralisms,
and there is no evidence that Walter ever read it. The choice
of this book for a lively, strong-willed boy of eighteen who
studied enough to make superior grades but spent most
of his time on the farm even then, simply indicates that
Walter's mother was one of the several women who did
not understand the capacity and determination of this man.

"He was no sainted angel," his son Tom told me once
when we were discussing Grand Pa 90+. "Remember, that
blue stein on the mantel is what he won playing cards when
he was in college."

In the fall of 1886 he enrolled at Asbury College. This
scholarly institution in adjoining Putnam County offered
intellectual lectures, debates, and programs almost nightly.
Walter's cousins, Fred and Lizzie Pochin, made brilliant
records there. But Asbury's scholarly blessings made little
impression on Walter Peden; he was more interested in Jack
Greene and Jim Egnor, who drove the mules that pulled
Greencastle's streetcars over the college town. The two
men later came to Spencer and started a little general store
which grew and prospered along with other town business.

Their families, like Walter's, were among the older settlers of the community.

Walter never mentioned any of his courses or professors or any scholarly experiences at Asbury. He always said (though he sometimes laughed when he confessed it) he considered the year a waste of good time he could have spent farming.

He never had any real enthusiasm for encouraging his own sons to go to college, although two of them did go for a year or so. But as Grand Pa+, he wrote to his oldest grandson, Joe, then attending Franklin College: "I was interested to read that you plan to attend Purdue next year. May I suggest you major in animal husbandry. Your grandfather often advised me that there was twice the reward in livestock husbandry that there is in crop production. In farming, one ounce of brains is worth a pound of brawn. The field of animal husbandry is much wider for the use of brains than the field of crop production is. With corn at $1.15 a bushel I was able this year, June and July, to put 11,000 pounds of gain on a lot of hogs at a cost of $7.27 per hundred weight. It took me seventy years to learn how to do it. While I was aided greatly by the agricultural colleges, I had to add the last vital spark on my own studies."

A month earlier he had written the grandson, "I can appreciate your lack of enthusiasm for college life. While I made the grades all right, as I look back some seventy years, I believe my year of college life was the least fruitful of all my ninety-two years. Born of a race of farmers, I took to farming like a duck to water. I think your comment on machinery is entirely correct. The depreciation and capital investment in machinery is deplorable. There is much less depreciation and more increase in value in livestock investment skillfully managed. If a farmer is mentally alert and equally gifted in crop production and livestock management, the livestock will return twice the investment compared to the crop investment. Backed by my seventy years of experience, for profit I would rather have the profits of the feedlot than of the crop production on a farm."

When his three grandchildren (Tom's son Mark and Dick's son and daughter) did go to college he was proud of them. His granddaughter started her college career at Walter's own alma mater. When she was still in high school he wrote her, "I note with pride you were second in your class of 269. You must be a throwback to your great-grandfather, Thomas Peden. Attorney Willis Hickam once told me that when my father was over seventy-five he was the most perfect witness Willis had ever had in a courtroom; his testimony was clear as a bell and no amount of cross-examination could shake it."

♣   ♣   ♣

Walter began his farming when horses and mules were the power for farm machinery and also mostly for transportation. Eventually he drove a car and shipped his livestock to market by truck, but he never had a tractor on his farm until he was in his eighties, and he never operated it himself.

In his mid-forties he had an adventure with a high-spirited driving mare that called for the use of all his ingenuity. He was not a large man. When he said he was five feet seven inches tall, people looked skeptical, and he never weighed more than 130 pounds, even in his youthful years when he ate heartily. What he lacked in physical strength he made up for, always, by ingenuity and a wiry, physical courage.

He was driving down Morgan Street one afternoon when the high-spirited driving horse became frightened and began to run away, kicking wildly. At every bound it kicked back savagely with both hind feet. It had already kicked away the dashboard and Walter knew he was going to be next. He threw himself to the buggy floor, and when the horse kicked again, he grabbed its left hind foot and held on tenaciously while the terrified animal ran three blocks farther on three legs before it stopped, exhausted. Walter, also exhausted, fell out of the buggy but was soon revived by the quickly gathering crowd of congratulators. The incident was written up in local and state newspapers; he received a letter of congratulations from a man in Washington, D.C., and fifty years later the incident was mentioned again in the "Fifty Years Ago" column of a Chicago newspaper.

In those farming years Peden Brothers were making money buying and selling horses and mules and exhibiting purebred Clydesdales in some of the fairs. By the time I knew Walter, the showbox, in which the purebreds' harness and brushes were carried to fairs, had been demoted and sat on a sandy field out behind the toolshed on the Rattlesnake Creek farm. I retrieved it and used it in the house to keep quilts and blankets in.

"Did I ever tell you," Walter asked one afternoon, "about Berry, the insane horse we had? It was in the days of livery stables. Berry was a magnificent animal, except that he was crazy."

At that time Walter had a partner, John Wilson, in the horse and mule business. Walter supplied the money and John went everywhere locating and buying the stock. "He rode in train cabooses to save money," said Walter, "and slept in the fire station. The firemen liked him and let him sleep there.

"One winter we had ninety mules on the farm. We kept the red-hot sales possibilities in town, in the red barn on Morgan Street. It had sliding doors with a small opening door in front. Whenever Wilson took a prospective buyer into the barn he picked up a buggy whip and cracked it, and talked loud and touched up every mule as he went past it. He said, 'I don't want 'em standin' there on three legs, sleepin', when I show 'em to somebody.'

"John was a good horseman, but even he didn't know

what to do with Berry. Berry was gentle as a dog, wouldn't bite or kick, but he just wouldn't stand tied to anything. We tried to work him, hitched him up with a big, gentle old mare. He just turned around in the harness and threw his front legs over her shoulders. The next time we hitched him up he laid down. We couldn't get him up. We tried sticks, pitchforks, everything we could think of. We even hitched another team to him and pulled him along the ground, but not very far because we were afraid we'd tear his hide. We unhitched the team and went off and left him on the ground, and Berry got up.

"We bought a horse trainer's book and studied it; that didn't help either. Berry wouldn't stand tied if we went off and left him. He would stand there while we watched, but he always fought the rope as soon as we left. Once we tied his rope to a rafter above his head and left him. When we came back thirty minutes later he had got one foot over the rope and was hanging there, with his head up.

"Hitched to a buggy, he simply began to run backward and there was no stopping him."

"It sounds to me as if he had claustrophobia," I suggested, and Walter stopped to laugh.

Once a man from a livery stable in Bloomington came to buy a horse. John and Walter showed him all they had except Berry. The stableman saw Berry, a fine-looking animal, and thought they were trying to hold something back from him. Immediately he wanted Berry. Walter told him,

"No. We won't sell him. You can't work him. He's crazy."
If he had tried he couldn't have thought of a better way to
whet the man's appetite for buying the horse.

"The livery stableman thought he was dealing with a
couple of simple farmers who just didn't know how to handle
horses," said Walter. "He insisted on buying Berry, so we
sold him finally, but with the stipulation that if he took him,
he couldn't bring him back." They tied Berry to the livery-
man's buggy and the happy new owner drove away proudly,
confident it was the farmers, not the horse, that were crazy
and he, a horse expert, would show them.

"About a month later I saw him," Walter told me, "I
asked him about Berry."

The man said, "Don't mention him! I don't ever want to
hear his name again!" In the livery stable there were two
rows of horses, with a row of buggies in between. The first
time he hitched Berry to a buggy the horse started backing
and they couldn't stop him. He backed into every buggy in
the row and wrecked every one of them.

♣   ♣   ♣

After leaving Asbury College for love of farming, Walter
did not go immediately to the farm, but spent a couple of
years in the West, especially in New Mexico, where he
worked with cattlemen and ranch hands; and with his customary insatiable interest in what was going on he picked

up a good deal of information about Billy the Kid, from talking to Pat Garrett, and made it a point to see the courthouse in which the famous gunman had carved his initials. Walter endured the record blizzard of 1888 when the cowhands slept in a log cabin and snow sifted in through the cracks upon their blankets. "It was the worst blizzard that ever hit the West," he liked to say proudly. "All through the night we heard cattle thumping their heads against the cabin, having drifted in the blizzard. Cattle move with the storm. Horses put their heads against it and go into the wind and ultimately come out better than cattle. In the morning we could hardly get the cabin door open; a steer had drifted against it, got down and couldn't get up. It was dead by morning."

Two fellow citizens from Spencer were in the West at the same time and place, Walter said. The sheriff was one, and Dr. John Sloan the other. The morning after the blizzard Dr. Sloan had to amputate the leg of a young cowboy, and the only place to do it was at the butcher shop. Dr. Sloan gave him some money and said, "Go get two bottles of whisky, one for the boy and one for me." Walter always related happily that the boy lived and was even able to ride horseback and drive cattle afterward, by using a special kind of stirrup.

The sheriff was a man Walter had known in "Jerden" Village in Owen County. "There had been a great deal of horse stealing and the cattlemen were pretty much worked up over it. One rancher had eleven stolen in one night. They organized a posse and went after the horse thieves. When they picked up a trail they were still so mad they were determined to take the law into their own hands.

"They finally caught up with the three thieves—an old man with a white beard, a young man about thirty, and a boy fifteen or sixteen. The posse took them to the nearest cottonwood tree and told them they were going to hang them," Walter related. "The old man said, 'It doesn't make much difference if you hang me. I don't have much time to live anyway, but this boy is young. He's made a mistake, but give him another chance. He has life ahead of him.' "

Walter said, "I decided I didn't want any part of the execution and I left. They hanged all three of the thieves. It was the way they did in the West."

A happier story was of the morning when the cowboys, waking in their cabin, saw three men riding toward them, and one cowboy said, "Here comes the preacher and two men with him." Someone asked, "How do you know it's a preacher?" and the cowboy said, "Nobody else rides a horse like a preacher!"

But of all the things he saw or did in those years in the West none made as great an impression on the young Hoosier farmer as the epitaph he read on the gravestone of a cowboy. He quoted it afterward many times in conversation and letters.

One cold December day in 1958 he wrote me, "I have not

been in my usual health for some weeks. For the first time in my life I did not feel like going downtown. Nothing serious, just the burden of ninety-one years of living.

"Summing up these years I think of the cowboy. He had been a cowhand for many years and had made many a drive; had driven 3,000 steers from Old Mexico to Montana. He had helped move his herd across the great rivers from the Rio Grande to the Powder River in Montana. The time had come to die. His fellow cowhands asked what they should inscribe on his gravestone. His reply was: 'Just say, "He done his d————." '

"This is what I have done for ninety-one years. With love to you and all, Grand Pa at 91 +."

He mentioned this epitaph so many times I think perhaps he sometimes felt he would like having it on his own gravestone in Riverside Cemetery.

♣ ♣ ♣

One reason Walter's eyes always looked so large and blue and luminous was that one always saw them magnified by the thick lenses he had to wear. Early in his middle years his sight began to fail from cataract on both eyes. Even before his oldest son was out of high school Walter had been almost blind at one time. In that year, in order to know what kind of stand his planted corn was making, he went out to the field and crawled along one row, counting the distance and number of sprouted grains in each hill.

He finally had one eye operated on; the operation was successful and the doctor gave him instructions about taking care of the eye, but he neglected to follow the instructions and consequently lost the sight of that eye again. In later years he had to have an operation on the other eye. It also was successful but he always had to wear highly magnifying glasses. to read with, and in addition he used a reading glass held in his hand. The frames of his spectacles made no pretense of being fashionable. They were round, silverish metal and the shafts held them on by curving behind the ears. When the nose piece broke, or the shafts broke or bore too heavily on his ear, he wrapped the place in layers and layers of adhesive tape until finally the spectacles looked like some kind of structure rather than mere spectacles.

When he was telling a story that deepened his feelings, either of tenderness or merriment, his eyes looked even larger. Telling his best-loved stories, his voice took on a velvety understatement; the more moving the story seemed, the more simply he spoke. Telling a funny story, he had a habit of looking down until he got to the explosive point of the story, then suddenly looking up and into the listeners' eyes and exploding into a quick little laugh himself. At such times his eyes turned up slightly at the outer corners. It was as definite as the curve of a mouth in a smile. His second son, Paris, had eyes that did the same.

Paris was killed by the accidental discharge of his own

gun one Sunday morning within sight of the kitchen on the Rattlesnake Creek farm on which Dick and I were then living. He was only twenty-six and Clara never fully recovered from the grief of it. When Paris didn't come back as soon as he should have, we had all gone out and walked and called to him. It was Dick's unhappy lot to find him lying face down and dead on the grass beside the fence which he had started to cross, having first carefully laid down his loaded gun. It was Walter, however, who when he heard the news threw himself on the ground and drew himself into a little curve of suffering, like a small, wounded wild creature, and lamented, "Oh, what shall I tell his mother?"

Years later, at Thanksgiving dinner at Dick's house, he said quietly, "In eighty years you get accustomed to grief."

During Christmas week one year, we went to the house on Washington Street and brought Walter and Clara to have dinner with us at the farm. It was a beautiful, still December morning, the farm fields here were snowswept and serene. Along the road that runs past the back side of this farm, and is the short-cut between our community and Spencer, we saw a deer in our clover field. The children eagerly insisted on being let out in the hope of getting close to it, while the four parents watched. The deer bounded away, a lovely, graceful, fleet creature, leaping easily, and was soon out of sight beyond the snowy slope. Perhaps it was the sight of this grace and the white morning that inspired Walter's memory. At the dinner table he told us the story of old Mr. Clay and the white heifer.

"All this happened a long time ago, fifty years or more, I reckon," he said. "I was a young man then and had sold a lot of fine cattle on the Indianapolis market. I was feeling pretty good, of course. Young, you know. And sitting around talking with John Clay, the head of the commission house."

Mr. Clay had come to America from Scotland where his father had lived all his life on a cattle farm. In Scotland, Mr. Clay told Walter, the stock farms were large and might change hands two or three times a year, but the tenants did not change when the landowners did. They went right ahead, looking after the cattle and land in the same way under the new ownership. When a tenant got too old and frail to work any more he did not leave the farm. The landowner was expected to supply him with a little cottage, a small vegetable garden, and other such small comforts necessary to him for the rest of his life.

John Clay's father had reached that age. As with all dedicated farmers, his love of livestock farming was undiminished. In particular, there was one young white heifer for which the old cattleman had great hopes. He knew his farming days were almost harvested, but told everyone he wanted to live until the white heifer "found her calf."

Every morning through that cold Scottish winter the old man took his cane and went out to see the white heifer. She was gentle and promising; every day he thought she looked

1 4 8

more strong and beautiful. Her white-coated skin was pliable, the hair thick and slightly curling at her face and over the shoulders. The old man's visit to her was his sustaining daily adventure. One morning, to his great joy, he discovered the heifer had safely calved in the night. It was a good calf; the white heifer made a good mother. Old Mr. Clay returned to the house, satisfied, and the next morning he quietly died.

It was one of Walter's favorite stories. His voice was velvety by the time he got to the last words.

*   *   *

In his farm operations Walter had to be the leader; he could not tolerate any interference with his plans, nor delegate any of the farm authority to his partner, even one who had money invested in the business. But in other interests he was a follower, more of a hero-worshipper than an actual doer himself. He admired men of military career, yet he never served in the army; he admired financiers and statesmen, yet never was willing to hold public office and only reluctantly a place of authority on a church or school board.

In his last few years he developed a great admiration for Alexander Hamilton, to whom, he said, the country owes a great deal for Hamilton's development of the United States treasury system and the dollar and Hamilton's help on the Constitution. In 1960 we gave Walter a newly published biography of Alexander Hamilton, and after he read it he wrote me, "I regret that I could not have read the story of Alexander Hamilton in my youth and had all the years of an octogenerian to think it over.

"Hamilton's government was, and still is, a republic. It took me ninety years to learn the difference between a republic and a democracy. In a democracy the minority have no rights. In a republic the minority have about as much or as many rights as the majority.

"It was rank heresy for Wilson to claim that the American government was a democracy. All my life until Wilson's day I never heard of the U.S. being a democracy. Our form of government since its foundation has been a republic and is yet. Notwithstanding Wilson's ignorance of our Constitution." (Also notwithstanding Walter's wife's being a Democrat and a great admirer of Woodrow Wilson, whose framed photograph she set in one of the glass-doored cabinets in which she kept her most treasured old glass goblets and compotes.)

One of Walter's real-life heroes was his uncle, Stanley Meade, a Civil War veteran who lived on Hillside Avenue and made his attractive back yard a refuge for birds. Stanley Meade's wife, Amy, and Walter's mother, Sarah, were sisters.

Stanley Meade had run away and joined the Union army when he was fourteen years old, misrepresenting his age. He didn't really look more than fourteen in the photograph where he stood holding his musket, which was several inches

taller than he was. He was a color bearer and served in some
of the bloodiest and most important battles, was captured,
and spent some time in Andersonville prison. His Civil War
experiences were the high point of his whole life. He was a
gentle, lovable, and stately-looking old man. In civilian life,
every year after the war, he put on his Union army uniform
for all the patriotic and Memorial Day parades. Walter
spent many happy hours listening to Stanley's war stories
and could tell them himself in detail afterward. Stanley
Meade was president of the Riverside Cemetery Association
and managed it well. At his death Walter was appointed to
this responsibility, and with his usual thoroughness, he informed himself completely of all the financial and legal
aspects of the care of cemeteries. Once he wrote me, "An
important matter on which I wish to write you is the care
and maintenance of the cemeteries of Indiana. Perhaps you
are not aware that the statute governing the care of cemeteries reads that it is the duty of the county to appropriate
a sum relative to the size of the county, to care for and maintain every cemetery in it. Is your local cemetery receiving
any money from the county commissioners?

"Every year the Owen County board of commissioners
publishes the amounts the various cemeteries receive in
Owen County." He greatly admired the somewhat unusual
system the Riverside association had, by which a permanent
income had been built up, preserving the capital and using
only the interest on its invested money for its maintenance

The "Roll of Honor" is a plaque in the Riverside Cemetery commemorating the Owen County men serving in various national wars. One of the names is that of Peter Withem, a Revolutionary War soldier who was one of Walter's heroes. He was, in fact, one of Spencer's heroes. In 1960, for some reason, the town suddenly became Peter Withem-conscious and held a parade and program in his honor. There was a speaker, band concert, flights of planes and "flying boxcars" and marching units of army bands, color guards, and Legion veterans. Peter Withem would have been proud if he could have been there and someone could have convinced him all this was in his honor.

"Now there were two Peter Withems," explained Walter afterward. "The father was old Revolutionary Peter—we called him that because he had been with General George Washington at Valley Forge and fought in other Revolutionary War battles. He died in 1845 on his farm three miles west of Spencer. He was ninety-two and had asked to be buried wrapped in a winding sheet. The snow was deep on the ground. John Hyden (Homer's father, and probably that's why Homer always liked to put his Spirit of '76 fife and drum corps into a parade) brought Peter's body to town on an ox sled for burial in the old part of Riverside. They gave him a military funeral with fife and drums and the firing of a final gun salute.

"A good many years later they wanted to put a marker on his grave and they got to diggin' around the records to find out just where the grave was. In all that time there hadn't been any marker for old Revolutionary Peter. They could find only two people who had been at the military funeral and they weren't much help—they'd only been fifteen-year-old boys then, but were grown men now and couldn't agree when they went to the cemetery to point out the exact spot Peter was buried in. One said it was in the northeast corner and the other said it was the southeast corner. They couldn't agree, so poor old Peter didn't get any marker.

"But there's a gold star after his name on the Roll of Honor because I had one put there. When they were making up the list I just knew nobody was going to buy a star for old Peter Withem, so I did.

"Peter's son was named Peter Withem, too. I never knew old Revolutionary Peter, of course, and when I knew his son, Uncle Peter as we all called him, he was an old man.

"His farm joined ours, and every year I went up and made a call on Uncle Peter and Aunt Mary. They lived in a one-room log cabin that had a big fireplace and no windows at all. One hot July day I went to pay my annual call, and Aunt Mary was cooking beans in a big iron kettle in the fireplace. A log was stuck into the fireplace and that end was burning, but the other end extended away out into the room. I said, 'Aunt Mary, would you rather cook on the fireplace or on the range?' She said, 'On the range, but Peter's too old to cut wood so I cook on the fireplace.'

"Living in the one-room cabin, they had raised ten boys and all of 'em that were old enough had served in the Union army. There wasn't any stairway in the cabin, but in one corner some cleats had been nailed across a pole and that was the way you went up into the attic. Uncle Peter had gone up there to take his nap, Aunt Mary said, because the flies weren't so bad up there. He came down, and we took a couple of chairs outside and leaned back against the cabin to talk. Uncle Peter had a little scraggly farm, a garden, a cow, and some chickens that were walking around in the yard that afternoon.

"I said, 'Uncle Peter, what do you feed your chickens?' He said, 'Nothing. In summer they catch bugs and eat grass and lay a few eggs.' What they ate in winter, I guess, was their own lookout.

"I asked him how long he had lived in the cabin and he said, 'Me and the old woman come here in 1836 as soon as we was married and we've lived here ever since.'

"There was a hole in the front door and I asked him about it. He said, 'Well, one of the boys was home on a furlough in 1865 and he was cleaning his gun and it went off and made that hole.'

"This visit was in 1896. Bryan was running for President on the free-silver issue and Uncle Peter was impressed with him. Up to that time he had been a rank Republican but he was mightily impressed with Bryan's free-silver speech . . . you know it ended, 'You shall not crucify mankind upon a cross of gold!' Uncle Peter knew the presidential issues of the day and discussed them with intelligence and a lot of spirit. And he was patriotic . . . all those sons in the Civil War, you know. He was very proud of his father's Revolutionary record.

"He had one son who was blind and he said he was going to leave the farm to him because he figured he'd need it worse than the other boys; they could get along.

"With all those sons in the Union army, naturally Uncle Peter had strong feelings during the war. There was a schoolhouse not far from his cabin in those days and it was generally suspected that several men of the neighborhood were secretly allied with the Knights of the Golden Circle. They held meetings in the schoolhouse and nobody knew what was really going on. But Peter suspected and it made him mad as a hornet. He made plans to catch them.

"The schoolhouse was set on a hill so that the front of it was right on the ground, but the back of it was high enough above the ground level for a man to crawl under it. Peter crawled under it one night and listened and found out his suspicions were right. So he talked John Hyden into going with him, and they went back the next night. The men meeting in the schoolhouse had posted a guard in front and when he saw John and Peter he ran inside and locked the door. Peter was so mad he shot through the door. The shot splintered the door and the Knights swarmed out through the windows. John said, 'Peter, you mighta killed

155

somebody, shootin' in there that way.' Peter said, 'I wouldn't 'a cared if I had.'"

♣   ♣   ♣

By 1903, when Walter married, he was already well launched on an expanding farming career managing three of his father's farms. Howard was managing the Rattlesnake Creek farm. Their oldest brother, Jesse, worked in the bank. Walter and Howard produced and sold livestock, especially hogs. They sold and delivered a hundred tons of hay a year to livery stables and to people in town who had delivery horses or driving horses or a milk cow in town but no hayfields. It was long before mechanical haybalers were available, of course; the loose hay was forked out of the field onto the horse-drawn wagon and loaded from the wagon into the town haylofts. The wagon was often higher than the barn loft and therefore required difficult down-lifting.

Howard said that in those days Walter's idea of a light Saturday afternoon at the Pottersville farm seven miles out of Spencer was to start to town at noon, with seven wagonloads of hay to be delivered and unloaded with pitchforks. The wagons were all loaded from the hayfields on a Saturday morning. The hired men drove the wagons in, unloaded, bought their groceries, and drove back home—a fourteen-mile trip in all, from Saturday noon on.

In appearance, Howard greatly resembled his grand-

156

father, Levi Beem. He was short, stout, heavy-featured, and bald in his later years. He liked to dress up and seem leisurely after a day's work at the farm. He spoke formally, but said he always felt the lack of a college education. In all the final farm decisions he acceded to Walter's authority. When Walter's sons were old enough to work on the farm, Howard expected a good deal of them, but taught them more about farming than Walter took time to teach them. Walter, restless, energetically intent on his own plans, was impatient. If there happened to be a patch of bull nettles in the way of a barefooted boy who was sent to "head off" a runaway cow, it made no difference. Walter expected the boy to wade right into the nettles.

In summer, when the boys went with the men to the farm every day, Clara packed their lunches and Walter's together. At noon Walter always opened the dinner basket. If there was pie, it was on top, of course, and he picked up every piece and bit the tip off of it before he set it aside to be eaten at the end of the meal. That habit annoyed his sons almost unbearably, but they never had the courage to demand that he stop it. He was tyrannical in those hard-working, tense years. The boys could have appealed to their mother, who was loving and indulgent. They could have asked her to pack the lunches separately, but they all knew she disliked packing any lunch at all, and often packed a light one, but always gave them a good supper at night. In those mornings, when she got the family breakfasts, she baked biscuits every morning. She kept the flour in a drawer of the kitchen cabinet. When she baked biscuits, she first put some lard directly into the flour (having salt and baking powder in it) in the drawer, worked it with her fingers, then poured in milk and kept on mixing and finally lifted out a ball of wonderful, light biscuit dough that baked into delicious, flaky browned biscuits. And often she sent biscuits-and-sugar sandwiches to the farm. When her son Richard was married he told his wife, "Don't learn to bake biscuits; I was brought up on biscuits, good biscuits, too."

Howard's mother, and later his wife, packed his lunch separately. "In the afternoons," Dick said, "we raided Howard's dinner bucket. He knew it and didn't care. I think Grandma used to put in some extra for us, maybe."

At home, Walter was often worried and irritable. When the boys came to kiss him good night, interrupting his reading, he rattled his newspaper impatiently. If one of them ate an apple in the living room after supper, the noise annoyed him. He never gave any of his sons a calf, pig, or colt because he always felt that half of all the stock and feed belonged to his brother Howard. For by the time the boys were old enough to go to the farm, the bank had been forced into receivership and Walter and Howard were joint owners of the Rattlesnake Creek farm. The other farms, and all the livestock, had been sold to pay the bank's depositors.

Walter's oldest son, Richard, was four years old when the bank failed. "We had a wall telephone in the kitchen," he said years later. "The day the bank closed, Walter came home and sat down on a chair under the telephone and cried." All the stock was loaded in Spencer and shipped to Worthington to be sold because Walter thought it would sell better there than locally. He went along to the sale, and the administrator paid him $25 to get into the sale ring and describe the stock as it was brought in for sale. Some years later the older brother, Jesse, moved his family to Indianapolis and lived there the rest of his life. Walter and Howard remained in Spencer and went into partnership on the Rattlesnake Creek farm. It was natural that Walter would be edgy. He was faced with the financial problems of that agricultural day which could have made a farmer edgy. Besides, he had to adjust to one farm after having managed three. There was always the danger of flood in spring and market loss at any time. He had a house to buy and keep up in town, a family of four boys to bring up—though they should have been considered an asset to the farm operation—and he had a partner's ideas to subdue. The farm was a hard mistress, and Walter gave it, for the rest of his life, his devoted attention. He was inherently an optimist, never carried a grudge, and in the hard, nervous, harassing farming years I suspect probably the greatest source of comfort to him was the work itself, by which he put his farming beliefs into execution against all opposition.

♣   ♣   ♣

A few weeks before his death in 1962 he said, unasked, "Well, I guess if I had my life to live over I'd still be a farmer."

♣　　♣　　♣

Farming, always a hazardous occupation, was just as full of danger in the horse-and-buggy days as in the mechanized era. When his oldest son, Dick, was about eleven years old and helping on the farm one summer, Walter injured his left hand badly. With the help of one hired man, Raleigh Ooley, Dick and Walter were stacking hay in the upper barn, using the track and hayfork, which is a savage-looking prong even when it is hanging still. Walter was in the loft, receiving and placing the huge forkfuls of hay as the rope pulled them in, along the track at the comb of the barn. It was a hot day and, as always, hotter in the ·hayloft. Walter lost his balance and started to fall out of the loft. Instinctively he caught at the moving hay rope which dragged his hand to the pulley at the loft door, tearing the flesh off two fingers.

He had to come down a rickety ladder, and by the time he reached the ground floor he was bloody and yelling for Raleigh. Dick, terrified, kept asking Raleigh, "Will 'e die? Will 'e die?" Raleigh, about as high-strung as Walter, finally shouted, "Well, no, he won't die!" All this time they were getting Ginger, the patient old driving mare, out from the stall and hitching her to the buggy. Raleigh took Walter into town to Dr. Sloan, but the eleven-year-old boy stayed on the farm working and worrying and wondering all afternoon how the fatherless family would get along.

"We lived in the goat house then," Dick has said, "and when I got home that evening Walter was sitting on the porch, reading a newspaper, and his hand was in a sling against his chest." From that time on, even after his hand healed, when he walked along the street Walter held his left hand close to his chest, with the elbow bent as if protecting his hand, and his head slightly bowed as if talking to himself, as in fact he often was.

♣   ♣   ♣

His first son was born in 1904, and by the time the baby was old enough to sit up, Walter, with a kind of teasing, practical ingenuity brought in an enormously oversized horse collar from the farm so Clara could set the baby in it, a kind of forerunner to the modern play pen. It probably fanned the child's inherited farming yearnings so that in time he took over Howard's half of the farm.

As soon as they could, the boys all began going out to the farm. They all loved it, growing up in the family illusion that Rattlesnake Creek farm was superior land and, if not conquerable, was at least tameable.

On hot summer days when the boys were working at the farm, Walter allowed them half an hour to go swimming in the pool in Rattlesnake Creek below the hired man's little house. "We never had a watch," Dick said later, "and we worried so much about being late getting back to the field that we never really got the enjoyment out of swimming."

By the time he had become Grand Pa+, or actually before, Walter had mellowed. Most people are more indulgent toward their grandchildren than toward their children. It is not a matter of loving the grandchildren more, nor of having less a feeling of responsiblity for them. It is, in a way, a tentative chance to recapture something. And then there is a natural affinity between a first and a third generation. Walter tolerated things from his three grandchildren that he would not have tolerated at all from his sons.

Once when we had been visiting there in the afternoon he decided for some reason not to come to the door to tell us good-bye. His grandson Joe thought he ought to come and finally said, "If you don't Grandpa, I'll pick you up and carry you. And I can do it." Walter laughed, replied, "I know you can, Joe," and came. And he endured the children's jokes with real pleasure. One Sunday afternoon, having just acquired a de-scented skunk for a pet, we took her over to Spencer to show her to Walter and Clara, who had not yet heard about her. Joe opened the front door quietly and let Petunia go in by herself. She ambled swiftly, close to the floor in natural skunkly gait, toward Walter on the sofa in the front parlor, and he jumped up with a roar. When Clara mildly called in, "What's the matter?" he yelled, "There's a skunk in here!" but he quickly forgave us all for our hilarious laughter at his expense when we came in, and Joe explained.

He was particularly fond of his only granddaughter, Dick's daughter Carol. In his later years he made a point of giving her the pearl-handled knives and sterling silver forks that had been a wedding gift to him and Clara. He wrote, "I only regret I have delayed the gift until there is so little left to give you." He often mentioned her especially in his letters, but once, when she was four years old and suddenly threw herself impetuously into his arms, he was genuinely embarrassed, laughed, and didn't know what to do with her.

"I would never have let him get away with that biting off the pie points," Joe told his father, but Dick only said gently, "He was different then." There was a great difference, too, between Dick's viewpoint as a father and Walter's viewpoint as a father.

♣   ♣   ♣

When he was ninety-two years old, Walter led Dick's white Shorthorn bull, Jupiter, in a parade at the Owen County Fair, and we were all watching, proud and somewhat apprehensive. It was a long parade down a hot street, but Walter stepped along briskly with long steps, confident, happy in the showmanship of fine cattle. The big bull followed along, tireless and biddable. When the parade was over and I ran out to congratulate Walter, I took his hand to lead him to the shade. He laughed and said, "You make me feel so decrepit," and then gaily told me about Annie, the hired man's wife, and the time Walter had a good bull which he exhibited at a series of fairs.

It was about fifty years earlier, he said, but fairs were a good deal the same as they are now. "Judges, too," he added, chuckling. He had several good Shorthorn cattle that year and a Scotch herdsmen named Andy. Together they had made a tour of county fairs, scooping up a good share of the prize money and ribbons.

At one fair Andy came to Walter after making a tour of the competitive entries, and said, "We're going to get beat today. There's a man here with a lots better bull than we've got." He went away to find the hired man and get the bull groomed for the show ring. Presently he came back smiling. "I've figured out how we can win today," he said. "We'll let Annie lead the bull in. She's pretty. The judges won't see anything but Annie and we'll win."

"It happened just as he said," laughed Walter; "the judges just walked right over and handed the ribbon to Annie. And the man with the other bull was mad as a hornet. He had a much better bull and he knew it."

After the parade was over and the white bull was back in the tent, Dick and Walter sat down on a cot there, where Joe slept at night in order to be where he could take care of his fair entries. Dick told Walter he'd had an offer for one of his best steer calves and was undecided what to do about it.

Walter exclaimed at once, "Sell it! Sell it! You can go to Franklin and buy another one."

Dick said, "But this is an extra good calf and both of our children want a good steer to show at the 4-H fairs, too."

Walter exclaimed impatiently, "Sell it, sell it! Why, you could get $250 for it. You can't afford to take that kind of money out of the business." It was a basic philosophy he had about farming. Farming came first and everything else after that. It was indicative of the difference between his farming philosophy and Dick's. In Dick's system, a boy's love of farming was an important, long-growing crop to be tenderly nourished and cultivated. In Walter's system, he would have spared no expense or effort to finish a steer to perfection, would have given a pig whatever feed, supplement, or shelter it needed toward yielding a profit. "It explains," said Dick at breakfast the next morning, "why he always sold the best calves and the colts we liked best and all those things."

It explains also why nobody should ever have expected him really to delegate any of the authority of the farm to someone else. As, for example, in the two years when Dick and I lived at the Rattlesnake Creek farm and owned half of it and Dick worked in town, Walter was still the manager. To me, daughter of an orchardist, a farm meant vines, brambles, fruit trees. I planted strawberries on a sandy, vine-taken hillside that had not been cultivated for fifty years and had become a squatters' paradise for cutworms. The strawberries took hold and yielded abundantly, but raspberries planted in the same hillside winter-killed both years. I had planted grapevines in an unused small hog lot adjacent to the strawberry patch, and cleaned out the long-abandoned hog house for a garden house. The grapes had been in a year and were growing well, and a row of zinnias next to them were prospering giantly when Walter suddenly decided to replevin the hog house and lot. Without consulting anyone, he sent Dick's hired man to dig up the grapevines and transplant them elsewhere. But in order to make the morning pleasant for me, he came to the kitchen and did make it pleasant by a long, absorbing discussion of Abraham Lincoln, while the hired man dug secretly, screened by the giant zinnias.

This did not mean Walter did not love me. It meant only that he regarded me as one of his children and therefore my farm plans were secondary to his farm plans. We were always good friends. He was unfailingly courteous, affectionate, and admiring of me, and also, I think, of the wives of his sons Mark and Tom.

♣   ♣   ♣

One of the problems of Walter's creek-threatened farm was the groundhogs digging in the levee that to some extent held the water off the fields. Walter and Howard fought groundhogs for years, poking gas-saturated rags into their dens. And yet, surprisingly, the groundhog of weather repute, "Mr. G. Hog," as Walter called him in letters, was one of his favorite and most often mentioned characters. In his letters he seemed to have almost a neighborly attitude and respect for the groundhog.

Once he wrote, "The groundhog is quite a VIP in Indiana history. A few years ago the Indiana legislature in joint session came up with the decision that February second was Groundhog Day. So Mr. G. Hog shares with George Washington, Abraham Lincoln, Charles Darwin, W. E. Gladstone, and many others whose birthdays are in February."

In another year, still thinking of the groundhog: "Sometimes I think I might have made my mark if I had been born in February, too. Valentine on February fourteenth and Mr. G. Hog on the second.

"Naturalists tell us there is one groundhog to every acre in Indiana.

"I have a book that shows there are 29,000 persons in the U.S. that are ninety-five years or older. That averages one to every 27,000 people in America. Mark Twain wrote that anyone living to be a hundred years old was generally not known for doing anything else. So I do not want to live to be a hundred. Grand Pa 92+."

But one other year he wrote, "I wish I could have been born in February. When it comes to birthdays, February is the greatest month in history. To my mind it is the greatest month in American history."

♣   ♣   ♣

While Walter was growing from an impatient young farmer into Grand Pa 90+, the pattern of farming was also changing. Mechanization swept across the farms, driving the old-time farmhand before it like Indians before the pioneer settlers.

The agricultural population declined as the urban population increased, and small family farms began to erode away into large farms, like unprotected topsoil into the rivers. Indiana moved from a basically agricultural state toward a highly industrial one.

On the farms, the hoofprints of workhorses gave way to the pocked trails of steel-rimmed lug wheels on farm tractors, and these in turn were obliterated by the wide tracks of soft-rolling rubber tires on tractors, wagons, hayrakes, balers, grain combines, trucks.

In Walter's later years commercial trucking greatly shortened the time and widened the scope of livestock shipping as practiced by his grandfathers, Levi Beem and Jesse Peden, and his father, Thomas.

Thomas Peden drove cattle to market from the Mc-Cormick's Creek farm to Cincinnati. Walter drove cattle from all of his father's farms to the railroad in Spencer. Hogs, too, were driven to the railroads before commercial trucking caught up. Hog-driving required skill, tact, and sweat, but in 1958 Walter wrote me of "fond memories of the days I spent with the pigs seventy-five years ago. A fat hog travels at a gait of one mile an hour to the very minute. I have timed them on many occasions.

"Cincinnati and Louisville were the only hog markets open for Indiana farmers 120 years ago, and since there were no refrigerators, these markets were open only in winter.

"About the time of the Civil War there was opportunity for high adventure in marketing hogs in Louisville. The hog drovers always took a wagon or two along—a sort of hog ambulance—to pick up the slow hogs that could not keep up with the drove. The high adventure was for the anti-slavery men of the North to conceal a husky slave in the bottom of the returning hog ambulance across the Ohio River and start the slave on the underground railroad to Canada and freedom. It would require a large volume to record the history of the hog from the lowly swineherd of the Scriptures to the great Armour packing company handling ten million hogs a year. Long live the American hog!"

We went to visit Walter one afternoon when he had been ill. He greeted us in a spritely way at the outset: "Well, I'm feeling a little better. The cattle did better than I expected." Around daylight the day before, he had loaded nine cattle into the stock truck and gone on with the driver to finish a pick-up load in the neighborhood and then on to the stock-yards at Indianapolis. He was home by three o'clock that afternoon and the check from the commission house was in the next day's mail.

"He was lucky," Dick told me. "He accidentally hit the best market that week. Cattle have been off every day since."

A farmer counting his assets has to count in a certain amount of luck. About the only thing that remains unchanged in farming, as it becomes increasingly efficient and modern, is the uncertainty of it. There is never any definite, sure answer to its problems. It is an eternal gamble, despite the government's effort to help. The gamble somehow seems to be part of the charm for the dedicated farmers.

One Sunday afternoon when Mark, the city grandson, was home from Miami University he came down to go "caving" with Joe, the farm grandson, and some of his fellow students from Franklin College. On the way to Boone's Cave in Owen County, they stopped at Washington Street to show Walter the football helmets they intended wearing in the cave. They had affixed carbide lamps to the helmets, and Joe set his helmet jauntily on Walter's head.

Walter told them how the Owen County cave got its name. "Mr. Boone came up from Kentucky, before the Civil War, and bought the farm. That was before anybody knew it had a cave on it, of course. In Kentucky Mr. Boone was a slave-holder, but he didn't really believe in slavery, so he sold or freed all his slaves before he came to Indiana, which had been admitted to the Union as a free state. It was, actually, why Mr. Boone wanted to come to Indiana. Several of his slaves followed him to Indiana and stayed on the farm with him.

"I knew two of them, Sylvia and Brad. When Sylvia was about thirty years old she used to walk from the Boone's Cave farm to a farm on the other side of Spencer and do a day's washing for the family on that farm, and then walk back home. In all, a trip of around fourteen miles. And for that day's work, she received fifty cents."

Some of Walter's stories he liked to tell in about the same way that some people like to recite poems or sing the same songs over and over, in the same way Clara liked to sing "The Old Rugged Cross." These stories were familiar and comforting to him. Others he liked to tell because they stirred up facts he wanted to keep in his memory. These he liked to tell in somewhat the same way a workman looks over his tools to make sure they are all there and properly sharpened or oiled.

"Your mention of Homer Hyden and his drums," he wrote in April, 1953, "reminds me of the story of probably the world's greatest drum.

"Sir Francis Drake, one of the world's greatest sailors and the first Englishman to circumnavigate the globe, in 1580, had on board a drum. On Drake's return to England his drum was placed in the British museum where it remained for more than three hundred years. In World War days the great German battleship *Graf Spee*, was a terror to the commerce of the high seas. Finally two British cruisers (the *Ajax* and the *Exeter*) met up with the great battleship, off the east coast of South America, and in one of the fiercest of naval encounters the cruisers sank the *Graf Spee*.*

"A year or so after this encounter the two British cruisers were in an English harbor for a general overhaul. While there, the British navy gave the officers and men of the

---

* Three British cruisers attacked the *Graf Spee* off Montevideo on December 13, 1939. They did not sink her; she was scuttled by her own crew.—R.P.

two cruisers a triumphal parade like the triumphal marches in ancient Rome. To lead the March of Triumph through the streets of London and cross London Bridge, they got out the Drake drum."

And then he had some stories he told just for the pure fun of it . . . stories of real people, from real life, like the story about old Billy Hinton. "For years Billy was a janitor at a country church and one day he returned a box of matches to the groceryman with a complaint. He said, 'For years I've used one match to light both lamps in the church. I strike a match and light the first lamp and then walk across the room and light the other lamp with the same match. These new matches are too short; they burn my fingers before I can get to the second lamp. Now it takes two matches to light the church lamps every Sunday night.' He wanted his money back and the grocer gave it to him."

Some of Walter's heroes were the unrecorded men who engaged in livestock farming in the hard way, in the early days. "Let me tell you about the East brothers," he said one Sunday afternoon, happily. "All this happened back around 1870, but I don't know what years exactly. I knew the East brothers; in fact, one of them later owned a 750-acre bottom farm and offered to sell it to me for $100,000. It had a $40,000 mortgage on it and he was afraid of losing it, but he didn't. He kept it and sold it later for $125,000.

"He had started from simple beginnings. When Ed East and his brother Pink were fairly young men they were traders, lived down around Worthington. Their mother, then around ninety years old, lived with them. They were sort of gypsy traders then. The way they did was to start out horseback, from Worthington, and ride around the country buying and trading cattle as they went, and gradually making their way to the Indianapolis stockyards where they sold whatever cattle they had left. It took several days for each trip.

"When night came on they just stopped at whatever farm they came to and arranged with the farmer for feed and shelter for their stock overnight, and then rode on the next morning. At the stockyards it was always late afternoon by the time they finally got all their cattle sold. Then they had a seventy-six-mile ride back home to Worthington. In winter it was a hard, cold trip through snow, slush or mud. Pink used to tell me about it afterward. It was always late, he said, by the time they came through Spencer, with twenty miles yet to go. Pink told me, 'We used to look in through the windows as we rode through town and see the people sitting in their warm, cozy homes and we wished to the Lord we lived there instead of having twenty miles further to go!'

"When they got home they put their horses in the barn where their ninety-year-old mother had already thoughtfully put feed and hay in the boxes for the horses. Oftentimes, Pink said, they were just too tired to go any further after they unsaddled the horses. They just laid down in the clean hay and slept the rest of the night, and in the morning their mother came and called them to breakfast.

"That was cattle business the hard way."

♣ ♣ ♣

"A fat steer," he told us once, "could travel three miles an hour if it wanted to, a lean cow maybe four; but in the days when farmers drove their cattle to market, the drivers and the stock also went along at a slow pace that was comfortable for the stock. In Spencer, cattle were driven into the stock pens and left there overnight, to be loaded into the trains the next day. People who lived close to the pens could hear the bewildered cattle bawling all night in the unaccustomed new place. In those early days the citizens of Spencer were fortunate if the cattle being driven through the streets did not break and run and get on the lawns and yards."

One of Walter's ambitions started with his father's triumph in the cattle business in 1871. That year Thomas Peden drove two oxen steers to the Cincinnati market and sold them for twelve cents a pound. They were large and netted Thomas seven hundred dollars, which is an outstanding record for almost any farming era. Walter had kept this in mind all during his own hog- and cattle-feeding career, hoping and intending sometime to equal it.

Finally he did, in 1950. By that time feeding systems

and market transportation had changed greatly. In December, Walter called the stock truck and sent two steers to the Indianapolis market. They weighed a total of 2,260 pounds and sold for thirty-two cents a pound, paying off to the Thomas-topping record of $723.20.

In feeding his steers, Walter explained, he had combined the best features of his father's system with improved ideas of his own. His steers, unlike Thomas's, had never done a day's work in their lives. They had been pastured on bluegrass until they were eighteen months old, then they spent ninety days in a field of unpicked corn where they could eat as they pleased. (This was a practice Walter considered an excellent feature of his Grandfather Levi's harvesting system). When Walter's steers went to market they went quickly, comfortably, in a rubber-tired truck, instead of plodding along on their own leisurely feet all the way.

That day, Walter achieved one of his dearest farm ambitions. He wrote us a proud, happy letter about it.

♣   ♣   ♣

When Walter and Howard were farming together on Rattlesnake Creek and specializing in hogs as they did for fifty years, they sent their hogs to market a carload at a time, in July and August, when the market was good.

A carload was too many to haul in farm wagons. If a farmer had only half a dozen hogs, or a few calves, he usually hauled them in a wagon into Spencer and shaded them with leafy boughs cut at the farm and laid across the wagon bed. But before they finished the three-mile ride from the Rattlesnake Creek farm this way, the leaves were wilted, the hogs hot and panting.

When the Peden brothers sent fifty or sixty hogs, the stock had to be driven in, on foot. It was a trip with many hazards. When Walter's sons were big enough to help they had to help, and Dick says, "We were always apprehensive the night before a hog drive. We never got much sleep, for worrying. The hogs had to be got to town early, before the heat of the day set in. At the rate of a mile an hour, it took three and one-half hours on the road, even if all went well."

Walter always told them he wanted to be at the farm, with the hogs up and ready to start the drive "when it's just comin' day." Dick told me once, "It still gives me cold chills just to hear that expression 'just comin' day.'"

On those hog-driving days Howard brought the buggy to Walter's house in the chilly, dark hours before dawn. Walter sat on the buggy seat with Howard; the two older boys, Dick and Paris, "rode the back axle," which means they stood up behind the seat; the youngest boy, Mark, crouched on the floor beside the seat, and they arrived at the farm in the dark.

Some of the instructions Walter gave them for those drives finally achieved the stature of proverbs: "Never argue with anybody when you're driving hogs." They gave the right of way as much as possible to cars and buggies they met along the road during the hog drive. One of the boys had to walk along the side of the drove, with the special assignment of closing the neighbor's farm gates and barn doors as the hog drove went past, because a reluctantly walking hog was likely to duck in for refuge to any opening he saw.

"Don't crowd a hog," was another proverb. "You've got to let 'em take their time." They had to be watchful that the hogs did not overheat and die, or fall down a steep grade and break their legs, or get lost in the tall horseweeds and wild rose bushes that grew high as the buggy wheels along the roadsides. And the drivers had to keep looking back for laggards. If a hog grew tired or offended, or overwarm, he pulled off into the weeds and stayed there until loneliness impelled him to go out and rejoin the herd.

By the time they reached Quarry Hill, which was also called Porkhouse Hill because of Thomas Peden's earlier meat-slaughtering business there, they began to meet early traffic coming out from Spencer and men going to work at the stone quarry. On one side of the road there hedgeapple trees offered thorny refuge for the recalcitrant hogs and scratches to the boys who had to run in under the limbs and force the hogs onward.

On the other side of Porkhouse Hill a steep grade was concealed by weeds, and there it was too bad for the hog or young driver who happened to roll down that steep grade against the tin cans, barbed wire, and other debris hidden there.

A third, and enforced proverb of Walter's, was, "If you're heading a hog, you've just got to head him, no matter what you run into, sand burrs, bull nettles, or whatever is there."

Having gathered speed down steep Porkhouse Hill, the hogs ran straight on into difficulties where the railroad tracks began. Five sets of tracks there made difficult hurdles for the tired, breakable legs of fat hogs. Local trains, waiting on the siding, added to the nervous confusion by letting off short, sudden gusts of steam, frightening the tired animals.

A little farther, the drovers met women coming to work at the clothespin factory. The women, as confused and distressed as the hogs, didn't know which way to turn to get out of the way of the advancing army of hogs. "They just ran everyplace, scared to death and screaming," Dick said.

But this was the end of the ordeal. The wide-open gates of the railroad's stock pens offered haven to the weary animals. There they were fed, watered, left in the shade to rest all day until the stock-hauling trains came in the evening.

The train was the I and V that left Vincennes early in the evening. It stopped all along the way to hook on loaded cars, filled with livestock intended for the Indianapolis market, and it reached the Indianapolis stockyards early the next morning.

At the Indianapolis stockyards, unloading was easy; the

pens were built out close to the tracks. All the trainmen had to do to unload was to slide the car doors open and push the hogs down into the pens. The farmer-shipper did not, therefore, need to go along to the market. The commission house to which he had consigned his stock looked after it from then on.

Having got their hogs from the farm into the stock pens early in the morning, Walter and his crew went back that evening, and by that time there was a 42- or 46-foot stock car put off for them, which they bedded deeply with nice, clean straw. They used the railroad's "pinch bar" to push the car up to the chute, and the hogs went in onto the deep, clean bedding. The men sprinkled them down with a hose until water ran out of the closed car. The loaded car was left then, with the hogs in it, until the I and V arrived late that night.

"At that time of the night," Dick said, "the train crew didn't care how much noise they made, just so they didn't injure the livestock. Cars were coupled together with loud banging and rattling. Calves bawled, hogs squealed. Everybody in town knew just when the stock run finally pulled out of Spencer, and nobody expected to get any sleep until the last sounds died away as the train passed through 'the Narrows' at the outer edge of Spencer. Then even we boys could relax and go to sleep."

♣   ♣   ♣

By the time he was in his nineties, Walter Peden had become quite a celebrity in little ways. People liked to listen to his stories and were beginnings to say somebody ought to compile them into a book. He was frequently interviewed and photographed. He liked it.

"I had quite an experience at the stockyards this week," wrote Grand Pa 91+, in 1958. "The president of the stockyards had written me twice inviting me to call on him. In one letter he said, 'At long last I know what name is the oldest among the patrons of the market: Peden. The record and accomplishments of the last three generations must be most gratifying to you.'"

He had written Mr. Chambers, the president, that "the great triumvirate of the livestock industry is the farmer-feeder, the central market, and the packer." This comment interested Mr. Chambers, and when Walter visited him in his office at the stockyards, he took a picture of him to hang in the office, which was a deep satisfaction to the lifelong livestock farmer.

One of his favorite newspaper reporter-photographers was J. D. Burton, a Bloomington newspaperman. Mr. Burton photographed him in November, 1960, at the polls, in company with an eighty-six-year-old acquaintance, "Army" Joe Clark. The two men were beaming at each other. Walter, a lifelong Republican, hadn't missed voting in an election for seventy-one years. Joe, a lifelong Democrat, has spent most of his life in the army but told Walter, "I never had enough education to get any further than captain."

Although Walter was careful not to be nominated for any public office, he had been, by this time, secretary of the American Shorthorn Breeders Association and was then president of the Riverside Cemetery Association, and a member of the Methodist Church board.

He had spent so many years in Owen County and Spencer that he knew the locality almost as well as he knew his own farm. He knew the people and their families and businesses. He watched the farms grow, diminish, change owners and farming patterns. He watched Spencer businesses begin and grow strong or fade away as sons went into them with their fathers or moved away; he saw the changes wrought by two world wars, and his youngest son Tom put on the navy uniform to participate in the second one. He knew the spoke factory, the clothespin factory; the "corn parchies" kitchens, and saw sculptor Viquesney's *American Doughboy* statue become popular for placing on courthouse lawns; he knew the E. T. Barnes dahlia farm where it was believed more than a thousand varieties of dahlia were grown. He knew the Calvin Fletcher mansion at the outer edge of town through all the years when Mr. Fletcher sent a team and surrey to meet every incoming passenger train because it almost certainly had his guests on it, and many, including James Whitcomb Riley, were well known nationally. He knew the twenty-eight-room mansion later when E. Chubb Fuller was publishing a little farm magazine there, *The*

Agricultural Epitomist, which gave its name to the hill on the road near it. And he knew the *Epitomist* when it became C. A. Taylor's *Farm.Life* and prospered, becoming for many years the life blood of Spencer employment, with its circulation of over a million copies a month, and finally became a casualty in the depression of 1929, when Walter's own farming operation survived by a mere straw. He saw the county fairs, the poultry shows.

He knew when both the Spencer National Bank and the Exchange Bank were robbed at the same time in the 1920's and an Indianapolis newspaper reported in a banner head with two-inch type, "Bandits Rob Spencer Banks in True Wild West Style." He saw new churches built, and donated the hauling of stone as his contribution to one. He saw the new schools rise, and in 1911 watched a new limestone courthouse replace the old brick one that had, in 1828, replaced Owen County's first, log courthouse. He saw the hitching rack and horse-watering trough disappear from the courthouse square as cars, trucks, and tractors replaced horse-drawn buggies and wagons, hearses, delivery trucks, and farming implements. He had watched the town pave its streets, so that people no longer walked in mud or fell over livestock asleep on warm sawdust fills in the streets' holes, or left their buggies and cars stranded in mud when they could not drive farther. He had watched the street lights come on along the streets. He read with interest when the people of Owen County bought the land on his grandfather's

McCormick's Creek farm and donated it to the state to become part of Indiana's first state park. Walter watched clothing styles change, and told me, "I can tell the boys from the girls because the boys' blue jeans have hip pockets on them."

In that amount of time a man's convictions change, except the basic ones. He mellows, and acquires the beginnings of wisdom. By the time he had become Grand Pa 90+, Walter was beginning to be aware of the real importances. One of these was the land, and man's use of it.

♣   ♣   ♣

In his reading he was alert to the connection between Owen County affairs and those of the state and nation and world. When he read in the paper that Harold Macmillan had been appointed Chancellor of the Exchequer of Great Britain, he wrote, "I hand you some clippings relative to the promotion by Prime Minister Churchill of Harold Macmillan to the third highest position in the British Empire, that of Minister of Defense. Thus placing Macmillan in direct line to succeed Sir Anthony Eden as Prime Minister of England. The fact that Macmillan's mother was a Spencer girl is making world history for Spencer this week."

"P. S.: A representative of the United Press called me this week for any information I might have about Nellie Belles."

He knew Nellie as the daughter of Dr. Belles who was buried in Spencer's Riverside Cemetery, just about where the early Beems had planted their first corn crop. Nellie had lived in Spencer in her girlhood, and, Walter said, "She was a great lady." Of her half sister Flora he said, "She was my first sweetheart."

The more he thought about it, the more he thought Mr. Macmillan ought to come and visit the town where his mother had lived. On his trips to Riverside he sometimes went to look at Dr. Belles's tall, narrow gravestone shaft.

The thoughts boiled and simmered in the restless, logical mind of this mentally alert, frail-looking, ninety-year-old farmer until finally, with characteristic forthrightness and letter-writing candor he wrote Mr. Macmillan, suggesting he come and visit his mother's girlhood hometown and grandfather's grave. He sent the letter, in his direct Hoosier thinking, to Number 10, Downing Street, London.

"It was seven months before I got any answer," he said later, and laughed a small chuckle about it. "I learned I should have sent my letter to the American Embassy, but I never thought of that. I just hauled off and wrote the Chancellor himself."

The reply, months later, came from third secretary, N. E. Armstrong. On gray paper, embossed with the seal of Great Britain, the letter said, "Dear Mr. Peden, The Foreign Secretary is so fully occupied with his official duties it has not been possible for him to reply personally to your letter. I have therefore been asked to thank you on his behalf, particularly for your very kind thought in sending him the photographs of Dr. Belles's home and grave."

Walter never knew whether his suggestion had any influence in bringing about the visit which occurred in 1956, but in any event it was a high point in his life, an exciting page in the history of the little county seat town of Owen County, Indiana. Walter was invited to a grand reception given for the Chancellor in Indianapolis. He was pleased, but declined the invitation, saying, "I feel the burden of ninety years." But when Mr. Macmillan came to Spencer on this "Sentimental Journey" as the press called it, and visited Riverside Cemetery, and the farmhouse where his mother had lived (and, looking in through the window of it, had exclaimed, "It seems so little!"), Walter was in the attendant crowd. The people of Spencer held a picnic supper for the Minister of Defense in the Redbud shelter area of McCormick's Creek State Park, not far from Wolf Cave and Thomas Peden's big barn. Walter was photographed in conversation with Mr. Macmillan. In the photograph most often printed, he was standing in his characteristic storytelling pose, looking down and smiling and, you felt, just ready to look up into Mr. Macmillan's face and laugh his little short, crinkly laugh. The photograph appeared in many newspapers and magazines. So many people wrote Walter afterward that he said in a letter to me, "I had to buy some better stationery."

Even as late as three years after the visit, he wrote: "Mr. Percy Wood, long-time correspondent for the Chicago *Tribune*, called at my home today. He has been stationed in Judea for seven years. He was not flashy dressed, but well dressed. The best-dressed man I have ever met. Mrs. Abrell saw him coming and said to her husband, 'The Pedens are sure going to have company today.'

"The object of Mr. Wood's visit to Spencer was to write a feature column for the Chicago *Tribune*. Subject: the mother of England's Prime Minister, her girlhood days in America. He is going to Bloomington tomorrow to interview President Wells of IU about Macmillan's visit there in September, 1956.

"With sincere apologies for burdening you with all this hot air, Sincerely, Grand Pa 90+."

I would have bet the farm he told Mr. Wood the cowboy's epitaph.

♣   ♣   ♣

Walter was not a musician. I never heard him sing, and I think he never attempted to study any musical instrument. But he was pleased that two of his sons, Mark and Tom, had excellent singing and speaking voices, and pleased that his three grandchildren played in their respective high school bands.

He had enjoyed only moderately, in his earlier farming

days, the music provided by an Edison phonograph and thick flat records Clara bought in her determination to educate her sons culturally. By the time Walter was writing his 90+ letters, the Edison had long since given place to radio and TV. Phonographs were electric and records were high fidelity. Sometimes when we visited him Dick and I took along a small portable phonograph and some of Walter's favorite records to play for him.

One of his favorites was a gospel quartettes's singing of "When they ring dem golden bells." The one he asked for most often, however, was "The Cry of the Wild Goose." A somewhat surprising choice, it was a haunting, wild ballad popular at that time, and he liked some lines enough to quote them sometimes: "My heart knows what the wild goose knows, and I must go where the wild goose goes."

Once we took along two albums of Civil War music. One, "The Confederacy," and the other, "The Union." In addition to the record, each album had pages of history, illustrated with photographs. Walter enjoyed these, asked to keep the albums to read, and wrote me early the next morning: "I wish to thank you for the entertainment you put on for Clara and me last evening. . . . I was greatly interested in the Union version of the musical review of the one depicting the songs of the Union Army. After you were gone I picked up the songs of the Union Army. I just could not lay it down until I had looked at every picture and read every word of it, and then to my surprise it was midnight.

"I enjoyed every word and picture in it. It is a rare book that will entertain a nonagenarian until midnight. Every page and picture was interesting to me.

"With love to you all, and particularly Carol, Grand Pa at 92."

♣   ♣   ♣

He wrote me many letters. His handwriting was always legible though slightly unsteady-looking, and the lines often crept up toward the right-hand corner unless he wrote on ruled paper. His y's and g's turned back to the left in a long loop under the line and many of his capital letters began with a rounded loop like a baling wire bent loosely around a stick. He mailed his letters regularly in government-stamped envelopes. His words were never crowded in against each other. The page gave the impression of someone taking pleasant time to express himself without haste, but without unnecessary words. To find one of his stamp-embossed envelopes in the mailbox, with my name or my column name on it and his return address in the corner, came to be such a pleasure that I always regarded it as a good omen for that day.

In January, 1961, he wrote, "It is three o'clock in the morning. I cannot sleep tonight so I thought to improve the time by writing to you. Some years ago I took a course in reading, relative to the lives and habits of the race known as the Laplanders. No geography has ever been able to give the definite boundaries to Lapland. It is a region lying above the Arctic Circle. There are two types of Laplanders, the fishing Laplanders and the Reindeer Laplanders. It might be of interest to Carol to learn they have schoolteachers but no schoolhouses and no licenses to teach."

It was his last letter to me. He was beginning to feel always too weary to write, though he still enjoyed talking and retelling his stories. He was still cheerful, and a visit with him was still a pleasure.

He was unable to attend Clara's funeral in October of 1961. The last night we went to see him, which was slightly more than two weeks afterward, and by this time he was in Jen Reapp's kindly refuge, which had long ago been Calvin Fletcher's mansion, he was too weak and ill to be out of bed. We all talked. He told me again about Captain Slocum's trip around the world in a little fishing boat and later on asked, "Do you know what is the greatest responsibility of the Supreme Court?" Holding a glass of water with a drinking tube in it for him, I said, "No." And he told me it is "to make the decision, after a meeting."

Presently his third son, Mark, and his wife came and we all stayed rather quietly awhile. I had been sitting beside his bed and I moved away to make room for them, and presently he asked, "Where is Rachel?" I was greatly touched and honored by this affectionate compliment. Mark and his wife went away presently, intending to come back later. Dick and I stayed on for a while. Presently Walter told his son Dick good night and then said to me, "Well, Rachel, I guess that will be all." Reluctant to leave him, I asked, "Is there not one more thing I can do for you, Walter?" He said, "No, I'm going to sleep now." So I kissed his forehead and we came away.

The next morning I learned it really had been, as the farmer probably had wished it to be, a dignified, loving, not at all mournful good night. A final good night.

As soon as I learned this my mind whirled back immediately, like a telephone dial released, to one colorful October afternoon a year earlier when Dick and I had taken Walter and Clara for a little drive in the country. We had stopped at a country grocery store and Dick had gone in to get some ice-cream cones. While we waited, Walter, in the front seat, turned around and asked me earnestly, "Do you know what is the greatest blessing on earth?"

"Hogs?" I suggested flippantly.

His blue eyes were large and luminous behind his thick spectacles and his voice was velvety with the conviction of his thinking: "The fact that men can die, and leave a place for a new generation to come into possession of the earth."

A long-time farmer, loving the land and acquainted with it through success and defeat, he had learned some of its wisdom: how one harvest, departing, lays the foundation for the new one to follow, in earth's eternal pattern.

♣   ♣   ♣

The Fulness of Maple Grove

THERE was nothing spectacular about the morning; it was just pleasant, a sunny, all-but-chilly October morning, and I was writing in the kitchen when Frank Bell phoned to ask Dick to come and help him with some calves.

As I went up to the barn with the message I was so taken by the charm of the morning I wished I could bottle up some of it for winter enjoyment, or to send as a Christmas gift to a particularly loved friend.

Nothing unusual, nothing dramatic; just the farm on a sunny autumn morning. A wire-covered coop on a chunk outside the barn, containing a Bantam hen and eleven baby chicks hatched from a nest she had stolen out in the hayloft. They serve a vestigial interest for Dick, who as a child used to raise chickens in town where he could not have cattle. He had a pen of Bantams, and had them so circus-trained that when he stood in the doorway and cracked a whip they jumped, like acrobats, from one perch to another.

On the way to the barn, I had passed the walnut tree from which now the huge walnuts are fallen and ready to gather, because this year for the first time, and goodness knows why, the kernels are good, filled out with plump edible richness instead of dry, crinkled paper. Against the fence lay a five-foot-tall, unpainted cross from a float the Reverend Mr. Ed Skirvin had built on one of the farm's wagons to go in the

Fall Festival parade at Ellettsville a couple of weeks earlier. The float was reverent, with signs advocating "A closer walk with God," and the Reverend Mr. Skirvin had worked hard, up in the toolshed, sawing, hammering, and otherwise putting it together. (It won a prize in the parade.) Perhaps the bare cross released some of its dedicated feeling into the pleasant October air to make the day significant.

Also it was the birthday of my dear neighbor, Iris Stanger, but that was not unusual; she has had one every year all her life. From the pond above the barn the geese screamed their scorn, having observed me come up and search everywhere for Dick. This is not unusual either. Their continual scorn provides me with a great deal of amusement and prestige.

The sunlight was warm-looking against the old red of the painted barn and the old gray of the unpainted corncrib and toolshed and against the mottled gray of the concrete slab silo. I went past this fruity-smelling tower which was filled before Labor Day and opened a month later, so great has been the drought effect on pasture.

Sparrows were twittering and chirping as gaily as if they had not heard of a coming presidential election, and if they hadn't they were fortunate. Although, of course, if Americans could not hold one every four years they would also be twittering and chirping—or worse, chattering and swinging from trees, or still worse, accepting it quietly from deep under unmowed grass.

The sunlit air had a sweet smell of October, coloring leaves, wood smoke, dew-washed morning, old warm boards, farm living. Nothing dramatic, nothing spectacular, but all overflowingly pleasant. And I had the same majestic joy the farm boy must have felt one morning when, four years old, he exulted, "Oh, there's so much things in my proudness! Every new thing is beautiful to me in the morning!"

♣   ♣   ♣

This is a small farm, of the species family farm, now generally considered becoming extinct. In an era of mechanized farming and an overpopulous industrialized world, little hope is held out for its survival. The question is thought to be not whether, nor how, but merely how long, O Lord?

The chief crop on this farm is feeder cattle. We keep around 167 cattle and raise corn, hay, and silage to feed them.

The farm contains 239 acres, which is 109 more than we had when we first came here a little over twenty years ago. In those years the pattern of farming has changed greatly in the nation and almost completely in this community. When we bought the first 130 acres here, the farmers were in the final, polishing-off stage of the changeover from horses to tractors. They were shortening the tongues of their old horse-drawn corn planters, manure spreaders, and mowing machines, so they could pull these with tractors. Later they traded in the obsolete implements on new ones designed from the beginning for tractor power.

Electricity, bathrooms, school consolidation, church re-modeling, the second and third farm tractor on the farm, the second farm car, the hay baler, corn picker, grain combine, and field chopper have come since then. The neighborhood "grapevine" telephone that was maintained by neighbors who rang each other by code and paid a small "switchboard fee" was already competing with the Ellettsville exchange and soon vanished from Maple Grove farm homes.

The fields on this farm were poor, badly fenced, eroded, and hungry. We also were poor, though not eroded or hungry. The fields were hilly, underlaid with limestone, subject to sinkholes. In every field was eloquent opportunity to demonstrate the value of soil and water conservation and tender, loving land care. In one field was a gully so deep I was afraid to drive the tractor close to the edge. Dick drove closer and got into it. Carr Stanger, plowing in his field across the road, had been watching and came with his tractor and pulled ours out. Dick plowed the gully full of topsoil from the field and it went off in the first rain. But after the field was terraced, he filled it again and it stayed healed.

There was a small woods, about twenty acres on the hill-top field; there were brushy fence rows and weedy corners to provide good wildlife cover. The house was run-down, shabby; the neighbors cordial, observant, and each one as interesting as a new book.

All around us were other small family farms, most of them occupied by members of a family that had owned the land a long time. The road ran between this farm—then known as "Benny's old place"—and the farms of two Stanger brothers, Clint's 127 acres and Bent's 109.

Clint's married son, Carr, and his wife, Iris (who has an AB degree in geology and taught high school geography before she married a farmer), lived with Clint and Eaglie. Bent's married son, Ira, and his (Ira's) wife, Monta, lived with Bent. It was the local pattern; when a son married, the family made the back porch into a kitchen, built on another room or two, and shared the house with the young people.

When the parents were old, there was someone in the house to care for them.

By the time we moved here, Clint and Bent were both old men, both still taking an active part in the work of their farms. They were blue-eyed, friendly, liked to visit, and each had stories he liked to tell of the community's history and people. When they butchered their "meat hogs," Dick butchered ours with them, and afterward went down to Clint's to help render lard in the big iron kettle in the wash-house. It takes a slow fire to render lard and makes a good time for a long, leisurely visit. Clint told about his early days of farming. His mother's farm was small, so he and Bent had cropped other land around. They rented some land from old Tom Owens one spring, and were eager to get at the plowing. Tom said it was too early, the ground was too wet and would be cloddy if plowed then. Clint said, "I was on the road this morning and I saw other farmers plowing." Irritably, old Tom exclaimed, "One fool makes forty more!" Clint always laughed when he told that story.

Slowly the farm we had bought began to become ours, and less slowly we became a part of the community. When our children were small and we were building up the farm, the community and the farm were our world. Farmers met often then, at church or at the country school, at birthday parties in their homes, at club meetings and church suppers, silo fillings, butcherings, hay balings, farm sales, and they visited each other in their homes more than they do now. When a woman was in the hospital with pneumonia or a new baby the neighbors went to help. When an old man was ill for weeks in his terminal illness the neighbors took turns sitting up with him through the nights; when a farmer met his neighbors in town it was like meeting a fraternity brother.

In those years of family life on this small farm we went through all the customary experiences of getting acquainted with wildlife, weeds, all kinds of poultry and pets, worms, birds, moths, butterflies, frogs' eggs, tadpoles and turtles, leaves, kites and marbles, sleds, bicycles, ponies. We went through the era of cap guns and cowboys, bubble gum, school buses and PTA, Brownies, Girl Scouts, 4-H clubs, and Future Farmers. We studied teachers, farmers, ministers, and farm machinery. We had caroling parties, hayrides, school and church programs, radio, TV. The children camped in the back yard under a tent made of paper fertilizer sacks, saved their money and bought a real tent. Spelunking, swimming, fishing, baseball gained momentum. We terraced the fields and fertilized them, built new fences and farm ponds, remodeled an old barn, and hauled away the debris from the one that burned suddenly one rainy morning. People came to visit us. I began to write a newspaper column.

Gradually the farm fattened; the old house straightened its shoulders and lost some of its haggard look. The farm boy and girl outgrew the school bus and went on to college.

Having known and loved deep woods in my childhood, I soon discovered the joys of the little woods on the hilltop on this farm. It gave us mushrooms—edible morels to eat and beautiful scarlet caps and orange shelf mushrooms and others to look at. It gave us sassafras roots for tea, wild blackberries for pies and jelly and philosophy; papaws for guests who like them, walnuts, glimpses of wildlife and flowers, snail shells; and a small demonstration of the way limestone breaks apart underground, swallows the soil above it and makes a cave. It gave us places for solitude, for thinking, a place where we could go and sort out our values and lick our spiritual wounds clean. It offered a place to walk with congenial companions and gave us, finally, a wide viewpoint. The wooded hilltop is high above and behind the farm buildings, which on a farm are customarily referred to as "the improvements."

The fields in front of the woods were the first with which I established an affectionate rapport when we came to this farm. The understanding began that first spring, when I planted a little potato patch up there. Dick plowed a little space in the hillside field where the three-year-old farm boy and I could plant all the sprouted potatoes. This always seems as much an act of mercy toward the potatoes as a hope of harvest from them. It took all afternoon, up to time to get supper. The boy was little and tired and went to sleep in my arms as I carried him down the hill. It was pleasant, an expression in miniature of a farmer's relationship with the earth.

The hilltop field had an outgoing personality and spoke

to each of us in different ways, to the same purposes. "If I can just get back to the cornfield after a hard day in town I feel all right," Dick said once. It was a good field in which to fly a kite or ride a pony or find an arrowhead. The blackberry patch in the woods was a good place for a farm woman to go if she wanted to talk aloud to herself . . . nobody was likely to embarrass her by overhearing her in that hidden place, though actually why should it be more embarrassing to be caught talking to yourself than singing to yourself, which many women love to do? And certainly, if you're not on speaking terms with yourself, you need to do something about it.

In those early days when Dick drove through the woods on the tractor he got off and set sticks beside the mushrooms so that we could all go back later and find them. And I have known the farm boy to go up to the hilltop field and simply run, to work off a disappointment an eight-year-old was finding almost too great to bear.

Benny built his house at the foot of the hill, I suppose, because the water was there. Or perhaps because his parents' old brick house was already there. Or perhaps because, as I soon discovered, a walk up to the hilltop was a pleasant escape into a broadened viewpoint.

Carol discovered this early, too. We went up on the hilltop together one afternoon. She was four years old and wore a little red-and-white checked bonnet my mother had just recently made for her. She put her small hand in mine and

I resisted a desire to squeeze it too happily. At the back step Rose and her pup jumped up to follow. Beyond the first fence we were joined by the tame ewe and her lamb, and as we went up the hill we were three congenial mothers with our three youngest children.

At the top of the hill I sat down on a stone outcropping under the walnut tree, and Rose laid her head in my lap. Rose would leave her feed any time for a caress. Carol threw off the bonnet and she and the pup played ball with a green walnut. The ewe taught her lamb the glories of grass.

Looking downhill, I saw how the view of the house was erased by the lofty maples surrounding it. I could see the barn and on out to the east field where the other barn had burned. I could see the road running uphill in front of our farm toward the small, old white church which was almost hidden by its gnarled hard maples and oaks. I could see Ralph Lewis's little stone block house; and across the road from it, across six and a half miles of hills and valleys and dimpled farm fields, I could see the tops of the tallest towers in the university town, and smoke rising from some of the towers. Looking eastward I could pick out the tops of pine trees at Jim Bell's tall house, and not far from it was the shine of sunlight on Clyde Naylor's new galvanized barn roof.

The hedge east of the road shut off the sight of Monta's green-roofed small house and Clint's old one, but I could point out these places to Carol. I could show her Fred

Dutton's farm and Alec Ulmett's on the highest hilltop. We could see John and Leota Dunning's house where just the day before I had been frying thirty slices of beautiful pink, home-cured ham for silo fillers and feeling flattered because John had told Leota, "Let Rachel fry the ham. I like the way she does it." From our hilltop we could not see the deep hollow we have to go through to get up to John's house on its hill. At the crossroads was Fanny's small white house with Fanny's weedless, flower-garnished garden. We could see as far as Earl's apple orchard beside his white barn and silo, and after that the woods back of us in our farm cut into our circular view and took out a wedge like a piece of pie. But in the gap, we knew, were John Fielder's neatly remodeled white house and not far from it the new cedar-red one built by his dairy farmer son-in-law, Emmett Baynes. The pie ended just to the right, and we could see Russell Fyffe's cluster of neat buildings beyond our down-sloping clover meadow.

In those days, for my column's sake, I never went anyplace without pencil and paper. The farm always inspired something to bring back. That day it inspired Carol. Presently, on the top of that slope where the sense of country life was deepest and richest, she suddenly stopped playing ball with the pup, stood up and stood still, looking down the hill, and made up a psalm of rejoicing which she sang to herself, and I copied as much of it as I could: "I like this home with green fields and horses and little woods. I like this home better do I like any homes. I like the ponies and the cows and the trees and the mountains and the car. I like the daddies and the little girls and the little boys, and the red shoes, and the tractor, and the hay. And myself."

* * *

But no matter how much a farmer might love it, a farm of only 130 acres was too small. Farming was growing steadily more mechanized. The farmers took to the big machinery joyously; it was powerful, a flattering extension of their own strength. It was quick and efficient, but also expensive. Farming required a great deal of machinery, and to pay for the machinery required more land. Farmers on small acreages rented supplemental fields wherever they could, often several miles from home. On spring and summer mornings there was always some hardy early starter whipping along the Maple Grove Road on his tractor, going to some sharecropped corn or soybean field, "farming on the road." Other farmers took town jobs, did their farming after job hours and on weekends, hired their hay custom-baled; these were the "sundowners," the "moonlighters," the "weekend farmers." Tractors now were equipped with lights, so that fields could be, literally, plowed and tended at night. Farm boys liked this kind of farming; there was an excitement about using powerful, loud-voiced machinery in the fields at night, when the community was dark and people asleep, a kind of thrill about the way the tractor's headlights lit up the dark surroundings as the tractor swung around at the ends of rows. The larger, level fields lent themselves best to this night farming.

Dick's ancestors were farmers. As a boy he had been accustomed to a larger farm, although his father did not live on a farm. With only 130 acres now, he felt "boxed in." From time to time we looked for larger farms in other communities. By the time Carol was a freshman at DePauw and Joe was a senior at Purdue, we discovered Monta and Ira had decided to sell their farm and move closer to their married daughter.

The possibility of being able to buy land adjoining ours had never occurred to us. Bent had built the house on his farm. Ira, an only child, was born there. Monta had lived in it since she married Ira forty-three years earlier. I couldn't imagine the community without them living there.

It was at a meeting of the Women's Council in the remodeled church that I heard this news. "Are you really going to sell your farm?" I exclaimed incredulously to Monta.

"Well"—she turned her forthright dark brown eyes on me—"he asked us, and Ira made him a price, and if he takes us up we'll have to."

The man's offer was an opening wedge, but he was reluctant to pay Ira's price of $200 an acre, which was fortunate for us. We figured that since Ira's farm touched ours, the east road running between our field and his cornfield, buying it would save us the cost of moving, and we could afford to spend the saving for the land. Moving is expensive; farmers say "three moves is as bad as a burnout."

Ira's house is a small, one-story dwelling of no particular style, covered with imitation brick siding. After his father's death Ira had cut down on his farming operation and given his full working time to carpentering. He belonged to the union and worked for contractors. "He brings home his money from town and puts it into this farm, and we can't tell where it's gone," Monta had told me, sometime earlier. It was the usual farm comment.

She helped out by raising and selling strawberries and chickens. She kept a big flock of White Wyandottes and sold dressed chickens and eggs. Once a week she went to town to work for one of her friends at housework. She enjoyed this as an outing. She also enjoyed her strawberrying, gardening, flowers, care of the chickens, her church work, guests, family gatherings, and her housework. She liked color, activity, perfume, TV, singing, sewing. I've had bouquets and vegetables, strawberries, zinnia seeds, good times, advice, news, and deep comfort from Monta's house, and although we were happy to have their land, we regretted losing them as close neighbors.

Ira never complained when he came home from a day's work in town and Monta wanted him to take her someplace. He is little and bald, has a big car and likes to drive it. He is companionable, likes a visit with lots of laughter. He enjoys telling jokes and news, and even if the joke isn't very funny he has a good time telling it, which entertains his listener, and the more the listener laughs for whatever reason, the more Ira laughs also. The upshot is everybody can have a great deal of pleasure from a small joke. This is typical farm thrift.

Ira never complained when Monta asked him to make home improvements, such as pine paneling in the living room, cabinets in the kitchen, or a bathroom in one corner of a spare bedroom. In return, she never complained when he came in with mud on his boots. "It's his home, too," she said fondly, "and I'm just glad for him to get in."

Monta's henhouse and brooder house were halfway between the house and barn, and at night when some predator —raccoon, skunk, or fox—raided the henhouse she could hear the outcry of the hens. She had lost several hens to one invader one spring and so decided to stay up all night and keep watch. "I heard roosters crow on every farm in this neighborhood," she told me later; "Joe, your Bantams crow every hour on the hour." The marauder did not come on the nights she stayed up to watch. It came again, just at bedtime, one night later on. Ira was in the bathtub taking a bath. Monta, sitting on the bed, had just taken off her shoes, when the chickens began their uproar.

"Ira, that thing's back here after the chickens," she called, and ran out without stopping to put on her shoes. Ira got out of the bathtub, dripping, grabbed his gun and followed. The invader had got away by the time they got to the henhouse. As she walked back to the house, stepping gingerly on the cindery path, Monta noticed Ira for the first time. "Why, you're barefooted, too!" she exclaimed.

On the December evening when we went down to discuss buying their farm, Monta was pleased. She said, "It'll almost be like keeping it in the family. And you have a boy to help you, too. 'Course, we lost our boy, but maybe he wouldn't have wanted to stay on the farm. So many of 'em don't now, seems like."

When she said that, I remembered the time some years earlier when we were walking together up to the church on our week to clean it, and she told me about their boy. He was less than six months old, a big, healthy baby, when he suddenly became ill and died before even the doctor realized his condition. I have seen his little grave in the Maple Grove Cemetery. Monta said earnestly, "I walked up here every day that summer. If it hadn't been I was afraid somebody would see me . . . it being so close to the road and all . . . I'd have dug him up, I just wanted to see him again so bad."

We bought the farm in December and Ira gave Dick immediate possession of the barn and sheds to store machinery and feed in, and the fields to put steers on. Monta and Ira planned to hold a sale in March, disposing of their hay, grain, machinery and stock, and some household things they wouldn't have room for in the new place.

In June, before the strawberries were gone, they moved. Dreading it, I went down that morning to tell Monta good-bye. To my relief, she was already gone. The house was clean. The pink, polka-dotted curtains were clean at the kitchen windows. Ira and three movers were pitting their frail humanity against the long freezer which was full of packages of meat, fruit, and vegetables Monta had put into it. They had taken off the lid to reduce its weight. They were busy and I didn't want to waste their time (at $6.50 to $8 an hour for movers) so I came on home. I could call Monta and tell her good-bye over the phone, which would be easier. Or I could see her when she came back to pick the last of her garden and take up starts of iris and lilac for the new place.

♣   ♣   ♣

"There's eyeball-bustin' work to be done wherever you look," said Dick, staring out one rain-studded morning; "nevertheless, it seems peaceful this morning."

It is characteristic of a farm to be able to put on this peaceful look in each of its greatly contrasting seasons.

Winter is not my favorite time, but there are winter scenes I remember as the very portrait of peace. One in particular, not long before. It was snowing in the morning, the kind of snow God probably had in mind when He first created snow and later created Currier and Ives and painters and photographers and writers to try to capture it, and little wild animals to make tracks across it, writing their diaries for that day.

Snow was falling softly as if from a coarse sifter being turned from very high above the earth. It had been going on a long time; the leafless trees were whitened; weeds and tangled raspberry canes in the garden had become a great heap of foamy white lace. I looked through the back porch window where snow lay on the ledge making a white frame for a living picture of sparrows outside in the east yard. They were energetic, cheerful and busy. A group of them hopped along the swept walk, eating crumbs. One sparrow created a miniature snowstorm when he alighted on a delicate peach twig. The twig quivered under his weight, the sparrow rose, snowflakes sparkled and fell on the snow-topped woodpile under the peach tree.

Under the big swamp maple in the east lot the gray geese and white Pilgrim ganders gathered silently. During winter nights they sleep in the open-faced toolshed, and often in the night they think of new expressions of scorn and at once utter them. ("We are the watchdogs, we geese. We saved Rome.") That peaceful morning they walked on the clinging, moist snow and were still. They looked thoughtful, as if contemplating the sense of peace that pervaded the whole farmscape.

Snow was also falling on the red-and-white cattle in the east lot, and they were unconcerned about it. Some were standing up, others lying in the snow as comfortably as if on lush, summer grass. Snow falling through the sunless morning air dimmed it to pale gray and made all the cattle look dark. In the December nights, when anybody opened a door or walked through the yard, the cattle bawled as if they

wanted to call a summit talk. But on that snowy morning they were as quiet as painted cattle in a winter canvas.

A sense of deep, total peace filled the morning, a peace so profound it was almost disturbing.

I realized to my astonishment that if total peace ever actually befell the whole world all at one time, it would be the most spectacular sight mankind has ever seen. Nobody would be able to believe it, or, perhaps, even to survive it.

♣   ♣   ♣

We went one evening to buy some Bantams from Mr. Almond, who has a little chicken lot near the edge of town. As we walked out to his coops, Dick carrying a flashlight for him, Mr. Almond said enthusiastically "I'm going to tell you something—they're nice."

They were nice. Dick lifted one little yellow hen out of the coop. She had been asleep, but now she sat gently on his hand, bothered somewhat by the flashlight's beams.

"I picked these out for you from a flock of forty," Mr. Almond went on happily. "I'm going to tell you something—they're dolls."

We went on to another coop. Every time he began a sentence with this happy preface I expected the revelation of some great, basic poultry truth. Mr. Almond does know Bantams, as he told us he did. So does Dick. He also knows what Bantams he wants. He wanted seven. Mr. Almond wanted him to take all of them.

"I'm going to tell you something," said Mr. Almond; "you need 'em."

"I don't want so many white ones; I like the colors," answered Dick gently, lifting out a little red-and-gold hen. I wondered why Mr. Almond didn't begin to see the light. But the sparring went on while we chose and sacked seven hens and Dick paid for them. At the last, when we were sitting in the car with the window rolled down, Mr. Almond leaned against the frame and said, "I'm going to tell you something—they're nice, and you're here and you need 'em. Take 'em all."

I wanted to lean forward and say "I'm going to tell you something—when he doesn't say anything, it means you've lost the argument," but Dick thanked him and drove away.

🌲   🌲   🌲

"I can't shut the white Bantam keep-rooster up with the rest of the flock now," Dick said one April evening; "the other will kill him. But if I shut him outside, something else will get him. Something has been snatching at the geese; I saw feathers where it almost got one."

"A fox?"

"Could be, or something smaller maybe. This is the time of year when the small predators are getting ready to breed. They're hungry and need more feed than in winter."

Romance and danger in the poultry yard are equally signs of spring. Before we got the Bantam hens, the two roosters had been like Damon and Pythias. The evening Dick brought home seven little hens marked the end of this fraternal dream. After that, Damon and Pythias still saw eye to eye, but only in combat. The war went on between them inconclusively, first one winning and then the other, and hope springing eternal and misleading from day to day. One morning I saw whence came the hope. The white rooster came past the house, walking cautiously, head bloody but unbowed because if he had bowed it he would have been totally unable to see with his swollen, almost closed eyes, where he was going. His feathers were shadowy with blood and mud. Bedraggled and shamed, he had only a vestige of determination left. As he passed the lilac bush one little white hen came running behind him. She was small, and she was only one, but she was faithful; she was just enough to keep a vestigial ambition alive, and the war reflammable.

♣ ♣ ♣

There is another, less romantic, but equally dependable sign of spring on the farm, and I observed it later that morning.

A robin ran along the edge of the yard, looking sleek and carefree while I, earthbound, paused at the door to envy him his wings. While I watched, suddenly he stopped, lifted one wing and gave his whole effort to scratching his underside with his long beak. To itch like that, and to be able to scratch, is obviously greater bliss than to be able to fly.

It was spring in the barn lot, too, and Dick called me out to watch the new calf run in the lot beside the barn. This was the first calf from the new white Shorthorn bull. She was a pretty little thing, blocky, alert, brown-red with a nice sprinkling of white over her shoulders. Enough to call roan and to remind me of the way red-brown clay looks when it is mellowed, filled with frost and crunchy-dry on late spring mornings.

The calf ran vigorously, for the pure joy of running, as new calves always do the first time they are let out of the barn and discover the joy of outdoors. Finally she stopped and stood at the fence, licking the post, the wire, the ground, inquisitively getting acquainted with everything. The mother in shaggy red winter coat was aware of us watching her calf. She ate with enjoyment, but watchfully. And she itched!

She reached back along her shaggy covered flanks and licked her coat. A dog bites his itch or combs it with a claw-endowed foot, but a cow merely unfurls a long rough tongue and applies its brush-power. With it she can reach most of her far-distant places; what the tongue cannot subdue she consigns to post, tree, wire fence or wheat drill, or anything left where she can rub against it. Looking past, beyond and around her, I saw that all over the pasture cattle were licking, rubbing. Even those lying on the ground were rubbing the sides of their heads against the high, tough crowns of last summer's orchard grass.

All winter the chaff, dust, seeds, and debris had lodged in their coats, held there by the same protecting oils that keep their inner skin waterproof and insulated. Now that the roots of new hair were beginning to push out the old, the cattle were overtaken by a tremendous, blissful itch by which nature helps accomplish their shedding. Spring was bound to be just around the corner . . . the corner of the barn against which another cow was rubbing, rubbing, ecstatically rubbing.

♣ ♣ ♣

They were becoming a nuisance to him, and besides, foxes were catching some, so Mr. Bowman ("Bo," Monroe County Soil Conservationist emeritus) gave us his three Pilgrim geese: Priscilla, Miles Standish, and John Alden. Pilgrim ganders are always white, the females gray.

At first they lived in triumvirate harmony. Then romance struck and John Alden incestuously took his mother, Priscilla, to wife and ostracized the older gander, who thereafter walked alone in dignity, pretending to be merely thoughtful and to prefer solitude.

Presently a sad peace was accomplished between the two ganders; a fox caught Priscilla. "It was the thinnest, mangiest fox I ever saw," angrily declared Dick, who had discovered it crouching under the henhouse and shot it. "His tail was as bare as a rat's, and his backbone showed through his skin." The fox was probably better off dead, though of course it was not in his nature to think so.

After that, Dick went to a sale and bought two gray geese, the Pioneer mothers (one lame), thus restoring harmony and population explosion in the goose department. One day one of the Pioneer mothers laid an egg and started to sit on it. The flock then turned against their former neighbors, the ponies, cattle, Bantams, and people. Whenever anyone went near the toolshed where the nest was, all the geese ran forward, hissing, heads lowered and threatening, to protect the sitter. When the sitter left the nest for her daily exercise, she covered the eggs with loose straw. Eventually she hatched eight dusky-gold goslings and all the flock assigned themselves to protect them. At night they gathered around the second goose, by that time sitting on her own nest. After a few nights of such companionship she decided a share of the goslings belonged to her, and so abandoned her sitting.

The clan instinct is strong in geese. So is the sense of authority. They elected themselves ruler over the young white bull and made a practice of nipping him smartly in the flank when Dick let him out of his stall into the open lot. He was afraid of them and sometimes fled, scuttling back into the security of his stall. But one day, I don't know why, he suddenly turned and showed them his horns, and after that they left him alone as if they failed to see him.

The Pilgrims are dirty in the barn and cluttery in the lot where they shed feathers, and beautiful on the pond where they swim majestically. We like them partly for the animation they give the farm and the humor, but also for their beauty. When they fly they are magnificent: wide, strong wings outspread, shining in the sun. The trouble is they fly only when they want to.

One day my sister Nina was here (who says, "I have to come once in a while to get my feet on the ground," but actually because we love and need her and she loves us). It was a difficult day and we were walking over the farm for comfort's sake. I wanted the geese to show her how beautiful they are in flight, but they would not oblige. We chased them. They ran into the fence corner, where the gate has wide slots between its boards, but they would not rise and fly over. They tried to squeeze between the boards, and so we were able to catch Miles Standish and stroke him.

When they express their proud aloofness or scorn, they can stretch their necks up to great height and hold their heads high. When they want to threaten, they can lower their heads, stretch forth their necks to an eighteen-inch length. Caught that day, Miles Standish shrank his neck down to the shortness of an ordinary hen's neck. He trembled, and the hard core of his pompous white body was surprisingly small inside its depth of smooth deep feather. The feathery softness of Miles Standish's throat makes all other softness comparisons obsolete. "Soft as velvet," "soft as new falling snow," "soft as bread sponge," even "soft as a horse's muzzle"—all are inadequate. For days afterward, my fingertips remembered the softness of Miles Standish's throat.

Released, he ran back to the flock. They collected in their

exaggeratedly dignified way and exchanged experiences.
Then with poise restored, they assembled at safe distance
and again began to express contempt through their all-seeing,
ever-open magnificent yellow eyes.

♣   ♣   ♣

We heat this house with bottled gas, but in the kitchen
we have a Franklin stove in which we burn wood, cut on
the farm. It is a luxury, just as homemade bread which used
to be everyday farm fare is a luxury now wherever it is
found, but the pleasure of the open fire with its faint, ever-
present, ever-pleasant smell of wood smoke are part of the
charm of the farmhouse. We eat in the kitchen in winter,
except occasionally, and the drop-leaf cherry table, covered
with a red-and-white checked cloth, drawn up near the open
fire, creates a sense of leisure. (The table, incidentally, has
lived in this community at least four times as long as we
have; it belonged originally to "the Woodall girls" and was
acquired only after a good deal of diplomacy by Dick from
Blaine Kerr, out of the old house where Blaine had let it
stay, abandoned, for many years.)

The kitchen stove produces ashes, and taking these out to
throw away I have a feeling I ought to apologize to Benny's
mother, whose brick house stood out in the yard by the
cistern, many years before Benny built the one we live in,
moving the old Wampler one-room schoolhouse down from

the field across from the church, and adding rooms haphazardly to it.

Benny's mother lived on this farm in that thrifty era when women saved the wood ashes all winter in a hopper out in the yard. In spring they ran water over the ashes and thus got lye, which they combined with the winter's accumulation of bacon fryings, meat rinds, rancid lard, tallow saved from times when the wild dogs got into the flock and killed sheep. From all this fat and lye, farm women made soap. It got the clothes clean, sweet-smelling, especially the boiled white clothes. At Ira's farm his mother, Evvie, took the washing out to a creek below the barn where there was plenty of clean water handy and plenty of wood to burn under the kettle.

In our convenient era of detergents that pollute the streams and sometimes emit thick "heads" of foam out of city water taps into the drinking glasses, nobody wants to make lye soap. Few people even want to use it even if they can get it. You can always buy it, as a novelty, at such places as the farmer's market on the courthouse square at Rockville, during the October Covered Bridge Festival there, and I buy it there for Dick. He likes to wash his face and hands with it. Few people have time to make it. Time is more valuable than it used to be and nobody seems to have twenty-four hours of it in a day any more.

In the earlier farming era the waste of one process was the foundation of a new product, as it is in the natural world.

Farm women dyed the family's wornout garments and tore them up into carpet rags from which to weave or braid bright new floor coverings. The scraps of new homemade garments were pieced into quilts. It was time-using and could have been tedious. It was creative art, relaxing and sustaining. Surplus apples were made into cider or apple butter, or dried. Surplus cider turned into vinegar in a big barrel. Surplus milk was made into cottage cheese.

Farming, an accumulative process, is essentially based on a policy of conservation. But in the beginning, pioneer farms were created by a waste of forest that now seems appalling.

The policy of thrift is not practical, nor much practiced any more. Waste is a calculated part of today's progressive economy, and there is a frightening amount of it as a daily part of the simplest, frugal living. Waste keeps everybody busy; it makes jobs; it uses up time. It creates markets for products. It also uses up our natural resources—land, water, minerals, wildlife—far too fast. It keeps jobs for people so that everyone can live well and pay taxes and help support everyone else, and nobody has time to use waste or by-products, except perhaps farmers who still haul manure out to their fields, regardless of how much commercial fertilizer they buy.

Still, thrift was a good policy, and man should delve more deeply into its possibilities, and learn how nature, apparently madly extravagant, is at heart almost penurious in her thriftiness. And in the long run, note well, nature wins.

🌲   🌲   🌲

If the time should ever come when farming is no longer essential for feeding people, the metaphor it has given the language will probably immortalize it to the society of humankind. The ordinary language of farmers, often ungrammatical, is just as often deeply poetic.

"The expression came to me suddenly in a time of great need," Dick said; "it was that spring Clint had been so sick, so long—all winter actually. 'Course he was old and knew he wasn't going to get well and we all knew it too, but Eaglie and Carr and the family couldn't bear to talk about it. Clint had been talking to me . . . I had gone that night to sit up with him . . . you remember how we all did that for weeks, and for Uncle Bent later, too . . . and he had been talking about Eaglie and the farm and what would happen to them when he died.

"So I said to him—and I don't know how I happened to think of it—'Clint, you can't die now; we've wintered you!'

"He just opened his mouth and laughed and laughed . . . you remember how blue his eyes were . . . and that was the end of that gloomy talk. When I came home early that morning he was feeling pretty good."

🌲   🌲   🌲

From radio and TV news it seemed obvious that the affairs of man, large-brained, fire-wielding newcomer to earth, were in a crisis. A listener can stand just so much of this and then it is necessary to escape. I went up to the pond back of the barn, hoping to get a photograph of a frog.

There in the sun-warmed shallow water the life cycle of frogs was going on as it has gone on for eons in sun-warmed water, long before farmers took over dominion of earth and water.

The pond that day was rimmed with soot-dark tadpoles. About as big as watermelon seeds, but thicker, they already had the incipient bulges of froghood. Having neither legs nor feet, they were able to move rapidly, propelled by long, tapering tails set edgewise. Sound did not disturb them, but my hand's shadow on the water sent them scurrying away. The calm approach of a bluegill no longer than my finger also disturbed them. A dragonfly with long blue body and two pairs of gauzy wings held straight out from his sides like the wings of early airplanes did not disturb the tadpoles, neither did the long-legged spider that paused on the pond's surface, collapsing his legs without even getting wet.

I reached into the water and brought out a tadpole that was nearer froghood than the others. He was gray and white with distinct frog markings on his back. His tail was nearly transparent. On the east side of the pond I found a clump of frog's eggs, small black beads, each encased in its separate transparent bubble and all held together in a mass the size of a child's fist. Individual beads stirred as if wishing to break free but the mass held firmly, anchored to the roots of a grass clump under water.

Frogs were sunning on the bank. I walked softly, but they dived into the pond with sudden clunks—except one that was too deep in contemplation to hear my steps in the grass. When he saw me he dived into the water with a small surprised squeal, equally surprising to me. Camera in hand, I stepped softly and searched intently, but when I had the light properly in back of me, I was never able to get near enough for a photograph. Wild creatures instinctively know about the use of light angles and shadow concealment. Their survival depends on knowing it.

If all the pond's tadpoles lived to become frogs there would be far too many for this pond, probably for all the ponds in this county. Many will be eaten by bass and blue-gill and the turtle that we suspect lives in this pond. It is their assignment. It is why nature produces such lavishness of tadpole. But nature will also make sure enough survive to keep the race of frog going. That also is their assignment. Thinking these thoughts, I walked on to the dead elm beyond the pond, noting that a grackle has taken over the flicker's nest there. In the natural world, life is a ceaseless process of invasion and resistance. Survival is a point of balance somewhere in between, but where? And how? I wondered suddenly, is this generation of man comparable to the tadpole or to the frog?

   ♣   ♣   ♣

Opportunity knocks more than once, but when it knocks with a tractor, once is all you need.

Dick offered to bring the tractor and break the garden before he went down to Ira's to drill grass seed. We were going to disk the surface, and not plow it.

"It will take me five minutes to get there with the disk," he said, "then you come out and tell me exactly how you want it done." The garden is a small area of the raspberry patch and always embarrassingly identifiable by the weeds that overtake it. But it is essential. No matter how many luxuries a farm woman may have, her life is never whole without at least a small garden.

The saving of human energy by use of machinery is never more apparent than when a farmer breaks the garden. He used to plow it with one horse and a walking plow, and afterward harrow or drag and roll it. Now he can go in with a tractor and disk, choosing a time when the soil is at perfect state of moisture, friability and mellowness, and warmed-throughness. He can cut it up three times in less time than his wife can locate the hoe and rake and her packets of seed.

The disk cuts up and covers tender new weeds, but a little disking is enough. "The disk is the most dangerous tool on the place," Dick says. "It can ruin the soil texture."

I watched him deftly turn the tractor around in the little

garden space. When he finished, the soil was dark brown, fine and fragrant to a shallow depth, just right to plant in.

"Good-bye," he said, sitting on the tractor seat. Gratefully I kissed him good-bye. It had been exactly thirty minutes from the time he got up from his noon nap to the time he had pulled out of the garden, detached the disk, backed the tractor up to the wheat drill and wagon so I could drop in the coupling pin, and was starting down to Ira's field. The grass seed and fertilizer were in the wagon behind the wheat drill. This is indeed the golden age of farming.

Invariably weeds overtake my garden before I get out all the crop, but I love it just the same. I love it on the day when the earth is prepared and I can take off my shoes and walk barefooted on the fresh, moist, sun-warmed soil. I love it when I put my shoes back on and begin to work, marking off rows and putting in seeds, and almost forgetting to stop in time to start supper. I love it when the first bean sprouts appear, the little bowed green heads first, then the two little green hands held up above the face. A garden makes me feel useful, poetic, comforted, overworked, justified for living, luxurious. I always promise to be faithful to this one, but every year the weeds are more faithful than I. After all, they have nothing else to do, of course. Once every summer I pull them all, but weeds can work full time at regrowing, and I cannot work full time at destroying them. The way weeds can come on in the late days of August and make a complete life cycle before frost is as comforting as it is astonishing.

In this survival-conscious civilization it is comforting evidence of earth's ability to adjust itself to what it has. A plant that can use three months' growing time if it has it or can capsulate its harvest into five weeks if it has to, is likely to be able to make a foothold against other odds if necessary and could probably prevent earth's denudement. For which all gardeners should give thanks to weeds.

Besides, such is the generosity of nature that even with the weeds, we always have enough of the importancies . . . green beans, onions, radishes, green peppers, tomatoes, cucumbers, squashes, dill, and cress. And sweet corn.

The chief harvest of my garden for me personally is the therapy of working in it, and the acquaintance of my neighbors from the natural world that I meet there.

One April afternoon, having a grief to deal with, I went about it as farm women have always done, working outside. Fortunately the yard was in extreme need of raking, grass trimming, lilac pruning, stick gathering, iron-chair moving. Some blocks in the walk to the barn needed releveling. This walk is built of old silo blocks. When the children were little they hid "treasure" (bits of colored glass, marbles, stones) under certain of the blocks and honored me by telling me the numbers under which the treasure would be found. Turning up a block that day to level it, I found three blue-and-white glass marbles.

The vegetable garden invited me to plant the radishes. There were horseweeds to be pulled out of the strawberry patch, the rhubarb needed to be dug around and fertilized with barnyard gold. This cooperation of the farm in time of human need adds greatly to its value per acre.

Even your private vegetable garden is a public spot and there "you meet such interesting characters" as I discovered at a later time in the season. All around me great numbers of insects were working out their problems, having survived the winter either as individuals or as eggs laid last summer by parents that paid no further attention to them, that did not survive the winter nor expect to.

There were monarch and viceroy butterflies, looking much alike, but not enough ever to convince me the viceroy is able consciously to imitate the monarchs for survival's sake; there were dusky swallowtails, mosaic-bright checkerspots fluttering around the deep-throated small flowers of lavender sweet rocket, that had spread too abundantly all over garden and yard.

Most butterflies tarried hardly long enough for a real sip, but a hummingbird moth lingered thirstily over one after another. It was about the size and shape of a bumblebee, with a slightly squared head, but its gold and black were less velvety than the bumblebee's luxurious colors. The moth's tapering body ended in what resembled a flounce on a long, narrow skirt. Its gauzy wings vibrated constantly, held the body suspended between two blurs. The real hummingbirds always come elegantly to sip from the flowers of althea in July.

I took up some sweet rocket plants to transplant, experimentally, into the narrow, shady space north of the porch step, a place that has never accepted any plant with much grace. While I raked away the mulch, a sooty-winged Diana fritillary (blackly blue wings with long white marks on them like daisy petals along the border) alighted on the stone. She stayed there a generous length of time, opening and closing her wings against each other, like the covers of a book being blown open and shut. The underside of the book covers were marked with orange and brown spots. When the book covers were closed, the book was harp-shaped; hers may have been a music book.

When I carried the mulch out to the garden I found there a gold beetle, of a scarab outline and enclosed in a small round transparent bubble. It was resting on a heart-shaped wild sweet potato vine leaf (unwelcome in the garden, but rampant there just the same and a beautiful leaf). His underside was as black as the F-sharp key on a piano. I broke off the leaf and put it into a plastic specimen box to take into the house, and the beetle clung to the lid as if glued there. The next morning, however, it had taken time to eat four neat holes in the leaf.

There aren't as many beetle watchers as bird watchers, but this is not the fault of the beetles. They come obligingly in great variety of shape, style, and color and all with one passionate, consuming aim, to survive and increase.

For pure body interest, the ox beetle with curved horns

and large chitinous, ridged body is a collector's item. For a striking use of color that surely would impress an interior decorator (even one as gifted as Indiana's Everett Brown), one could consider the big, loud-buzzing clumsy May beetle, green and gold, harmless even when disturbed from its feasting on overripe wild blackberries which a farm wife has come to take.

On the way home from the July blackberry patch she is likely to discover tumblebugs, and they are well worth studying. These large, dingy-colored beetles can provide a farmer with an enlightening half hour, as they roll their spherical wealth cooperatively along the dusty, bare ground. One

pushes, with his front feet on the ground and his hind feet braced against the dung ball. The other rides on the ball, instinctively using the principle of weight and balance in giving traction—knowing without instruction the principles high school boys learn in 4-H tractor maintenance: that a tractor pulls better when equipped with wheel weights.

♣   ♣   ♣

The housebound farm wife finds ways of getting out on a fine day whether she has time or not. I had important writing to do that morning. I had taken the typewriter into the fastness of the dining room; the necessary papers and privacy were lying four inches deep all around it. So how did it happen that when I "came to" I was out in the garden digging a hole in the winter-mellowed earth in which to set the winter's last remaining onion, which had sprouted?

My brother, the onion!

In the darkness of a brown paper sack in the utility closet the onion had sensed the return of spring and sent up its pale yellow sprouts like flattened tubes. The onion had to sprout even if it shriveled and died without ever getting close enough to earth to put down roots for nourishing those pale, bent-over flattened tubes.

A farmer knows that persistent yearning for a touch of the earth. The need of it is as persistent in man as in the onion. My brother, the onion!

♣   ♣   ♣

Some farmers would say a farm is like a jealous woman and demands all the attention; some say it is like a child who wants to be loved and included. The strength of the family farm is in this sharing . . . as when Carol was a little girl

233

and we were having important company and she sat beside me and whispered, putting her hands on my arm, "Will you look at me, too, some of the times, and smile and talk to me, too?"

On the family farm everybody shares the work, the food, the company, the car, the grief or the glory, and the family cold. When the children were little and Dick had a cold bad enough that it kept him in bed upstairs, the children went up and sat on the bed and read to him and let him play with their toy tractors and cap guns. At mealtime I carried meals up to all of them and they ate as happily as if on a picnic. When Blaine Kerr came at noon to ask modestly about bringing one of his cows here to our bull, I sent him upstairs and carried up ice cream to everybody.

The flu, however, is somewhat more serious and sometimes almost demands isolation.

"For a person who doesn't have the flu it must be pure jet-propelled you-know-what to live in a house with three people who do have it," I said to Dick, having of course first coughed, blown my nose, and wiped my eyes.

"Well," he said, being cautious because he knew all he said might be used against him later when inevitably he would be just as odious and fluent as we were then.

"Considering how much of American family life is spent with colds and flu," I went on, "every house plan ought to include a coughing room, where a person could go in privacy to cough and blow his nose and sneeze."

"I think probably you're right," he said, thinking probably of the blessed barn to which he could soon escape. For while it is true that cattle do cough—a mild elegant belch that brings up stored grass from one of the cow's three stomachs, to be chewed again before being swallowed down into another—and they also bawl and snort and bellow, and kick and butt and horn, and sometimes even "mash" a farmer against the wall if he gets in their way; and also they like to block the way to the water trough or feedway, they do not "clear their heads."

They have subtle ways of harassment, but they do not blow their noses, nor ever grab a cleaning tissue and stand with eyes ecstatically narrowed to mere slits, mouth half open, inviting the dynamic explosion of a sneeze that will transform a by-stander temporarily into an air missile.

"Well," said Dick tolerantly, being now coated and capped and almost ready to leave, "I think maybe all this bull-heaving is unnecessary . . ."

"What is bull-heaving?" I asked, and at once we were nostalgically back in the horsepower days of farming when farmers were known by the idiosyncrasies their horses kept.

"It is an expression of frustration," happily explained Dick. "Horses suffer from frustration the same as people. When a horse is kept stall-tied instead of standing loose or running free in the pasture, he gets bored. Sometimes he pulls back and sucks air into his stomach and roars and pumps and pulls his stomach in and out."

It sounded like a horse's idea of doing push-ups, I thought. Dick tied a final string around his waist, for warmth's sake. "It's not the ordinary heaves," he said. "Charlie used to have heaves. I always thought that was caused by scar tissue on the lungs." By now we had both forgotten the coughing and head-clearing coming steadily from both upstairs bedrooms.

"There were cribbers, too," Dick continued, "and the weavers. Bo used to have a weaver. That's one that just stands in the stall and weaves back and forth, back and forth . . ." He began to demonstrate as he talked. I had never seen him attempt the twist before, especially when swathed in winter coats. I was so fascinated I just stood there and forgot to finish my sneeze.

♣   ♣   ♣

Land is a living, breathing, changing personality. It is restless, seemingly fragile, yet surprisingly tenacious. When it speaks violently, as in an earthquake, everybody has to take notice, but much of the time it shows its restlessness in small ways. After a rainy April night I noticed that where moles had tunneled through the yard under the sod, the tunnel had acted almost like a water pipe. The loosened earth had been washed out by the night's rain and into the driveway and there caught by stones and held at the first level. But that much soil had got that far in its restless way toward a river, a sea, or other distant place.

Perhaps the unity of nature is expressed by the willingness of land to travel in water.

The fragile soil texture of a woods makes that an unsuitable place to pasture livestock. Our small woods on the hilltop is fenced with barbed wire to keep cattle and horses out. Horses like to take bites out of the tender bark of young trees. The sharp hoof of livestock is a menace to winter-softened sod or leaf mold at any time. In late winter a farmer watches his diminishing supplies of hay and silage and estimates the time " 'til grass comes" and he can turn the stock out to pasture.

The purchase of Ira's farm gave us eighty acres more of woods, wooded hills, and creek fields. There are magnificent trees in the woods. In between the hills, and cut through by creeks, are stony, thin-soiled fields. On top of one steep hill a ten-acre field was going back to brush because the road up to it through the forested hills was too steep to get machinery and fertilizer there easily. The last time Bent and Ira raised a crop on the hilltop it was corn, and the wagon turned over on the way down the hill.

Dick and Joe decided to clean the brush from that field, which our jovial neighbor, Warren Fyffe, at once named "the Klondike." It took two tractors to pull the wheat drill up the steep hill. It took two tractors, two power saws, and a brush hog several days to prepare it for seeding to oats and grass.

A considerable amount of money and work would be

required, as I knew, to fence the steers out of the larger part of Ira's woods which that spring blossomed out in all the wild flowers I have ever known, and more besides. In one small grassy prong at the foot of the hill were dense, extravagant patches of long-stemmed blue, purple and white violets, as if produced on some kind of a dare.

One afternoon, walking in the woods I discovered trillium, squirrel corn, tight buds of fawn lily, bloodroot, fragile anemone, May apples holding their green-brown umbrellas just ready to open . . . reminding me of the old-time umbrellas farmers used to put on their spring wagons and now use on tractors, and people use, more sophisticatedly, over beach tables. Along the hillside I found great variety of other plants beginning to come up and I bitterly resented every cattle track I found in the woods. Not many had gone that far yet, fortunately. On another hill I found bulbs that had been trodden out of the paths along the hillside where cattle had walked. Cattle never bolt straight up a steep hill, but wisely take the long way, slowly winding down or up.

Depressed by the exposed bulbs, I went down to the creek and crossed it, and paused there to pay homage to a majestic hard maple at the foot of the hillside. Near it is a papaw thicket, and one of spicewood. Back of it is a fallen tree where in summer we had found cup-sized ruffly orange-colored fungus as large as our old-fashioned water goblets and shaped almost like morning glories. On the ground near there we had also found thick, round grayish-brown boletus, the size of old-fashioned sugar cookies. I had intended to walk all the way to the Klondike that spring afternoon, and might not have got back until late, but good fortune intervened. Beside the creek was a large sycamore with a forked trunk, and there I discovered a young Hereford steer with his head caught between the forks of the tree.

I could not get him free alone, so I hurried up the steep hillside and back to the toolshed to find Dick. He came and deftly freed the captive. He said gratefully, "I probably never would have found him away down there. He would have died."

A horrible death, of thirst and despair, I thought, and was doubly grateful. I figured if the steer were worth $125 I could ask half of that to be spent for steel posts and barbed wire to keep the cattle out of the woods. It had been a profitable afternoon's walk.

I never go into the woods without finding some reward. It may be actual tangible treasure to bring home, or it may be the joy of walking there with some appreciative friend, or it may be and often is simply a message from the earth, a deeper understanding of the earth and myself and my neighbors, human or wildlife, that inhabit that place.

Or it may be a column.

   ♣ ♣ ♣

The next morning I was still thinking of the durable, fragile, and persistent lives I had seen in the woods. In the clear swift-running creek were many kinds of stones that had been tumbled along by water for ages and miles. There were old bleached snail shells washed out by winter's restlessness, and mud-colored rough-textured geodes that sparkle like diamonds when broken open, disclosing their crystalline interiors; there were sharp-edged pieces of reddish chert and yellow and gray flint such as Indians used for arrowheads; there were the flat disks of sea-lily stalks, long ago petrified, that grew before glaciers swept over this land. And in the hillside above the creek, where cattle had made their narrow path down to the creek, small bulbs had been uprooted and were lying about, turning darkly pink from unaccustomed exposure to light.

All this had impressed me deeply. I thought of durability and endurance, of how suffering is essential and inevitable in the pattern of life, and a part of the beauty. I was going to write a column about all this.

The telephone interrupted me. It was Edna Fielder, a neighbor whose daughter, Gledith, was my son's first schoolteacher at the one-room country school in this community. Edna has brown eyes, an affectionate, happy laugh. She enjoys having company and likes to cook. She always cooks the silo-filling dinner for her son-in-law, Emmett Baynes, when Gledith is teaching. She has always loved to read and taught all her five children to like it. When she reads, she likes to lie on her back on the sofa, and all her children grew up believing that was the normal position for reading.

Edna had called to tell me she was planning to fly by jet plane to Paris within a few days. The high point of her trip, she said, would be to go out to a place five miles outside of Paris and see the spot where during World War II her son's plane was shot down above the English Channel. His name was John. He was her oldest son and was named for his father. There were five American men in the plane and they were all lost, four in the English Channel, one on land.

We talked awhile on the telephone. I wished her a good trip, and when she hung up I went back to the typewriter. Durable. Persistent. Fragile. Love, death, war.

It was time to write my column, but all I could think of was how will this lovely, quick-laughing, warm-hearted woman feel when she finds that spot, five miles outside of a foreign capital, which all these years and for a terribly great price, has belonged to her?

♣   ♣   ♣

All through the year on a family farm there are enchanting tokens of weather, bird, insect, fruit, livestock, flower, tree, beauty, and human love. Sometimes, in fact, the beauty of earth is almost too much to bear.

January fields have sometimes the look of an old green rug that is faded to greenish brown and bare in spots, as in front of the bureau where one walks more often than in some other places, and still bright green under the bed where it has not been much trodden upon. All the same, even with that threadbare look the fields when wet with a light January rain have a clean-swept, comforting look, however shabby. They look serene, untaxed—partly because you know they are resting, partly because you don't feel any driving need to be out there harvesting or planting or fighting something. The rain brings up the green in the lichened north sides of the tree trunks and they look as if somebody had cleaned a paintbrush there.

All you really need to do, at any time of year, is to take time to look at it to realize how beautiful is an untroubled piece of earth.

And everywhere, if you need an example, you will find resilience and quiet evidence of courage. I saw one, on the way down to the mailbox one spring morning. In a winter storm a large maple limb had been bent, cracked like a stick of kindling across a fire builder's knee. Falling, the limb rested horizontally across the branch below. In April a few weeks later a sturdy twig on it had expanded its leaves fully, in contrast to the tentative, timid buds on other branches waiting for the right, warm season. It was as though the broken branch understood it could not survive the year and therefore wished to make the most of what life it had left, spending its all extravagantly out of season.

♣　♣　♣

As soon as we had taken possession of Ira's farm we wanted to show its fields and woods to friends. And there were places on it we wanted to explore, not having ever seen them before we bought the farm.

Often I rode out with Dick on the tractor to the fields back of Ira's barn or on up to the Klondike field. From the wagon's height, as I rode past a grapevine-filled hackberry tree one day, I saw a dove's nest in the tree. It was sloppily built of sticks and bits of pennyroyal and there were four eggs in it. Then suddenly one morning, the eggs were gone. They had not hatched. The thief could have been an owl, a blue jay, crow, or something else. Man resents these natural interceptions of what he admires, but in carrying out his own plans he frequently intercepts the plans of birds and animals. The very possession of land is, in fact, a history of invasion. Indians were hunters and believed the land belonged to them. Settlers came in, to be farmers, invaded successfully, and took the land and believed it to be theirs. Industry now is invading agriculture and the small farmer is becoming a victim of the invasion in a changing era.

All that spring we took pleasure in taking our guests to see what we were doing to the new fields.

One Sunday Ralph and Polly West had come from Putnam County and Joe had come home from Purdue, bringing a fellow student, Calvin Cuppler, for the weekend. It was a spring day, a day when every living thing was probably glad just to be alive. We all got into the tractor wagon and rode past Ira's barn and on up to the Klondike. The woods we passed through was a garden of spring flowers, and we found morel mushrooms at the edge of the hilltop. When we reached the Klondike, Calvin and Westy looked over the field and complimented Dick on his reclaiming of the land from the brush. Westy reached down into the ground and picked up a blacksnake that had been run over and killed by the disk even before it had had time to emerge from its winter sluggishness and shed its skin. He lifted it out from its snug, unsafe death place and laid it exposed on the field. Within an hour it would be discovered by the telescopic-eyed buzzard already gliding gracefully above the field.

Calvin found an almost perfect arrowhead on the surface of the ground. Dick found the first mushroom.

All over the hillside, unmindful of the dove's eggs or disk-killed snake, were wild flowers, new grass, and up-springing weeds. The woods was a magic place, a place of beauty, but at the heart of its tenderness and extravagance was a hard core of discipline. Nature disciplines unceasingly, to keep the balance, and to make survival possible. She strengthens stalk and muscle by hardship. Sometimes I think there is as much of danger as of safety in numbers. Perhaps it was their very overabundance that made the passenger pigeons vulnerable to extinction. As for the dove, probably nature never intended that all birds should have equal success or equal pleasure, but only that all should wish for it and try.

We stopped to pick mushrooms along the hillside as we came back, and when we got home we had a gay dinner of fried chicken and mushrooms in the dining room. It is by stages like this that a new farm becomes owned.

♣　　♣　　♣

To impartial nature there is no "good" bird and no "bad" one, no "valuable" insect and no "worthless" one. She has uses for everything she devises and she has tasks to exact from everything, and none can escape her assignment.

In the bird world a fight is not a manifestation of hatred, but a clash of hunger against the courage that fear often calls up in the presence of danger.

A farmer considers a Cooper's hawk a bad bird because it destroys his poultry or the songbirds he likes and feeds. Therefore the farmer who saw a Cooper's hawk in the lot below his barn, eating some feathered creature, got a gun, intending to shoot the hawk. Even with the gun trained on this large, striking-looking bird, the farmer hesitated. He hesitated so long that if the hawk had not been overconfident or perhaps overhungry it could have got safely away. It stayed. Repeatedly, with its long beak it stabbed its smaller, feathered victim, pulling out feathers and tossing them aside. It looked around only carelessly as it continued stabbing. One shot killed it.

Passing by soon after, I went into the field to look at it. The hawk lay on the ground, the April wind slightly ruffling its pinkly tan underfeathers. The feathers on its upper body were gray. The head, slightly flat, like an eagle's, bore a thin line of green above the beak and a circle of green around each yellow, half-open eye. The beak was a cruel-looking weapon, strong, dark, fiercely curved. The hard, dark scimitar-like claws on its toes were even more savage-looking. A hawk has three front toes and one back toe on each foot. When one forward claw closes with the back one, they form a ring from which there is no escape. A Cooper's hawk can lift up and carry away a large hen if it wishes. The hawk had held its captive and killed it by stabbing it repeatedly at the back of the head.

The victim was a yellow-shafted flicker, possibly the one that had come all winter to eat from the feeder west of our kitchen window. A bird of splendor, larger than most songbirds, it wore a patch of red at the back of its head. The upper feathers were striped black and white, the soft, wind-shaken underfeathers beautifully polka-dotted. All along the side of the dark wing feathers on the underside ran a line of golden yellow. It also had a strong, dark beak and it also had been in the act of killing for food. When the hawk struck, the force and pain of it had caused the flicker's

246

beak to clamp shut so tightly that half of the moist, pink earthworm was still dangling outside, unable to pull itself in or out. An earthworm is a farmer's good friend. Traveling through his fields it helps aerate, enrich, and mellow the soil. But a farmer cannot hope to protect all the earthworms. He has to depend on the greater and more ubiquitous wisdom of the natural law that provides earthworms in such plenitude that great numbers of individuals can be eaten, but the species will not perish.

♣   ♣   ♣

The year before we bought Ira's farm, Carr tended Ira's cornfield. The corn on the level field along the east road was of such spectacular fineness, tall, blue-green, heavy-yielding that people passing along the Maple Grove Road drove slowly or stopped entirely to admire it.

When we bought the farm Joe was a senior at Purdue University majoring in agronomy. He told his father, "You'll either have to do right by that field or build a forty-foot board fence around it." Lumber being the price it was, it seemed cheaper to buy fertilizer and gasoline and do right by the field. Dick put $1,600 worth of fertilizer on Ira's farm the first year. Being a former Purdue student himself, and having a son to act as his "farm manager," Dick planted the cornfield according to the "Purdue Says" system, with the help of a large staff of unpaid local consultants, observers

247

and advisers, including naturally the former owner and the neighbor who had planted last year's excellent crop.

The Purdue Says system, as administered by the farm son, Joe, began with soil tests and continued with a series of letters home urging, reminding, instructing, and querying. Fortunately, Dick already knew a little about raising corn, having done it for twenty years or more. Fertilizer was applied generously at the right moment, including anhydrous ammonia applied by Mr. Splendor from his truck at the rate of 120 pounds to the acre, and Mr. Splendor staying to dinner with us that day.

The farm manager came home over weekends to work on the cornfield, and unfailingly rallied his boy friends around to help and join us at gay meals. Last year's cornstalks were disked in. This seemed for a time like a mistake, because the fluffed-up stalks were difficult to keep under the tilled surface. The cornstalk situation, however, provided the excuse for many happy consultations of the advisory staff. The cornfield is unfenced, lies right next to the road, and 'when any passers-by saw the consultants summiting, it was easy to pull off to the side of the road and join them.

At the planting time approved by the Purdue Says system the Lord also cooperated, sending a weekend of superb weather. The farm manager and his special consultants, Dick Francis and Tony Scherschel (both of them university students), kept two tractors going all night, preparing the ground.

Dick was entrusted with buying hybrid seed corn, borrowing a neighbor's bigger, better planter and drilling in the seed. Have faith in the land and treat it right, is the core of the Purdue Says system. And love the land, adds Maple Grove.

Agriculture is said to be the beginning of civilization. Whenever men begin to till the soil and mold fields and make requirements of it, industry follows. When they fight for possession of it, society is well under way. Art follows the tillage of the soil, Daniel Webster said.

Actually art exists from the beginning of land tilling. It is manifest in the lines of the tilled field. There is hardly anything more artistic than a well-tilled, fertile, disciplined field at any time. When freshly plowed, brown and shining and fragrant from its winter mellowing; or when newly worked down, fertile, full of promise and waiting to receive the seed; or when the first green sharp-pointed sprouts make dotted lines across the field, almost but never quite meeting at the distant horizon, and always beckoning on; or later when the blossoming corn scents the sun-warmed air and the long, warped green blades clash together in the rising wind, or gently in still, summer air; or when the corn picker rushes through a ripened field knocking the brown stalks about and some stalks fall and others stand waving their empty brown gloves aimlessly in the wind . . . I think all these times are art and beauty, and sometimes I wish I could reach out and put my arms around the cornfield.

Late near the end of a day that threatened rain, when Dick was plowing the last round of the cornfield, preparatory to "laying it by," I rode with him on the tractor. I took a firm grip on the tractor's gray fender with one hand and a firm grip on Dick's suspenders with the other, because the effect of watching corn cultivating is hypnotic; you could easily fall off and get plowed under with the weeds.

There are eleven steely bright points to the cultivator (four spearheads and seven duckfoots). The tractor rushes forward, roaring softly, and these sharp points split the brown, dry crust of earth in a smooth, darkening flow. They push small weeds over and uproot the shaving-brush clusters of volunteer corn that sprouted from an ear of last year's corn accidentally plowed under with the stalks. The tall, waving tender green blades of young corn plants are gathered close and gently drawn under a metal arch and protectively disciplined into passing between two metal walls called "clod fenders." The green line thus flows under the arch and then spreads apart behind it, giving the effect of rippling, flowing green water. It is spellbinding. A corn-cultivating farmer has to watch it so he can keep the wheels in exactly the right line. A deviation of half an inch is that much too close . . . corn planter wheels set just the right distance apart to co-ordinate the cultivator tracks; tractor wheels set at an exact spacing so that everything is mathematically in harmony. In agriculture, as in banking, baking, music, painting, sculpture, crossword puzzles, quilting, or poetry, mathematics is the foundation.

This may surprise people who thought weather was the basis of farming. Machinery is mathematical and impersonal. If a corn plant is out of line it makes no difference whether it is the best plant in the field; up it comes, uprooted by the shining steel point and covered into oblivion by the smooth-flowing, increasing brown river of soil.

The final kindness of corn to a farm wife is the test it provides for her farm affection. Silage is made of unripe corn; it is essential for succulence in cattle feeding. By spring, when it is nearly gone, it has a distinct odor. If in the last days of April a farm wife can endure the smell this late-lingering succulence imparts to boots, jackets, overalls that have even barely brushed by it, and if, smelling that smell, she is still glad she lives on a farm, then she loves the farm, and she is a farmer down to her farthest threadroot.

♣   ♣   ♣

Somewhere I have read that laughter and the use of fire are the two gifts that essentially set humankind apart from his animal neighbors.

The difficulty of remaining truly silent is something equally differentiating, I think. Humankind cannot be truly silent. Baby birds can freeze at a sharp cue from the mother bird and remain silent for a long time. What seems even more miraculous is that they know these cues from birth. Humankind has to have soft music to be silent to, and even then is not very successful at it.

Wakened at night by the stealthy, small rattling of paper in the kitchen wastebasket, I got up; but the mouse had heard my conscience rousing my sleepy mind to the investigation and had become still by the time I arrived. Until you have thus listened for a mouse, you cannot appreciate what a talent for stillness a mouse has.

While I waited for the rustling to resume betrayingly, I sat down and did some thinking about man's inability to be still. What other animal can jingle small coins so steadily in his pants pockets while speaking at a farm meeting, or rattle car keys, or click a fountain pen on and off interminably all through a tense committee meeting?

What other animal, even the huge-eyed, lovely lemur with its humanlike fingers can "pop" its fingers so steadily that the listener involuntarily looks on the floor for the mounds of chalk-brittle, broken-off fingers?

What bright-colored bird can so busily scratch its head, pinch its face, clean its fingernails or clip them with a metal clipper, or tear from its long nails the coat of bright red polish applied only the day before? What centipede could possibly do as much wriggling with all of its feet as a nervous human animal can do with one, while having to listen to a boresome conversation or wait half an hour in a doctor's office or bus station? Or what ruminant could possibly chew gum with the steadiness and infinite variety the human race easily manifests? Or cough, sneeze, rustle its clothes, open its purse and get out things and snap the purse shut with such modulations, crescendos and cadenzas? What round-eyed owl gets half as much good out of its spectacles, taking them off, blowing gently on them, wiping them, holding them up to look through, then polishing again before adjusting them on again?

There is probably no creature from whom noise can be so varied, automatic, or meaningless, yet from whom silence is as rare and difficult as from humankind.

Perhaps that is why silence is a magic word and the sound of it is so beautiful.

♣   ♣   ♣

For people who wake in the night with a heaviness of spirit brought on by the world news of the day, there is some composure to be had from listening to the simple, familiar, often melodious night sounds in the country. Farmers, being so well supplied with these, perhaps ought to take on the burden of national worry, as one farmer bales hay for another who has no baler. Custom worrying, with twine and one extra wagon included.

A farmer, waking at this vulnerable hour, is comforted by little sounds: the tentative brushing of pointed leaves against an old farmhouse wall, or the long, curling quaver of the small gray screech owl in the apple tree, the tinkle of rain against the window sill and the flowing melody of it in the eave trough, or even the sound of a cow expressing her night thoughts frankly, if she is far enough in the distance.

Listening does not dissolve the oppression, nor solve the problem. It merely makes the burden more bearable, as shifting a basket rests a tired arm.

Sometimes on summer evenings a farmer, sitting quietly on the back steps and listening intently, can hear the sounds of insect wings, a thinned-down sound, faintly like the sound of cattle pulling grass in the still summer nights. A tiny sound, the rustle of many tiny wings, it is the sound of summer's skirt swishing.

But most of the time the drama of the insect world goes on soundlessly, and except for mere chance you would not observe it. One night, by chance, I looked through the back porch window into the moonless darkness and saw a small, nearly square patch of green light glowing steadily against the glass. I recognized the firefly's light, but was puzzled that it did not go on and off intermittently as it normally does in midsummer evenings when fireflies rise up from the dampening grass and fly about, exploding into light like tiny firecrackers.

With the reading glass held close to it I saw the green light originated from the two lowest segments of a firefly's soft underbody, with a tiny bar of black between the green sections. From the lowest segment a new spurt of light spouted up at intervals like a fountain of green fire. Suddenly the square patch began to wheel and dance madly, and I understood. A firefly had blundered into a spider's web at the window and was held fast there, which created the steady glow. The dancing was made when the spider came down and stung; and the firefly made a frantic effort to free himself, creating a wild, green ballet.

He was hopelessly held by the tenacious, delicate spider thread. I went outside and took him down, carefully removing what thread I could remove. But it was already too late. The legs curled up like lifeless wisps of black thread.

It is hard to resist interfering with the natural world. And the reason it is so hard, perhaps, is that the human interferer wonders how far the rule of survival applies also to his world, and the world news suggests that it applies too far. He seeks further, for another rule.

♣   ♣   ♣

Actually how far removed is the human world from the world of our neighbors—the animals and insects? By what evidence does man support the belief that he is the choice, finished product of creation?

On all hands, all over the farm and in the woods, the life patterns of these neighbors make thoughtful suggestion for a farm observer to gather, store, and chew on later.

In July, when I was getting ready to set out some dried tulip bulbs from Easter's potted gifts, I went out into the yard and scratched away dry leaves and trailing ends of honeysuckle to make a place. Immediately there rose up from the disturbed ground a distinct odor, pleasant, woodsy, menthol-like. Simultaneously ants gushed forth from the spot; medium-sized ants having the amber color and transparency of bread-wrapping paper. They came in a confused crowd, individuals darting into and out of the mass. They ran over each other, pushed and dragged at the white capsule-like larvae lying close on the ground. I picked up a handful of the dry, crumblike earth they had run out of, and smelling it discovered where the fragrance was coming from.

The ants' nest, properly called a formicary, was saturated with the odor of formic acid. It is this acid that makes the ant's bite painful. The ancientness of ants is attested in the word "formic," which has come from a Latin word that meant "belonging to ants."

The dictionary describes formic acid as "a colorless, mobile, vesicatory liquid" of formula HCO_2H, but this does not at all describe the odor it gives the ant's house. Cool, summery, fitting to July, somewhat like the odor of wild bergamot in a deep woods.

Formic acid is also in the sting of bees, those cousins of ants so much better known than ants that their common name Hymenoptera more often suggests bees than ants. I

picked up a few ants, making no attempt to select a complete society—drone, queen, and worker—and brought them
into the house, along with a few of their larvae and two
inches of their familiar dry, crumbled earth (which remark-
ably did not pack down, giving me the thought that perhaps
formic acid would help a too-tight clay soil while humus
was being worked into it). I put all this into a glass and
watched. The ants continued to panic, tunneling into and
out of the soil and inspecting the quiet larvae. Gradually
they subsided. Finally, when they were resting, motionless,
on the surface of the soil, all the smell had gone from it.

I took them back to the now-abandoned formicary and
again they became wildly active—I could not tell whether
because they recognized their former home and were ap-
palled by its desolation, as a person might be in a war-ruined
deserted city. I left them there, feeling indebted to them for
some new land-treatment ideas and the memory of a new
smell, and also for a new adjective, "vesicatory." It means
"having the power to blister," and I set it aside to use in human affairs. It is bound to come in handy sometime.

♣   ♣   ♣

In late March, when Ira and Monta held their sale, the
ground had thawed through; there seemed to be no bottom
to the mud. Cars, trucks, and tractors left deep gashes in
the barn lot and fields. Trucks had to be pulled out with

tractors. For a study of mud in depth, the day made history even in a farming area.

But the earth is resilient, especially with some help from soil-conscious owners. Dick and Joe rolled the gashes shut, smoothed the sod. By the end of the strawberry season, when Monta and Ira were moving their household goods to the new place, the March wounds had healed. Grass had closed in again. "Grass," said John Ingalls, "is the forgiveness of nature." Grass is nature's coveralls. Grass is to the earth what the subconscious mind is to mankind. The power of the subconscious is greater than all the work lists and prod-dings of conscience a gardener can have. But the power of grass, I suspect, is even greater. All summer, whenever I dashed out to the garden by the raspberry patch for a last-minute cucumber or green pepper, or a salad's worth of fresh dill, my subconscious mind had silently pointed to the grass that needed pulling from around tomatoes, beans, and pep-pers.

"Yes, yes, I know. Sometime. Not now," my conscious mind had replied.

Suddenly one day I was out there pulling grass. It was as much of a surprise to me as to the garden. I had gone out to pick a cucumber.

When I came back in, some hours later my subconscious mind was smirking. The grass lay piled in a great heap, un-discouraged, biding its time. The noon dishes were still wait-ing to be washed.

While I washed them I thought of something else John Ingalls said which every gardener admits ruefully and every farmer rejoices in knowing: grass is immortal.

I respect grass; I love it, actually, and could spend fifteen minutes a day saying complimentary things about it. I love its various seeds and the feel and look of them and the way they flow through one's hands. I respect the way grass comes, unplanted, apparently from no place, asking so little. All you need to do is to move a board from the ground, or an oil barrel, or pull out some weeds and then, mercifully, protecting grass covers the spot of bare earth and feeds it with its own blades. By grass, I mean clover also.

Encouraged, it feeds livestock, which is the beginning of feeding people and essential in maintaining the soil. Grass holds the flesh of earth to earth's bones, which is the beginning of farming and housing, government jobs, business, gymnasiums, schools, churches, music halls, auditoriums, and places for red-winged blackbirds to build nests.

In one of the oldest readers I can find, Sarah Roberts Boyles speaks in a poem for grass, "Here I come creeping, creeping everywhere . . ."

Grass provides suburbanites something to take their minds off their problems by giving them something to mow. Without grass there would never have been any power mowers, and, as my music-teaching, piano-playing neighbor, Grace Lundy, says, "Nothing has made so much difference in the appearance of the country as the power lawnmower." Without the power mower, even with the blessing of rural electricity, people would never have flocked to the country in such starling-like numbers as they have.

I love grass for its fragrance also. A freshly mowed yard smells like a different place; a freshly mowed hayfield, especially one with sweet clover in it, or an upland field in which nature has planted a liberality of field mint or pennyroyal is one of the rewards of farming. The frantic days of haying provide one of the pleasantest times for farmers or farm visitors to remember. De-grassing the garden that afternoon, I pulled up several handfuls of what I call menthol grass because it smells pleasantly like menthol and I do not know its real name. It has a heavy blade, glossy and bright green above the surface of the ground, and pulls up easily, disclosing the white underground section thickening as if trying to develop into a bulb.

Many other kinds of grass I had pulled up and thrown into the heap, for a garden democratically welcomes them all and collects all. I had pulled up elbow grass that makes a new plant wherever its joint touches earth; nest-egg grass that pulled up readily, and although its long seed head looked green in color and immature, it had already ripened a little clutch of seeds that it dropped on the bare ground where they would prosper just that much more because I had removed the parent stalks.

The names of grass are beguiling to read: brome; orchard grass which makes fine eating for livestock but inspires a lawnkeeper to profanity on account of its high, bulging crown; witch grass, crab grass, and love grass. There are three kinds of love grass: ordinary love grass, sand love grass, and stinking love grass!

Best of all I love grass when it is hay.

♣　♣　♣

Let this be a lesson to people who think they will do on Sunday what they didn't get done during the week.

Sunday morning was dark and chilly. I was three columns late, so I decided to stay home from church and write them.

The typewriter was interrupted by the Maple Grove minister, who said the fuel oil line was broken at the church's stove, the church was cold; so could they meet at this house, which is the nearest one?

"Just give me time to get the typewriter out of the living room," I said. Dick was up at the barn doing his morning chores.

While the minister went back up to the cold church to summon his flock, I set a quick fire in the dining-room fireplace and took out the ironing board. Coming from a chilled building, the people were not critical. Besides, they were all neighbors.

The adult Sunday school class met in the living room from whence the typewriter had fled, leaving the games table to serve as a communion table. Faye Baynes and Delitha Cowden took their beginners' class to the dining room in front of the welcome flame. The minister's wife convened her teen-agers around the kitchen table. Mary Naylor took her in-betweeners upstairs to Carol's bedroom, which fortunately was somewhat in order, having been available to an overnight guest only a few days earlier.

When Dick came down from the barn he was surprised to find himself in church. He had never, so far as I know, attended church in overalls before. This is an old house, and although it has had church parties and church dinners here it has never had a worship service in it before, as far as I know, and it must have felt privileged. My only regret was that it happened on a weekend when both the farm children were away in school and could not share the honor with us.

♣   ♣   ♣

It was a new experience for the church, too, but this church (organized in 1876) keeps young by having new experiences.

The builders set up a one-room frame building, which has since been remodeled, enlarged with an entryway and basement.

It did not have a wedding until it was an old church; its first bridegroom was a young man then serving it as minister. Since then it has had several weddings. It has had many funerals, and many homecomings which it calls "Big

June." On Palm Sunday it held its first ordination.

The young man to be ordained was the son of Emmett Baynes, a dairy farmer in this community. At that time the son was a student in a theological school in Tennessee.

To the people of the community it seemed only an invocation's length ago that John Baynes was a little earnest, red-haired boy sitting between his schoolteaching mother and the witty, dark-eyed, quiet-faced deacon who was his father.

This is the pattern of children growing up in little country churches: first the mothers hold the babies on their laps. It is a mark of special talent if the father is able to hold the baby and keep it reasonably quiet during the hour and a half of services. Presently the babies have grown into little boys and girls, not quite tall enough yet for their heads to show above the backs of the long, gray-painted benches on which they sit between their parents and are given "something to keep them busy," which may be a Sunday school leaflet and crayon, or the mother's purse. Next they are trusted to sit with favorite aunts or grandparents. At four, a young man will sit in proud, smiling decorum beside the seventeen-to-thirty-year-old woman he has already invited to be his wife in the future. Later he sits with his boy contemporaries and whispers too much. Finally he brings his girl friend; and more finally, his wife.

At this ordination, surrounded by the affectionate good will of neighbors and relatives, John sat next to the aisle beside his wife and held their baby girl on his lap until it was time for him to rise and declare solemnly, "I respond to that call and desire to be formally ordained to that work."

How is a man different after ordination, and at what point does the difference actually begin? Is it at the moment when he kneels at the altar and is touched by the hands of minister and deacons . . . in John's case the hands of his neighbors and his father?

The service has the quality of ancient ritual about it. A listener, hearing the undertone of usual murmurous human sounds accompanying a country religious service, could not help thinking how vulnerable, how pitiable, how needful and weak, and yet how potentially splendid and strong is humankind.

The neighbor who made a benedictory prayer at the end of the ordination was, obviously, deeply stirred. For John, in my thoughts, I had the same reverent wish I would have for my children, my husband, myself, my friends, the people who dislike me and the people I do not know at all . . . one prayer, differing only in intensity: that he should discover his ability and use it in the way most useful to God and his fellow men and, it follows, to his own peace of mind.

♣　　♣　　♣

Levi Oliver, school bus-driving farmer, and Bob Judah, commercial artist in IU's geology department and president

of the Hoosier Hills Art Guild, had asked Mary Naylor if
the women of the Maple Grove church could serve a supper
to conclude a soil conservation tour during Soil Stewardship
Week in May.

The church had been in process of remodeling all spring
and was still as unfinished as Schubert's symphony. The raw
earth that had been removed to make space for a kitchen
and dining-room basement under the old one-room frame
building was piled up in the yard, but the kitchen was usable.
There were as yet no curtains up at the small basement
windows that were half above and half below the surface
of the ground and protected by a half circle of metal set outside like a kind of cup rim. The windows opened inside.

We had chairs and the long tables on which we always
served Big June dinners out in the yard. The Council needed
the money, so Mary immediately said yes, we could feed the
supervisors and country preachers of the tour.

They had planned to make a tour to farms on which they
would see the benefits of terraces, sodded waterways, farm
ponds, contour and strip crop farming, spillways. The country preachers should have no trouble finding texts for Soil
Stewardship Week. Verses showing how the ancient people
appreciated water and suffered from lack of it run through
the Bible like a creek threading through a green pasture:
"His soul shall be as a watered garden"; "He shall be as a
tree whose roots are planted by the river"; "the land lan-
guisheth because no man layeth it to heart."

The Council women appreciate the need of conservation. They were glad to help make other people realize that if the soil goes, we shall all go. They were also appreciating the importance of water. We badly needed rain. Strawberries were not growing to full size; tomato plants freshly set in the gardens were falling over limply and dying. "The little sauerkraut plants are turning yellow," remarked the young minister from California, looking at Mary Naylor's cabbages.

We expected the preachers to be thirsty after a day's dry tour so we had made a washtubful of iced tea. While we prepared the hot rolls, chicken and noodles, green beans, pickled beets, and other accessories before and after the fact of a money-making church dinner, we looked up through the dusty high windows in the dining room and hoped the darkening sky meant rain to come.

Mary Snooks brought clean white linen tablecloths and bouquets of flowers from home. We set the table prettily because a photographer was coming to take pictures for the local newspaper. Besides we hoped the ministers would remember the dinner happily and ask to come again the next year.

The men ate, talked, laughed, ate more, lingered at the table. The photographer came and took pictures and went away. In the kitchen the women chatted happily because a small rain had begun to tap against the basement windows.

We had carried away the dishes from the main course, cut the pies, and were just ready to serve dessert when suddenly the Lord let loose with a full-sized rain. It beat down on the unprotected raw earth piled outside the windows, filled the half-cup protectors and the half-cups ran over. Suddenly the pressure of muddy water pushed the windows open, inside. Water cascaded into the dining room, barely missing the Maple Grove minister sitting at the head of the table. The men leaped up and two of them tried to close the windows, but muddy water gushed down the concrete block walls and within a few minutes had flowed across the dining room to the furnace, to the kitchen floor, to the foot of the stairway leading up to the main room.

It was muddy water, like thin gravy.

The women sent the guests upstairs to the Sunday school rooms to wait for dessert to be brought to them there, and the men went thankfully.

Then the Council women took off their shoes and went barefooted through the two-inch depth of muddy water carrying plates of cherry pie and glasses of iced tea and cups of coffee upstairs.

Everybody laughed about it. "The photographer went home too soon," cried Monta gaily as she waded past me, carrying a plate of pie in each hand.

Barefooted, the women afterward sat upstairs to watch the conservation program. "The balance of nature on this earth is very delicate," warned the film at the beginning.

"Downstairs," said Prevo Whitaker, chairman, "you have just seen an example of the perishability of unprotected soil."

The Lord couldn't have planned a more convincing demonstration of the need of soil conservation.

Nor a better way to show how farm women combine reverence and expedience to meet an emergency.

♣   ♣   ♣

At one end of the flower-bedecked room John lay. Not as I remember him and prefer to remember him always, in clean shirt and overalls, always clean. John who drove his car into your yard at unexpected times, and got out slowly and walked slowly toward the house with a half grin waiting to break into a laugh, expecting a joke and prepared to answer in kind.

John the superb storyteller, acute observer, accurate rememberer, with the keen analytical philosophy and the widespread penetrating love of life and fun. Vigorous John, of whom his friends said, "He'll do anything for you or anything to you." He would go to fantastic effort to pull off a joke and could take one of the same dimension.

John who spent money and energy to improve his old house, and when his neighbor said mournfully, "I just hope you live to get the good of this," replied sharply, "I've got the good of it if I die as soon as I've finished it!"

He could make quick, angry, erratic decisions. He tore out his good fences without regret when he decided to stop raising cattle and start raising crops instead on his bottom fields that often got flooded in spring. He said, when he had a building problem, he just went to bed and the next morning woke up with the solution in mind. He changed the course of the creek across his bottom fields and tore down good sheds so he wouldn't have to pay taxes on them.

John, who in the days when money was hard to come by and he had a little income of $10 a month from a rented house, stopped and gave two months' rent to a neighbor whose barn had burned.

At the crossroads grocery, where farmers met almost as if at a clubhouse and everybody played jokes on everybody else and nobody resented it, John asked for a sandwich (which he always called a "savage") and wanted horseradish on it, and they put on so much that the tears streamed down his face while he ate it, but he never "let on" that he noticed. He said of a friend, "A good man, but high-strung; he'll go to pieces and fly like glass." When his wife, Leota, was away John cooked his own meals. "I fried eggs," he said, "and you can get enough of that." His language was beautiful in its farm expression; a canvas tarpaulin he called "a cavinas," and he said once, "The truth finally donged on me."

When he was late getting home to supper, Leota kept supper waiting and she and the two little girls, Audrey and Bertha Mae, waited to eat with John. John always kissed Leota good-bye when he left.

For a long time, when anybody said, "How are you, John?" he smiled and said, "Goin' in low gear."

The neighbors thought he had some premonition of death. He had got his house literally and figuratively in order; he had put in a bathroom and changed the stairway and put in a furnace and insulation, and built Leota a little sewing place she had always wanted. At a sale a couple of years earlier he had finally been able to buy an old Seth Thomas clock, something he had always wanted, and was delighted to find it in perfect running order. He liked to fish; he stocked his ponds with fish. He was big, and gentle in strange ways.

That last summer he had told Leota he wanted to get two things done before winter, to roof the shed on the "Far hill" and to get the creek banks sprayed. He told Leota one morning he wouldn't really care if death caught up with him when he was working alone, over on the far hill.

And that was where it came to meet him. He never got the creek banks sprayed, but he had almost finished the roof. It was on the same hill where, a year or so before, the tractor and a wagonload of wood had overturned and he came near being killed.

That final day he had eaten his lunch and was still sitting on the ground leaning back against a tree. From where he was sitting he had a wide, beautiful view out across his farm, and he was apparently at peace with everything.

Something vital, distinctive, and irreplaceable went out of the community when it lost John Dunning.

♣　♣　♣

Among the many businesses pendent from farming like charms from a bracelet, is the livestock sale barn. The auctioneer has usually been a farm boy; often he still lives on a farm and keeps some livestock there. He must understand farmers. He must know local farmers and be able to call them by name instantly in a crowd. He must know prices and how far to push a bid. He must have a good stock of jokes, even if they're old, such as the one in which he and his assistant hold up a log chain and he says, "It's got a crook on each end"; or when picking up some preposterous thing nobody is likely to want he says solemnly, "Now boys, it's not often you have a chance to bid on something like this."

He must keep the crowd entertained, hopeful, in a good humor and relaxed.

It's a help if the auctioneer can look, speak, or act like a buffoon, but in reality he must be sharp. He has to have a good carrying voice and be able to chant hypnotically, so he can do his thinking under cover of his chant. He must speak three languages simultaneously: one to the crowd, one to his assistants, and one to himself.

At a livestock sale or auction the only person who knows more than the auctioneer about what's going on is another auctioneer.

There is a new trend in auctioneering now. Time was an auctioneer went wherever the people lived, and sold their farm and household items there. A lunch was served by the women of some church. The new trend is for a well-established auctioneer to build his own sale barn and bring the merchandise there to sell. In these places the kitchen is an important psychological and economic asset.

We stopped one evening to see a new auction barn in a neighboring county on Gene Williams's farm. He had cried a sale that day on a farm where the people were selling everything. His barn, finished only three weeks earlier, was a spacious room, well lighted, capable of accommodating three hundred people in addition to a full day's sale of merchandise. It was clean, orderly, and that evening already full of antiques gathering for a sale to be the following Saturday.

Gene's wife bakes the pies and manages the kitchen at the new barn.

"Do you ever have anything you're afraid isn't going to sell?" I asked, having noticed that when an item isn't going an auctioneer is inclined to "throw in" something more, and when the bidder takes his purchase home he often leaves what was thrown in. Even if he is buying junk a farmer feels a little better if he gets something extra.

"No ma'am," Gene said promptly. "I never pick up anything that I have any doubt about at all. I have faith that as sure as I'm standing here I can sell it. And I always do."

True, he always does. In his enthusiasm that evening he was beginning to forget he was not crying a sale, and he kept addressing Dick and me and his wife and son Billy as "People," as he does the sale crowd.

"How did you happen to become an auctioneer?" I asked.

He had been a farm boy, and considering his unmistakable gift for selling I would have thought his parents would have known at first sight of him they had an auctioneer on their hands.

"People," he cried happily, "I was about fifteen and heard Fred Reppert cry a sale. I followed him around all day, spellbound, with my mouth open. I tell you, people, I think I caught all the flies there were there that day. I knew then I wanted to be an auctioneer."

But it was some time before he started learning it. First he spent some years as a tenant farmer. "I finally got tired of farms being sold out from under me," he said, "and I went to auctioneering school."

The selling brotherhood already established did not welcome the newcomer with open arms when he got back from school. It was pretty tough for a while. "But I tell you, people," he cried, and looked at Dick as if expecting him to nod or lift a finger in a bid, "I kept on, even if it was tough. Finally one day a woman named Job, bless her heart, came and told me she and her husband were selling out, going to Florida, and she wanted me to take charge of selling her stuff." It was a start, and with his unquenchable enthusiasm plus the help of his wife and his son, who also wants to be an auctioneer, he became established; and now, he says, he is "almost covered up."

♣   ♣   ♣

273

"There's a new trend in eating at farm sales now, too," Dick told me on the way home. "The coffee break has made itself felt there now. At the Dalton sale the men ate in the kitchen, then in the aftenoon a woman came out to the barn with sandwiches and coffee. I thought the cows would run over her any minute, but she stayed until she sold everything. A farm sale is like a committee meeting now; nobody can get down to business until everybody's had a cup of coffee."

♣   ♣   ♣

"Come over," said Ruth Fyffe, driving away after we had visited pleasantly at the road's edge in front of our mailbox. This is the traditional farewell greeting of farm neighbors who have met any time, anyplace. It is sincere; it is also a convention, just as when you ask somebody, "How are you?" you don't expect them to tell you.

In the modern changing pattern of life on a family farm this greeting is more of a wish than an actual expectation. When she stopped, Ruth had been on her way home from a job in town where she works three and a half or four days a week. She has weekends free. "I have to let things go at home to do this," confessed this immaculate housekeeper. She lives in the big, pink-roofed white colonial house her grandparents built on the eighty-acre family-sized farm adjoining this family-sized farm.

Her husband always has some cattle on the farm and a job in town. He is a good mechanic. Russell used to say, "I'll be out here with you fellows someday, milking cows." But now he has two town jobs. One, a welding job, begins at noon; the second begins at one o'clock in the morning. This system, by which owners of small farms are able to continue living on them, is one of the reasons the old-time pleasant custom of leisurely neighborhood visits died down to diminuendo. One reason the home economics club suspended in this community was that many of the women had taken jobs. Granted, too, there came a time when the extension "lessons" were merely a repetition of what most farm women already knew or could learn at leisure from the farm magazines.

One of Ruth's sons and his wife and children have parked a house trailer in the field just outside of the neat picket fence. This son and his young wife both have town jobs and they take the children to a baby-sitter as they go into town. The other son has a country place a short distance farther away. He has two children, both in school. His wife has held a town job since they were married, and he had a town job and also does some custom trucking in his spare time.

Ruth and Russell do not try to raise fruit or farm crops. Russell rents his fields to another farmer, but they always have a fine vegetable garden, neat as a washed meat platter. When I met her at the roadside, Ruth told me they had had guests from out of the state over the weekend and she had feasted them on the first fruits of the garden.

"We had new beets, new carrots, new peas, new potatoes, new green beans, and lettuce," she said, and smiled a smile of quiet satisfaction. Ruth is pretty and one of the kindest persons I know.

A garden helps the budget; even more important, it eases a country woman's conscience for leaving her house to take a town job. Also finally, it rests her spirit. Suddenly realizing it was nearly suppertime Ruth said, "Well, come over."

"Oh, I will," I promised, "and you come."

♣   ♣   ♣

Summer is that lovely season of overwork and garden abundance when every farm woman has too much of something and therefore her neighbor, who has none, has enough. A perfect policy for small neighborly farming communities, unfortunately difficult to apply on an international scale.

"The canning season has seemed endless," said Martha Weymouth, whose husband is a farmer and a government accountant. They live in a pleasant old farmhouse on a large farm in an adjoining county.

Martha, who is also a writer, had temporarily escaped from the kitchen to the typewriter to write a letter. "Today we'll use the last of the glass jars and I'm just about to say to the tomatoes, 'The rest of you just rot and see if I care.' Where I'm going to get jars for garden huckleberries I don't know, but these I just can't let waste. Besides, I do love gloating over my beautifully crowded cellar shelves."

At church Jeanne Morgan said, "I got rid of three bushels of green beans yesterday." She looked triumphant, as if getting rid of the beans were the reason for raising them.

"I've canned all the green beans and tomatoes I'm going to can," said Mary Naylor, whose canning for a family of six runs into the hundreds of quarts. The Naylors have three sons and a daughter and live on an eighty-acre farm. Clyde and the boys rent about 210 acres more in other places and spend a good deal of time "farming on the road."

"I'm freezing corn now," continued Mary, "and I'm not going to make any mixed pickle. We love it, but I made so much last year we have plenty left over."

Probably the reason farm women go on canning and freezing their garden's offerings after the cellar shelves and freezers are full is from a sense of *noblesse oblige* established when they planted their gardens. A garden is a truce with nature, by which gardeners have some rights, but not many, and these subject to recall without notice.

One rule is that if a tomato for example can put its heart into making a crop the least a farm woman can do is see that it goes to a good purpose. Of course she can count on the chickens or hogs to take it on themselves once every summer to help her dispose of the garden; the trouble is they always choose the wrong time. Nature feels free to withdraw from the truce at any time and give the whole garden to some of her other creatures, all of which are just as important to her as the farm wife is. The gardener may go out any morning to find that bean beetles have made a beachhead in the bean rows while she was in the house canning the late cherries. From nature's viewpoint even the best gardener is only a squatter and his lease is temporary.

"Mary was mad yesterday" said Clyde Naylor. "She was mad at Bart's sow that got into the henhouse and tore up things and upset the feeders and spilled the drinking water. Then she discovered Johnny's ducks were eating the blossoms off of the peas in the garden."

This is partly what is meant by a family farm; everyone in the family shares the consequences of what everyone else in the family has or does.

Mary, red-haired, brown-eyed, thin and wiry, is a tolerant and forgiving person, quick to express her opinions kindly. Vengeance would have overtaken Bart's sow and Johnny's ducks except that Mary didn't have time to dispense it just then. She had to get dinner for a haying crew. She is a good cook, quick and efficient, and likes for people to eat as if it were a pleasure. "She got us an awful good dinner," said one of the haying crew, who sympathized with her even though he laughed.

Mary is a graduate of Indiana State Normal School, where she majored in home economics. After that she taught a year or so but didn't like it as well as farm housekeeping. She is experimental and original in her housekeeping and gardening. When she plants pole beans she plants strawberry popcorn there so she doesn't have to set bean poles. When the beans are gone, the popcorn is ripe, attractively dark red and salable, so she makes some money from her bean supports. She makes decisions quickly and never regrets them afterward. She likes to watch television while she irons. "Of course I iron in a few wrinkles, but what's the difference?" she says, laughing. Every year Mary and Clyde go on a vacation by themselves and without telling anybody where they are going.

She is forthright in a way many women can envy. Once when she had dinner ready and Clyde and the boys were unaccountably and unreasonably late, she waited awhile, then took the dinner and threw it into the backyard. It takes courage as well as wrath to do that.

Mary is able to go to church every Sunday morning and yet serve a good dinner, promptly and without nervous haste, almost as soon as she and the family get home.

The secret of this efficiency she explained with a characteristic Mary Naylor laugh. "I just have the same menu every Sunday. It's beef and potatoes, green beans and carrots, and chocolate cake."

♣   ♣   ♣

No matter what else you do, your "image" is incomplete unless you collect something. It can be anything from old tractor parts to family history. You may not have anything to say about what it will be. The choice is something bestowed on you, as unsought as rain.

One year, in silo-filling time, I suddenly discovered I was a collector of persimmon pudding recipes.

In this farming community, the silo-filling dinner is about the last remaining harvest dinner. Farmers like it, even though they dread it. On that day an astounding investment in farm machinery—tractors, wagons, field choppers, blowers, trucks, cars—are gathered at one farm.

Thanks to farm freezers, quick-fuel stoves, refrigerators, packaged food, running water in the kitchen, and easier farm chores in general, the preparation of a silo-filling dinner is not the great chore it used to be. In an earlier day a farm wife's neighbors came to help because she really needed the help; everything had to be prepared that morning. Now, much of the work can be done long before; a farm wife has frozen pies, meats, rolls, and vegetables in the freezer. The women who come to help simply make a bright holiday out of a workday. The food is good, and of banquet-sized quantities.

Hazel Dutton had offered to help me get the silo-filling dinner that week and she suggested having persimmon pudding for dessert. (In addition, of course, to ice cream, and some kind of pie.) She has a persimmon tree in her yard, whereof the fruit is large, sweet, never puckery even before frost. "And I have some persimmons in the freezer, already put through the colander," she offered generously. "I'll bring you some when I come to church tomorrow. And I'll bring you Floy Reynolds's recipe. It makes a big pudding."

Floy is Hazel's fishing companion. Floy has a car and drives; Hazel does not drive. They fish together from different places, often at our pond back of the barn. Floy never eats the fish—she doesn't like it. But she enjoys fishing because she says it's relaxing.

"I can't get her to go anyplace else," says Hazel, "but if I just name fishin', she's ready to come."

On Sunday afternoon, therefore, I baked Floy's persimmon pudding recipe which fills two big pans with pudding and the house with a heavenly smell. Nothing can possibly taste as good as that recipe smells, baking.

The Judahs came. Bob, an artist, brought me a masterful oil painting of the old stone fence along the Telfer farm in this community. He had some writing planned for me to do for him. Mrs. Judah smelled the pudding, which unfortunately was not done enough to share with her, and she offered me her recipe, which is different because it is baked in a gallon crock.

I already had Monta's recipe, which is different because it uses bread crumbs and a cooked sauce "boiled to thin thickness," Monta says. And I had Aunt Hattie's recipe, which is different because it uses no spices, and Aunt Lois's, which is different because Aunt Lois was not like anybody else. And Bernice's, which is different because she lives in another part of the state, raises corn and hogs, plays the harp, travels to Europe, and sends me carbons of the round-robin letters she writes her family.

Hazel and I got out the recipes afterward and compared them. "How much is 'lump of butter size of an egg,'" inquired Hazel earnestly. "One woman got mad at me because I couldn't tell exactly. She thought I was trying to keep my recipe a secret from her." Hazel gave me her recipe.

The next week Mrs. Dixon of Lafayette sent me her recipe for Yankee persimmon pudding. A Farm Bureau bulletin provided me with two more; and at a meeting of IU faculty women, Dr. Kinsey's wife gave me hers. With all this richness, it was inevitable that I should become a persimmon pudding recipe collector.

This is Floy's recipe: 2 cups persimmon, 1 cup brown sugar, 1 cup white sugar, 3 cups sweet milk, 3 cups flour, 1 teaspoon baking powder, 3 eggs, ½ cup butter, 1 teaspoon cinnamon, ⅓ teaspoon nutmeg. Separate eggs, beat whites, add last. Bake at 325°.

        ♣   ♣   ♣

The hazards that won farming second place in the list of the nation's most hazardous occupations include fence building. A farmer's skin is thin protection from the rebuttal of the natural world as an unfenced area tries to hold its own against fence stretchers, barbed wire, farm machinery, grazing livestock, and chemical spraying.

When the hay baling paused for a second growth and the corn spraying was over, the men started stringing eighty rods of line fence along an area of Ira's farm that had not been fenced or tilled for several years. In such places the wilderness moves back in determinedly.

The men hauled rolls of barbed wire, fence stretchers, pliers, ax, hammer, fence "steeples," wood and steel posts in the wagon, tractor-pulled. Nature, to oppose this invading army, lined up an array of insects, water obstacles, and a list of plants like a chapter from Gray's *Botany*.

"There was one plant," reported Dick one day at dinner, "that stung so much if you merely brushed against it you could feel it for half an hour. It looked like an elm leaf, but it wasn't."

From curiosity and also because it was I who had wanted the woods fenced, I went down to interview that angry plant, which was, of course, wood nettle. While I was carefully breaking off two brittle stalks with my gloved hands I unknowingly stepped on some plants the tractor had run over. My ankles discovered my error immediately and remembered it for a full half hour after.

The sensation of nettle sting is like a prolongation of the beginning of a bee sting. The stinging keeps up, never developing into a real ache or breaking out into streams of blood, just gaining momentum and in addition acquiring the acute ecstasy of itch offered by poison ivy.

The nettle plants (cousins of the beautiful and harmless jewelweed) were from one to three feet tall, the leaves on long stems and set alternately on tapering, rounded stalks. The leaf is shaped like an embittered mulberry leaf, but instead of having the mulberry's graceful finial it ends in a sharp point as if it wished it could also stab. The outer edge of the leaf is notched into sharp sawtooth points. The under-sides are made fuzzy by numerous delicate hairs, menacing as the stinger of a wasp. They are set at irregular intervals, and point in seemingly haphazard directions. A fence builder, who has to follow a definite, disciplined straight line, can-not find any safe approach to the nettles.

What courage, or ignorance, it must have taken for the first hardy pioneers to penetrate American forests and carve out their farms without even a bottle of merthiolate!

♣   ♣   ♣

"If I get the corn all planted this week, I'll mow hay next week," said Dick at supper.

Hay. Roses. Last strawberries staining your fingertips fragrantly; Early Transparent apples ripe enough for pale green applesauce; cherries ripening with a ceramic gleam; robins hatching in the nest on the ledge of the back porch window; cardinals guarding the white rose bush. Red-winged blackbirds' nests beautifully basket-woven around four tall weed stalks in the hayfield and cut off by the mower; a quail's nest, full of eggs, discovered on the ground in time for a farmer to avoid it with the mower; a meadowlark singing from heaven's blue page; noon dinners in the dining room with the blue dishes and tall iced-tea glasses on the red-and-white tablecloth and the farm family and several additional young men and anybody else who happens by at noon, all eating hungrily, gaily; mornings early and evenings late; the evening song of the whippoorwill and the day-time concert of the mockingbird perched on some high place like the rim of the silo because he realizes what it does for his song; fireflies rising at dusk from the grassy yard; things well in hand and weedless in the garden; early tomatoes turning pale, preliminary to turning red; smell of hay curing; wind rising, ceasing; the continual inconsistency of hoping for rain because it takes 200,000 gallons of water to make a ton of alfalfa hay, and hoping for rain to hold off because it takes a day's good sun to cure hay in the long windrow; sound of people laughing, of men calling to each other across a field; of tractors hurrying in and out and around the place, and along the roads; big machinery running smoothly or creating an unnatural stillness when something breaks; at dusk the beautiful tiredness of a day's energy spent in a good task accomplished.

The haying episode is one of the busiest, most hazardous and pleasantest times of the farm year. A farmer continually matches his wits against weather, machinery, his own endurance. Only a free man could work as hard as a farmer must and does willingly in haying time. Only a free man could make the necessary sacrifices. When farmers cease to depend on their own strength, skill and judgment, either because they dare not act independently or because they need not, the land will suffer. History indicates that for a country, hunger is the price paid for loss of farm freedom.

In company with two cameras that would hang like millstones around my neck until they got attention, I went out to the alfalfa field where Dick and Joe and a couple of Joe's contemporaries, sons of neighbors here, were baling hay.

Dick was driving one tractor to the side delivery hay rake, turning the hay he had mowed the day before. The rake sidled along bashfully, turning the windrow in a long, curling roll that left the hay in a new row six feet farther west, with the underside turned up to cure in the sun's heat.

Another tractor pulling the baler and wagon was being driven by Richard Zellers, son of a former neighbor here and then in the Coast Guard and home on a thirty-day leave before going to a year's tour of duty in Alaska. While Richard spent his leave in the hot hayfields of Maple Grove, his parents were vacationing in the cool Northeast. It was Richard's choice. "The only bad thing about this vacation is going back," he said one day at dinner.

Joe, graduated that month from Purdue University and home on leave before going into National Guard training at Camp Knox, was on the hay wagon. I climbed up beside him. He was taking the green, sharp-edged bales from the baler's short elevator and stacking them on the wagon. Scorning the iron hay hook Dick and I always used, he grasped the bale by its brown, insect-proofed twines, gave it a fast swing, rested it almost imperceptibly on another bale, then tossed it up into place on the growing stairway of green bales at the end of the wagon. (Youth is a wonderful fuel, especially with the impetus of fresh release from the classroom.)

"This is the best hay we've put up this summer," he told me. "Always load the downhill bale first and then the others will fall into place." This hay had been cut when perfectly ready and had not been rained on.

"I finally got the wagons fixed the way I wanted them," continued Joe. "Did you notice those new boards in the back rack? Really holds the bales stacked now." No matter how efficient one farming generation is, the new one has improvements, and fortunate is the farmer of the first generation who has the youth on the farm with him and the wisdom to share the authority with him.

I got off the wagon and went to ride on the tractor with Dick awhile. He was in that supremely happy state a farmer goes into when everything is going well and he indulges himself in the belief that it's always going to.

Before I left the field, I took pictures of everything. Joe said, "Be sure to be watching when we bring the hay in. We're going to pull three wagons with one tractor. Be sure to get a picture of it. Jim May and Dick Francis are coming to help us put it into the loft. We won't be in for supper until late."

As I left the field I looked back, admiring the work, the field, the hay, the farm, the summer afternoon, life itself, and the American system of free agriculture. In the long run, the greatest reward about farming is that sense of personal worth a man gets from having authority over a portion of land. A farmer is "his own man"; whether he owns forty acres or four hundred makes no difference—except of course in the income.

♣ ♣ ♣

In this community agriculture is not the chief source of income nor even the best-known product of the land.

This is oölitic limestone land, source of Indiana's fine building stone which is used in homes, churches, public buildings all over the United States, and valued for its endurance and adaptability. Indiana limestone lends its simple elegance equally to straight lines or decorative, carved designs.

Limestone underlies the hills of the farms around here, including this one and Ira's, and crops up where the hills are washed bare. Not all of it is suitable for building use. There are stone fences in this community, durable dry masonry laid up by skilled stonemen many years ago, from flat stones struck out of the hillsides. One such fence encloses the Maple Grove church and cemetery. Some of the farms have fields enclosed with stone fences.

When the farms were marked off into fields, some of the early farmers set corner posts or gateposts of sawed stone with iron brackets for hinges. Benny had some here, and there are some at the roadside edge of Ira's cornfield next to the road and back on his fields. We like them, though few of them serve either fence or gate any more.

There is one stone post at the front corner of the yard here, beside the driveway. It has stood there, out of the way of buggies and wagons, neighbors on foot or horseback, cars, farm machinery, livestock, for close to a hundred years. It leaned slightly to the west, like an old man insatiably curious about what was going on at the field down the road.

When the county black-topped the Maple Grove Road one summer, the truck backed against the old post and broke it off. It was about thirteen inches square, stood four and one half feet above the ground, and probably weighed about six hundred pounds. No fence was fastened to it and no gate swung from it, but it was an old farm mark and we regretted its loss.

Comfort came from our neighbor, Hubert Brown, who owns a stone mill and loves Indiana limestone as heartily as Dick loves fine purebred cattle. "We can fix that," Brownie said, whipping out his stone rule. I doubt that

Brownie ever goes anyplace, even to the Episcopal church where he is an alderman, without his folding stone rule. A stone artist handles this rule as if it were something alive. He takes it out of his pocket with one hand and moves that hand quickly, gently, and the rule springs like a live cat, opens up and straightens out full length. It folds up dexterously in the same way and the stoneman puts it back into his hip pocket and smiles. It makes an admirable parlor trick. People gasp and marvel.

"We have a new epoxy," said Brownie, who never underestimates the potential of stone in the building industry. "It will glue that post together and you couldn't break it again in the same place."

He came again on Thursday with his wife, whose real name is Carol, but has taken the name "Sairy" because she lives in Sairy Stout's 140-year-old stone house, having first loved it back from the jaws of death.

On Thursday came also Bert Payne and Charlie Condra, stone artists who work at Brownie's mill and share his enthusiasm for Indiana limestone. They came on their day off, in the mill's red truck that has a powerful mobile lift attached to it and a sign painted on its door: "Not for hire." It was fascinating to watch those men set up the post, as it is always fascinating to watch skilled artists in performance.

Charlie measured, made penciled hieroglyphics on both pieces of the stone post. Charlie can carve stone or draw a straight line on it without using a ruler. Bert picked up an electric drill and bored a hole in the limestone as easily as an apple corer bites into a ripe pippin. They set an eight-inch hollow pin in the opening.

To mix the quick-setting new epoxy, Bert squeezed eight inches of butter-like paste into a small amount of syrup-colored liquid in a metal can and stirred it as if mixing butter and molasses for Dutch honey. The chemical reaction made the can hot. With the pin then firmly set into the long piece of the post, they hooked two loops of heavy chain around it, holding it hooklessly, by a slipknot. This ten-inch metal tool looks as if it might be the old rusty metal clasp taken from a giant's garter. The slipknot doesn't scratch or chip limestone, which is, in its way, delicate of surface even when seasoned. When first quarried out of the ground, limestone is called "raw" and has to be left outdoors, like lumber, several months to "season." Seasoning, weathering adds continually to its beauty and strength.

Now came the big test. We all held our breaths and Sairy Brown involuntarily gave a slight shove in air as Bert boomed the long piece over the stub, and the stone settled down in the joy of eternal reunion.

Watching these stone artists handle their favorite medium in that skillful, almost affectionate way, I thought in sudden revelation, This is the way that geologist felt, who was here last spring. He thought he had discovered good stone in our southeast field and wanted to lease it and do some core-drilling for a limestone-quarrying development. He had drawn up a suggested contract in which he referred to the soil there as the "overburden." To a stoneman, anything that hides good stone is "overburden." But to a farmer the overburden is the precious flesh of earth itself, and when we read the contract we shuddered and handed it back, unsigned.

♣　♣　♣

"Levi doesn't carry a club or stock whip or hotrod to load cattle," said Dick admiringly, the day after Levi Oliver had hauled a load of steers for him to the Worthington feeder auction. Levi lives on a small family farm near here, that was badly eroded until he became soil conservation conscious.

"He is the quietest cattle loader I have ever known. Most of 'em think they have to holler and scream and cuss and force the cattle up into the chute. Yesterday morning we just backed the truck up to the loading chute and I went into the barn and drove the steers into the nearest stall and before the last ones were in the stall the first ones had walked right on up and gone out into the truck. Neither of us had to say a word to 'em."

Levi has driven a schoolbus for several years, which may have developed ways of patience in him. On the other hand he and his wife have had children in school for thirty-five years which may have developed ways of patience on the school bus. Some of Levi's children have already finished college with honors. He is a supervisor on the local soil conservation committee and a faithful worker in the Baptist church. He has a soft voice and doesn't talk much at any time.

"Cattle don't like all this hollering and profanity," Dick went on, "it makes them nervous. Beating them around in the sale rings shows them off at a disadvantage, too, if the sellers just realized it. They're on edge, mad, and they get contrary. It doesn't pay."

"Do you think cattle feel depressed or suffer from moods?" I asked.

"Oh, yes." He told me about a feeble-minded steer that walked out on the frozen pond twice while the more intelligent ones sipped safely from the cold, thawed edges; about a feeble-minded calf that tried to cross a thawing terrace at full speed and bawling. "He fell, slid sixteen feet, scooping up mud all the way into the trough made by his opened lower jaw, until mud stopped the bawling." He told me about the cow that was ailing for no reason except moodiness, and after coddling and attention she recovered and stays all right as long as she feels she is a pet.

Finally he got around to mention of Old Jerse, the real pet, who likes to be pampered by being allowed to walk slowly. "We understand each other," he said. "I let her walk as slowly as she pleases and I never saw any creature that could walk so slowly."

A good cattle farmer knows his cattle as well and individually as a good teacher knows his pupils.

"I have one big Hereford that has arthritis in her hip and doesn't want to be touched," he said. "She raises a good calf every year. When I want to turn the cattle into another field all I need to do is open the gate and call 'sook-calf!' Just once. Wherever she is, she gets up and comes and the rest follow her. There's no use using a dog or stick to drive cattle. They resent it."

He stopped, looked me in the eye steadily, and then went on. "They resent it even more than anyone in your family does, but if you let 'em think it don't make any difference to you, they'll come right into the barn."

Is there really such a thing as a "dumb animal"? I was thinking. Dick went on: "Some of 'em like to stand in the doorway blocking the rest, and they understand blocking and guarding as well as any basketball player ever did. I'd like to show Branch McCracken how they do. And when a cow flips her tail, it's the same thing as a man uttering a cussword."

♣   ♣   ♣

"The Guernsey cow has a calf this morning," he told me a few days later, but his voice was not topped with the deep foam of warm pride and affection it has when he announces, "Old Jerse had a nice calf last night."

On this beef-cattle farm we keep two dairy cows for milk at the house, the theory being that one will be fresh when the other is dry, and if you don't need all the milk for the house, it is easy to put a calf on the cow.

The spotted Guernsey is one of those difficult personalities a farmer sometimes introduces by accident into his herd, and keeps there for goodness knows what reason.

"It will be nice to have milk from the farm again . . . all that deep rich cream to send to the Brotherhood meetings," I gloated, "and I can make cottage cheese my own way again, by pouring a teakettle of hot water into a whole gallon crock of clabbered milk."

"I'm never going to milk her again," Dick said firmly.

Cottage cheese, cream, and butter vanished as I listened.

"I never could milk but three quarters anyway. The left hind quarter is off, somehow. Unless you bend it down into a half moon it squirts out in a stream across the barn. Of course, with a calf or milking machine it doesn't make any difference. It's good rich milk, and she gives lots of it. I had two calves on her last winter and I'll put two more on her now."

"She's really a good cow," he admitted, "but she's so high-strung she's like a hysterical woman. She never butts a person, but she'll run over you. I've never struck her, but somebody has given her an awful flailing sometime or other and I will say she probably had it coming.

"I can forgive her everything but one thing. When she eats she never sticks her head in through the rack and keeps it there, eating like other cows. She just barely sticks her nose between the slats and snatches a bite of ground feed between her lips like a barber taking snuff, and spills it on the stall floor. Or if she wants hay, she grasps a few wisps and jerks it back between the slats and that knocks off all the palatable, green, tender leaves into the bedding and manure. One morning last winter I gave her a whole flake of nice green alfalfa hay. She snatched at it in that silly way and jerked back and threw the whole flake clear back against the barn wall."

He stopped for a moment, then said contemplatively, "I knew I shouldn't have gone to that sale the day I bought her."

♣   ♣   ♣

The bread man was telling me his troubles with the farm people along his route.

"Farmers are queer people," I sympathized.

"Yes, they are," he cried, as if he had long been wanting to say so, "and I don't like 'em!"

You have to love them, to like them. You have to live among them to understand them, and even then you can't be sure. Even now when I see Dick and Carr out in the yard talking earnestly and Carr picking up some stick to whittle, I expect to learn that someone's wife has run off or set fire to the barn. But when I find out, they are only discussing whether it's cheaper to grind your own corncobs with the corn or buy them ground from the feed mill, and add to the ground corn.

Or to hear Carr confess, "I sure let the skimmer leak at that sale yesterday, Dick. I should have bought that mare that sold for only sixteen dollars." Of course, he doesn't really regret it; he hasn't farmed with horses for nearly twenty years. It's been at least twelve years since he sold old Pat and Mike and everybody in the family cried. It's just that he likes to buy things at a sale if they seem like bargains.

"When Carr gets ready to go to a sale," said Dick one morning, coming into the kitchen and laying his work gloves on the kindling kettle by the Franklin stove, "he gets in a kind of frenzy. Usually when he goes past—to church or town or down to the bottom field to work—he blows the horn. But if he's going to a sale he doesn't slow down or even look around. He went by like that just now and I know he's going to a sale. I know just what I'm going to say to him. I'll just ask him innocently, 'Was there some kind of emergency at your place last Thursday morning?' He'll know what I mean."

Carr will simply laugh and cover his face with his hands. Later, some winter day when he sees Dick has the ear flaps of his cap down over his ears, Carr will look worriedly into his face and ask, "Do the nit flies bother you in winter?"

When giant foxtail seemed about to take Dick's cornfield

one summer, Carr asked innocently, "There's something I've been intending to ask you. Do you think corn does better with that cover crop?"

When Dick owes Carr money he says, "I'll just have to come down and board it out. Tell Iris to bake a grape pie."

The neighbors agree Carr is blessed with what they call "Stanger luck." Such as a hog getting well when anybody else's hog would have died, or cattle prices pulling out of a low just the day Carr sent his steers.

"Stanger luck," they all agreed the time Carr got stopped on the highway by a motor policeman. Carr was driving his old but useful truck home, slowly, along the highway. Just before he reached the place to turn off onto his small road, he was stopped by the highway policeman, who began writing him a ticket for driving too slowly, obstructing traffic.

In ordinary visiting, Carr can talk half a day, flatteringly or philosophically, without giving any real news he doesn't want to give, or committing himself in any way. He can throw the sharpest inquisitor off the track with his innocent, wide-eyed "I don't know." He didn't try to outtalk the policeman. He just sat quietly, waiting. The policeman had just begun to write when another policeman dashed up, paused barely long enough to say there had been a bad wreck two miles ahead. The first policeman tore off the slip without finishing it, and hurried off. Naturally Carr just drove on home. Slowly, of course, as before.

The day after he dehorned his steer, Carr said to **Dick**,

hesitantly, "Do you believe some people have the power to stop the flow of blood?"

"Never heard of it," replied Dick, startled. Carr was not joking. Like most of the local farmers Dick has no trouble believing in water witching, and wouldn't think of having a well drilled without first getting a water witch to "find the vein."

"Well sir," continued Carr, "you know, Dick, that steer just kept bleeding and finally I went into the house and told Iris to call Cassie Fyffe. I know farmers used to ask her to help 'em sometimes before she moved to town. So Iris called and Cassie asked, 'What's the steer's name?' " Carr stopped to laugh. "I said, 'Oh, he don't have any name; he's just a steer.' Then Cassie wanted to know, 'What color is he?' I told Iris 'red and white, spotted.' Iris told her, and Cassie said she'd do her best. And do you know, time I got back to the barn that steer had stopped bleedin'!"

♣   ♣   ♣

You can say, "I like people and therefore enjoy having guests at the farm." Or you can make a mathematical formula. There is an ever-increasing number of people, but the amount of land does not increase, therefore the amount of land per capita decreases, and one farm should offer both ownership and visitorship.

Everyone needs—in fact, must have—occasional reacquaintance with the land. It is one reason we need state and national parks. People can go to parks if they have no farm friends or relatives to visit.

Yes, they can. They could.

But if they did, farmers would miss one of the best parts of farm living. One of the farm's finest harvests is the pleasant memories it can give to children who live on it or visit it.

There is a vogue just now, in this era of the survival struggle of the small family farm, for small farms to become recreation places commercially. This, it seems to me, requires a specialized talent and actually places the farm in the category of hotel and resort business. Not everyone could make a success of it, or wishes to try.

The pond back of our barn is stocked with bass and blue-gill which we do not fish, but we like for friends and visitors to fish there. We enjoy seeing the farm through the eyes of adult or child guests. To watch a child's pleasure in your farm is one of the happiest ways to appreciate it yourself and realize new truths about it.

"Roosters don't have tails, Datie," five-year-old Jeffrey Lundy told his grandmother, between gusts of laughter. "They have feathers. Horses have tails!" He brought this fresh viewpoint with him when he visited the farm. He had arrived early for a day's visit and I was taking him up to the beloved hilltop. We hoped he might find an arrowhead on the way, so he was carrying a two-gallon grocery sack.

Midway of the field he noticed the young white bull grazing in the distance and entirely oblivious of us.

"Oh, my goodness," worried Jeffrey, "I hope he won't see this red spot on my T-shirt." The red spot was a spilled drop of plum juice from a piece of pie he had eaten before we left the house. "I'll cover it up with this sack, though, and maybe he won't notice." He was thus able to conceal the infuriating color from the young bull, which never so much as glanced up, and we got safely to the hilltop. We did not find any arrowheads, but the high point of the day's visit for Jeffrey came late in the afternoon when he got to sit in front of Joe on the tractor seat and drive the tractor up to the barn. Young or old, men visitors enjoy the farm machinery.

We went into other fields and into the woods that day. Jeffrey and I were picking up walnuts from under the trees back of Ira's barn when Joe came and told us his friends the Martez family (seven) had come. They had brought a picnic lunch with them, he said, but since they were good friends of his, couldn't I hurry back to the house and set dinner on the dining table and invite the Martez family (seven) to eat with us?

Fortunately it was still warm enough to use the dining room to eat in. Also fortunately, I had baked two pies and some ham. This is the stuff of which family farm life is made. I wouldn't change it for anything.

At these happy, unexpected meals I think of my brother-in-law Mirl Lundy and his good and true story: a large number of men had dropped in unexpectedly to a farmhouse for dinner. The farm wife, an elderly, fussy woman, had cooked up practically everything she had in the house or knew how to cook. It was a large meal, and tasty, but she was not satisfied. She fussed and apologized and kept opening more cans. Until finally one of the men said kindly, "Such as it is, Grandma, you've got plenty."

♣   ♣   ♣

There was one summer day graced with a number of groups of guests, all unexpected.

Half an hour before dusk of that day, Dick and I met at the back step, each still intent on reactions to the day. Dick, who in childhood dreaded the dusk "because that was always when the company went home," sat on the back steps, untroubled, watching the neighbor's steers in the field across the road. The state of the house never bothers Dick when guests come. He wisely enjoys the guest and ignores the state.

"Mr. Walz had more good ideas about hog raising than any farm bulletin I have ever read," he said. We do not raise hogs on this farm any more. He pointed to where the steers were walking slowly toward the neighbor's woods. "They're going down to get a drink," he said. The cattle went serenely, as in a world unmarred by an increase in taxes, or tragedy in Saigon, or the danger of Indiana losing its share of the Dunes.

I sat down beside him, holding the armload of clean dish towels I had just taken off the back-yard clothesline. They had been rained on in the night, dried all day in the sun, and they had a delicious clean smell. Clasping them, I thought of Mrs. Walz's clean, starched white blouse, her clean children, her husband's clean shirt. I know she must have left a clean house when they started out that day.

"Hereafter," declared Carol, suddenly coming out and dumping an armload of newspapers on the back porch floor, "if anybody wants to read the paper you have to do it on the day it comes." I remembered, wincing, Mrs. Jorgan gently removing a stack of newspapers from the sofa so she could sit there. Carol had a broom in her hand. She had just swept everyplace, chagrined that it had not been done before the Bolingers came, or at least before the Emersons got there.

She had also mowed the front yard and cleared away her sewing out of the dining room. "Don't lean back," she now warned Dick, "there's a great big green bug on your shoulder. Ugh!" Carol studied Latin in high school and German at DePauw, but when she speaks of insects it is always in the Ugh! language.

Dick stiffened, accepted the dish towels I dropped into

his lap so I could take the broom from Carol. He did not take his eyes off the steers. "Now the first ones are coming back and the stragglers haven't even got to the woods yet," he murmured. I held the broom above his shoulder and the bug walked willingly onto it. It was an immature walking-stick. When I shook her onto the walk the twiglike legs quickly dragged the soft body away.

As I bent to retrieve the dish towels from Dick's lap I noticed a large brown coffee stain on the pocket of my white blouse and cast a look of dismayed inquiry toward Carol. "Yes, it was," she said, "but I don't think anybody noticed except me. And Mary Jo McCracken was so fascinating I didn't notice it much."

By that time I had discovered the rip under my sleeve. She nodded, confirmingly. "But Marie Wright was pretty and charming, so don't worry. But believe me, I will never let the yard go unmowed so long again."

"Their routine is as natural as the way a colt can be sound asleep and wake right up when the mare goes past without a sound," continued Dick, still observing the steers.

"And I'll never get dinner again without first taking a bath and changing my blouse," I said. "And I'll weed the garden and hang out the clothes in the dead of night." Mrs. Walz had insisted on looking at the garden when I offered her some fresh dill.

"We can quit eating, too, so the kitchen will always be in order," suggested Carol. It was time for her to dress and get her French horn and go to town to play in a band concert, and Dick had to go to the barn. I went into the house.

In the typewriter, as I walked through the back porch, was an unfinished letter I had started that morning. It sprang awake, like a colt, as I walked quietly past. "Go on down to the woods and get a drink and forget the lost Lenore," I told it, walking right on. "If they had to wait until we get everything in order, the time would never come. And think what we'd miss!"

♣ ♣ ♣

Emmett Baynes's dairy barn near here burned one July morning with 4,300 bales of new hay in it. The hay may have caused the fire, being not quite thoroughly cured before it was stored. It is a common cause of barn losses. Old-time farmers—Bent Stanger for one—used to scatter salt among the bales to preclude the possibility of spontaneous combustion.

The smell of burning hay lingered in the air for weeks; in the evenings the smell drifted sociably across to adjoining farms like a farm neighbor who has sold his stock and therefore has time to visit his neighbors at chore time.

It was the second major disaster for that family in the precarious haying season. A week earlier, Emmett had been struck on the head by a swinging hayfork. In the list of national hazardous occupations, farming comes right after mining.

At the time the fire was discovered, Emmett and his wife and their young son, Ray, were all ready to go on a vacation trip. The station wagon was loaded and they were only waiting until Emmett could finish the morning's milking. He had arranged for a neighbor's son to do the chores for two weeks while they were to be gone.

He did not understand why suddenly the power failed and the milking machine stopped, until a neighbor came out into her yard and called down to him that his barn was on fire. They got out all the cattle except some young calves. To everybody's relief, Emmett had some insurance. His father-in-law, John Fielder, who lived near, had an empty barn and they moved Emmett's cattle there.

"He ought to sell out right now and go ahead with his vacation," said one of the neighbors who would have been defeated by a like blow.

"There's hardly enough level land down there for a barn, anyway," said another.

Emmett was small, wiry, agile. All his farming life he had gone from one farming difficulty to another, hopefully. He was a good neighbor, a soft-voiced, witty person, a good 4-H leader. At silo-fillings it was his job to work at the top of the silo because he was never afraid to climb. He met his emergencies nimbly, depending on immediate resourcefulness.

The burning of a barn usually sends a farmer into a state of mild shock, sometimes makes him afraid to be alone in daytime.

Misfortune seemed to stimulate Emmett. He postponed his vacation . . . they took it later. He moved away the charred rafters and old roofing and within a few days had made plans for building a new barn on the same site, using some lumber cut from his own woods and some seasoned lumber purchased from a lumberyard. It was never really a convenient site for a barn. It was across the road from his nice new house, down a steep muddy lane. The stone was so close to the ground it was hard to excavate for a foundation. Nevertheless, he built the new barn there and by fall was milking cows in it again.

♣   ♣   ♣

Lacey was born in this house about seventy years ago, she told me as she stood, smiling, on the back step. A small woman who smiles often and seems always about to break into laughter, she was wearing a small hat with colored snail shells sewed all over the crown of it. I liked her immediately.

She lives in a trailer now, in Florida. "I just wanted to see the old place," she explained. She had not been back since the death of her father, Benny, about twenty-six years ago. She said she had only a minute to stay. Her husband and grandson were waiting in the car and the grandson had to get back to the IU campus for a final exam.

We walked over the house, Lacey reminiscing happily as I asked questions. Where did Benny have the carbide tank buried for the gaslights? It was not buried, she said, it was in the woodshed (now gone). He got scared and took out the lights after he read about a carbide-lighted house blowing up. He left the pipes between the walls, though, and electricians met them in the ceilings when they wired this house for electricity, meagerly during World War II when electric cord came only by priority and you were asked to use the barest minimum of outlets.

In the dining room, my favorite room in this house, Lacey told me, "This was our living room. This is where everybody was laid out when they died."

By the time we got to our living room her husband joined us, intending, I think, to tell her to come on. "This was the parlor," said Lacey. "This is where I done my courtin'." She stopped to laugh and her husband said, "This is the room your father threw me out of. Only it was your mother that threw me out." In Benny's last years it was his bedroom. He died in it.

"The rooms all seem so little!" Lacey exclaimed, surprised, "but when I was a child I thought they were so big!" She remembered when her father went down to Beanblossom bottom, she said, and dug up young maples to set out in the front yard. They are giants now.

She remembered the smokehouse (now gone), and the blacksmith shop (long since gone). She remembered the old soft brick colonial house her grandparents lived in (gone). It was out in the yard by the cistern. It had deer's horns built into an outside wall, Lacey said. She remembered her grandmother's silk dresses and bonnets, the cherry table, and handmade cord-laced beds. Why did Benny tear down the brick house? She didn't know.

Benny's house, which they called "the white house," is eighty years old in the new part, a hundred in the part that was made out of the old Wampler schoolhouse brought down from up on the hilltop across from the church. After the grandparents' deaths a hired man lived in the brick house for a while and Benny's family used the kitchen of it for a summer kitchen. When her parents went to town (six and one-half miles took longer then with a horse and buggy than now with a car), Lacey and her sister "did things," she said. "Once we moved the summer kitchen into the white house." Another time they decided to fry a chicken. In those pre-4-H days even little girls could dress and fry a chicken. But first they had to run it down and catch it, and then chop off its head. Lacey held the feet and couldn't bear to look. Her sister, wielding the ax, couldn't bear to look either. When Lacey heard the ax strike she let loose, and the chicken, unharmed, took to its feet and flew, squawking.

"Oh, I wish I could stay longer!" cried Lacey, who like

anyone returning to a childhood home after long absence found it full of memories, like flowers waiting to be picked from a garden.

♣   ♣   ♣

Some came because they were neighbors; some because it was a fine October day, a good day to go to a sale, and the country for miles around in Owen County was picturesque. On the way to the sale we saw farm fields, little side roads darting off to little farms, small quiet cemeteries, an old two-story log house with windlass and wooden bucket at a well behind it. We passed a small pointed white church and drove up and down Owen County's color-swept hills.

Some came for the old-time farm items to be sold from the farm that day; stone jugs and apple-butter jars, glass cans, a cypress churn, ox yokes, sausage grinders, wood-burning stoves, coffee mill, horse-drawn machinery and more modern farm items, a tractor, cattle, chickens, corn, and baled hay. What everyone got, just for coming, was a glimpse back into a time when that farm could support a family. The glimpse made you wonder about the future of such farms.

The owners were selling because they no longer had the health or energy to do the work required by the farm. That this had been an effort for them for a long time was evident in the neglected appearance; piles of broken boards, pieces of machinery and clutter lay around all of the buildings and along unkempt fence rows. The family had lived on the sandstone farm since 1920 except for a five-year interval when they had "moved in with his father," who was then too ill to take care of his own farm.

They had gone through one mighty depression and numerous hardships. But it was apparent no one had ever gone out and neatened up the farm just from pure love of it. It did not have that look a farm should have after so many years of occupancy by one family, that look as if someone had told it, "Oh, Farm, I love you, I love every inch of you. I could never bear to leave you!"

The small house had no flair to begin with. As it grew old it had been neatly sided with a pinkish asbestos siding. It sat on a high knoll looking down into a narrow, jolty road, on through a thin line of young trees and down into a small cornfield on a neighboring farm. No power mower had barbered its grassy yard, but there was an old-time push mower in the sale. Beside the garden fence was a big brown glazed tile, the kind in which farm women used to plant flowers.

The barn lot was bordered by great beeches, leafless that day, and magnificently swathed in a silvery haze reflected in the delicate brushy ends of limbs.

In that heart-seizing landscape the 202-acre farm was like a hay rope, with a series of big knots tied in it. The many small buildings occupied the various knots. There was a Swiss-like small shed on one knot, occupied by two milk cows. There were more cattle in the old barn and in the more recently built one near it. Cream had been a major source of family income. The small lot between the barns, enclosed by a fence of horizontal sapling poles, was occupied chiefly by a large manure heap waiting to be hauled out to the fields that greatly needed this nourishment.

There was an empty, small log corncrib and a new metal one with corn in it. There were hog houses, a doghouse, a woodshed.

In the henhouse, white hens laid eggs and cackled as triumphantly as if they had heard nothing about any sale. In a locked smokehouse, of which one wall was green with moss at the base and rotting away, several joints of cured meat, wrapped in paper, hung from rafters.

Bean poles, still tied together at the top like skeletal wigwams, were still standing in the garden, twined about with frost-taken bean vines. The family had fed itself thriftily from the farm; the farmer, his wife, and somewhat frail son had worked hard.

They did things in the old, hard way; for example, carrying corn and water to the hog house on the knoll back up above the house. On one grassy rope knot all the long-abandoned, obsolete horse-drawn machinery had been assembled for a sale; a manure spreader, a riding cultivator, riding and walking plows, a hand-dump hayrake, two obsolete corn planters, two grain binders on which the wooden platforms were sagged and rotting away, wagon gears with wide steel rims on the high wheels.

On another knot was the usable horse-drawn machinery, the mower used that last summer for mowing the hay now baled and sweet-smelling in the low-ceilinged old barn. The newest note in the old barn was the "No Smoking" sign put up by an insurance company. The one modern piece of equipment, a tractor, sold for $600. In the barn stood three white horses; on the wall behind them hung brass-knobbed hames, harness, and ragged collar pads. One team and harness sold for $120.

In the kitchen, neighbor women were selling lunch, sandwiches, pies, coffee, iced tea (instant), oyster stew. "If you spill your stew getting out that screen door," cheerful Mrs. White told one farmer, "come back and I'll refill it for you."

The farmer's wife, dressed as if for company, in a dark plaid dress, sat quietly in the second room, waiting for the day to be over. Other neighbors went in and sat with her, rocking and talking in soft, solemnly cheerful voices.

The sale clerk sat at a small table in the front room and people went there to pay for what they had bought. The churn brought $12, ox yokes $12 each. The coffee mill, selling for $32, surprised even the auctioneer. One sausage grinder with bench and much rust sold for $3.50. The other, with no bench and less rust, brought $4. A corn cutter that several farmers wanted for nostalgia's sake brought $7.50 finally. A woman wanting an old-fashioned egg case with a square slat box and a handle on the lid for carrying the case, hesitated. The auctioneer "threw in" the old-time washing-machine wringers and she paid twenty-five cents for the lot and left the wringers there when she took the case home.

When we were ready to come home, Dick had bought a sausage grinder for nostalgia's sake and $3.50, and I had bought a two-gallon stone jar for fifty cents because I think they are beautiful and never can resist them.

♣   ♣   ♣

Ralph West's farm in Putnam County is eighty acres of the farm his father owned and lived on when Ralph was growing up, before housing developments began to nibble it away.

Westy's family is his pretty wife, Polly, who collects and restores old dolls, goes to clubs and university alumnae meetings, or can drive car, tractor, or truck for Westy, or even let him help her with the cooking in the kitchen or at the back-yard picnic grill.

Westy had come down to go to a sale with Dick one autumn morning and was feeling slightly guilty because he had left his corn picking.

"I'll get at it in a day or so, though," he told me in the kitchen, waiting for Dick. "When I start picking I won't stop until it's all done."

He learned to shuck corn on his father's farm in the hand-shucking, team-and-wagon era. "I used to be in the field by six-thirty and I picked two loads, thirty-five bushels to the wagonload, by one o'clock. I never went back for that third load; my father always said two loads made a day's work for any man. I took the first load to the barn and unloaded it and picked half the second by eleven or eleven-thirty, then I ate a sandwich and slept half an hour and finished the second load by one o'clock. In those days sixty bushels to the acre was good. Now a hundred isn't even unusual."

His father had a strict rule that the corn had to be shucked by Thanksgiving. A common rule with farmers is that the growing corn must be "knee-high by the Fourth of July."

"One year my father saw we weren't going to get done by Thanksgiving and he hired six men to help."

In those days Indiana farmers "shucked" corn; only Easterners called it "picking" corn. The shucking peg available in right- or left-handed models, the trained team, the phrases "shucking" and "bangboard" went out of the corn story when the tractor-powered mechanical picker came in.

When he shucked corn, Ralph took two rows at a time. His horses knew what to do, never got off the row, moved forward and stopped on command. The one nearest the un-shucked row was muzzled. "I never used a shucking peg," he said. "A hook is lots faster. When you take hold of a corn ear you brush down it with the hook, and that rips the husks open so you can break the ear right off. While I was break-

3 1 5

ing out one ear I never looked at the wagon. I looked at the next ear I was going to shuck. You can't make any time looking at the wagon."

In 1950 he bought his first corn picker. "I remember it," he said, laughing wryly, "because it was no good and I had to buy another right away." He does all his farming with the same drive and precision he used in corn shucking. He has quit raising hogs and raises only cattle. His farm is on a much-traveled thoroughfare close to Greencastle. He has had to move his fence back twice for widening the highway, so now his front-yard plum tree is nearer the road than it was when he built the house for his bride. The farm is tidy and well fenced, a hospitable, comfortable place.

♣   ♣   ♣

"Take the car," Dick suggested as I came out into the yard with a basket of things to store down in Monta's house, to which we began taking the overflow from this house as soon as Monta moved.

But I wanted to walk. Just as a prolonged diet of biscuits sets up a craving for lean meat or sauerkraut or fruit, a too-long while in the house gives me a hunger to get my feet, literally, on the ground.

So I walked down to Ira's farm, noting down there again how the wide circle of horizontal view changes now from day to day. Now late in October the distance seemed almost brown. With leaves gone from the trees, hills that were filled with green light all summer now were more open and revealed. All along the edges of pond and pasture, leaves had fallen. They were dry and curled up and blown into drifts.

At the last I came back slowly because it was the perfect time for walking slowly, too late to start the ironing, too early to start supper.

There is a place along the stony driveway where I always walk slowly to watch for a groundhog that has a hole in the ground there, under a buckeye tree. There I saw two quails. They came out of the cornfield and ran in front of me across the road to the groundhog's den and paused there, letting me look at them.

They did not seem afraid at all. They were full-grown, with smoothly dark brown bodies, pale stripes on their heads, and one wore a peak of feathers on the top. After I had stood quietly a few seconds to admire those two, I began to see others quietly becoming visible in the grass along the weedy fence row, under dangling wild raspberry canes, even against the edge of the groundhog's hole. The unmowed fence row had provided safe hiddenness for the large covey of these attractive birds, which are Dick's favorites.

The fence row separated Ira's road from a field on the next farm.

The rule is: when you stand on your own land, facing your neighbor's land, the half of the mutual "line" fence to your right is the half you are to maintain. If his cattle break through your half to get into your corn, there isn't much you can say about it.

In summer there had been wild raspberries, both black-caps and an unusual bright-yellow kind, in the fence row. There were more of them farther on where Ira's road becomes the public road, and our mailbox sits in front of the neighbor's fence, but there the highway keepers had sprayed the fence row.

All summer I had intended to dig up a start of yellow raspberries and transplant them into the garden, to see what fertilizing and hoeing and the easy protected life might do to improve their small size and somewhat pallid flavor. The highway sprayers got to them before I did, but fortunately for me and the quails and the platoon of red-winged black-birds, the blue bunting and the treeful of goldfinches that live along that road, the private fence row was not sprayed.

How tidy should a farm be? How cleaned off? I like to see the pastures mowed before winter. They look better so, even under winter's snowdrifts. But I think little corners and thickets, patches of weeds, and brambles add greatly to the charm of the land, providing shelter and food for the little wild neighbors to whom also the land partly belongs, without the obligation of maintaining any fences (except the invisible fences the quails maintain during the long, warm summer days by calling back and forth along a boundary to each other).

Another reward, more personal and selfish perhaps, is the sense of luxury to be had from seeing a portion of land from which a farmer has not been obliged to exact the last possible measure of merchantable harvest.

♣   ♣   ♣

And I can never get very enthusiastic about the efficiency of large-scale weed-spraying, either, whether in farm fields or along the highways and under power lines.

Nature the resilient, the relentless, the thrifty waster, nature the user-up, the waiter-in-patience—how does nature outwit man the restless, dominating, arrogant, ingenious, self-contradicting waster?

The first year Dick and Joe sprayed the cornfields on this farm, I went out late in summer to see a cornfield that had been sprayed to kill jimson. The spraying had not hurt the giant foxtail.

Jimson had been tall already when the spraying was done, the trunk and the first two branches had already developed to normal size. The nature of jimson is to fork into two smooth heavy branches, then each forks again and so on until a tall, ornamental bush has developed, having leaves shaped somewhat like holly leaves. The unpleasant odor of its foliage has earned this hardy annual the subtitle "stink-weed," but its deep-throated pale blue-to-white flower has a delicate fragrance, pleasant in the cooling evening air fol-

lowing a hot summer day. It is a pretty flower, flaring outward like a long, narrow, gored skirt and is pointed at the
ends of the seams. A lawyer who lives in southern Indiana
likes this weed well enough to want to plant seeds of it, and
indeed in its early history jimson was planted as a garden
flower. Its vice was simply that it was too willing. It spread.
Its heavy black seeds develop in a four-sectioned, thorny
and attractive pod the size of a Bantam egg. When ripe,
the pod opens like a tulip and the seeds come rattling out at
every touch against the plant.

Spraying in the cornfield had caused the later developing
jimson branches to break out into many small ones, with
the look of water splashing haphazardly when a stone is
dropped into a shallow creek. Leaves were curled at the rim,
and had turned a sickly yellow-green. The unnatural appearance was disquieting. No flower bud had developed, no
bloom, therefore there would be no seedpods and since
jimson roots do not survive winter, the spraying had to that
extent, wiped out jimson from the field.

Dick's father always told me, however, that a farmer
plowing a field turns under and covers weed seeds that will
be there to plague his grandsons. I do not know how many
years of spraying would be required to rid the fields of weeds
sprouted from these long-buried seeds. Nor does anybody
know what would survive the necessary number of spray-
ings.

Thoughtfully, as I walked along the corn rows, disturbed

by the deformed appearance of the jimson, I remembered a time earlier in the year when we had visited a small home greenhouse. Its owner, Hollis LaBaw, is a registered nurse, dedicated to alleviating suffering and illness, a kind person and gentle by nature. She told us she liked to experiment with new plants and plant foods. She thinks there is some unexplained benefit in setting her transplanted seedlings in tin cans, something in the chemical reaction of earth with the metal, perhaps, that is good for the plants. She was then involved in an experiment with carnations.

To some she had given a new kind of atomic plant food; beside them were others not given this food. The atomic-fed plants were larger, darker, slower to bloom than the others. It was a comforting recollection to have now as I walked through the sprayed cornfield. If man's sprays and bombs destroy normal plant forms, perhaps nature will find a way, patiently, after long time, to transform the evil into food and use it for new kinds of plants.

Change is an essential part of nature's routine, annihilation is not. Man's deadly instruments may yet turn out to be nature's surgical instruments of the future. Hope is, she will not have to turn them against man himself.

♣   ♣   ♣

"There are 40,000 fewer farmers now than last year," said the blithe young law student arriving at the farm just in time to eat Sunday evening supper with us.

I don't know where he got that statistic, nor do I intend to verify or disprove it. It may be the count was made when a number of farmers were vacationing in Florida and so were counted with tourists instead of with farmers. I have read myself that the farm population is only eight per cent of the national total. But in any farming community it is obvious that the ranks of farmers from the small family farms are steadily thinning.

These farmers can understand now how the Civil War veterans must have felt every year on Memorial Day when they got out their gray or blue uniforms to march in one more parade. Perhaps while there is still time, every farmer ought to set aside one pair of bib overalls (leaving the wad of binder twine and handful of fence "steeples" in the pocket) to wear in future thinned-rank farm parades.

The day for this parade should be June 21 because on that date in 1834 farming received a tremendous shove toward its present miracle-machinery era; Cyrus McCormick patented his new reaper. Horse-drawn, its principle was so practical that it has become the ancestor of today's prodigious self-propelled grain combine, and has led the way toward a whole new system of farming.

The French Academy of Science said Mr. McCormick had "done more for the cause of farming than any man living." In 1859 Senator William H. Seward said, "Owing to Mr. McCormick's reaper the line of civilization in the United

States moves westward thirty miles each year."

With one powerful machine, such as the one that picks and shells corn from the stalk and spits out the cobs back upon the ground, one young man can tend a great acreage by himself. "Farming is a lonelier job with all this machinery and only one operator," complained an old-time farmer. "The farmer is the captive of his big, powerful machinery," said another. But farming moves steadily in that direction.

If it seems strange, as one farmer suggested, that with all its marvelous advancement, the machinery industry has not produced a pitchfork handle that is warm in winter, there is a good reason. It could produce one, certainly, but the industry is not interested in producing a warm pitchfork handle. Its aim is to furnish machinery with buttons and levers that will eliminate the kind of farming of which the pitchfork is the symbol.

♣　　♣　　♣

The thin-soiled stony hillside in the pasture behind Ira's barn speaks casually of such things as time, immensity, change. The simplicity of its speech is what makes it significant, and at the same time so easily overlookable.

Near the top of the hill, about ten years ago I should say, a great chestnut oak fell over. It was dead when it fell, but with a bole thirty inches in diameter at the base it must have made an impressive passage between the other mighty trees still standing in the hillside. When the topmost branches finally touched the earth they had reached almost all the way down the hill to the creek's edge. And the torn roots, still holding their fill of the stony soil in which they had stood, now extended five feet above ground.

In all the subsequent years, rains and snows have not washed out the earth from the grasp of these roots. Looking at them one can see how they deviated, turning, twisting painfully, evading, going over and under and around the stones to get down into the ground to nourishment and water, and foothold.

The pieces of stone in that clutch of soil are also old . . . bits of preglacial geode, chert, mica, limestone, and sandstone. The tree itself is old. An oak is an infant at fifty years, a teen-ager at one hundred, middle-aged at two hundred. The fallen oak is not older than the soil but it is older than Ira's farm. When the acorn fell, from which this mighty tree grew, it fell on woods soil, deep, rich, dark, like the soil in some of the other parts of wooded hills near there. The oak knew hunters before it knew farmers. It knew Indians before it knew Indiana settlers who came with axes, their teams and plows, their tractors and brush hogs.

Looking at this fallen tree, I felt the awe one expects to feel in the presence of a great teacher.

Thoughtfully after a while I walked on down the hill to the creek. A log fallen across the creek there made a bridge to cross on if one felt adventurous, and the bank on the opposite side was grass-covered, sunlit. Beyond there another hill rose, still forested with big trees. I crossed on the log and sat down on the thick grass under a young sycamore tree.

The sycamore was in leaf, its sharply delineated furry leaves full-grown and already losing their infant powderiness on the underside. The old bark was peeling like badly sunburned skin, disclosing new bark, pale green and marked with the irregular white lines that will also split later, to permit the tree trunk to grow.

Continuity is aptly expressed in the life cycle of a tree's bark. I leaned back comfortably against the sycamore and listened to the sounds around me.

The ubiquitous plane, representative of today's conquering world; the rustle and song of unseen birds in the lower trees, crows and blackbirds more distantly in the cornfield. From that field came also the sound of a farm tractor. Above me was the whisper and soft laughter of wind among the sycamore leaves, and beside me the stillness of still waters.

In the creek earlier that spring, water had rushed and foamed and beat its fists against the restraining stones, but now sliding rapidly, twinkling in sunlight, rippling in shadow, turning the bare stones to a smooth inscrutable green, it went all in stillness. Even when I knelt at the edge and bent so close that my ear nearly touched the water, I heard only stillness.

There is a difference between stillness and silence. Silence is eloquent, but stillness communicates.

When I attended Indiana University my psychology professor (who always seemed more like a farmer than a professor, I thought), liked to tell us there are two instincts that govern man's behavior. One is the instinct for self-preservation which is the basis of hunger, the other is the instinct for race perpetuation which is the basis for sex. "Ontogeny recapitulates phylogeny," Professor Nicholson liked to tell us, as if a whole world were contained in that foreign-sounding sentence. And he explained it as a farmer might: "It means in his development, the individual goes through, in a way, the same process the race has gone through in its development." Professor Nicholson's final examinations began every year with the same requirement: "Define psychology as the science of behavior."

In the years since I studied college psychology, I have lived close to the land, observing it with loving diligence, believing what it told me, and asking it more. From this observation I have learned that there is also a third instinct, as inherent and persistent as the instincts of sex and hunger, and probably more urgent than either, though not as soon recognized. That is the instinct of curiosity, which drives man to search for meaning. From it rises his passion to understand himself and his relation to the earth and to their mutual creator.

In the natural world around him he observes laws that apply to this world and its creatures. Many of these laws, such as the law of predation, and nature's ways of keeping the balance, are painful to him, but inevitably accepted. And he suspects many of the natural laws apply also to him. Dimly, too, he senses the existence of laws that apply only, or chiefly to him, and impose on him a terrible responsibility not borne by other creatures. This vital instinct of curiosity impels him unceasingly to try to discover what it is that sets him apart from the other creatures with which he must share the earth. And what, if anything, actually sets him as an individual apart from other men as individuals.

This is one of the reasons he must return to the land; to consult it minutely again and again. To touch, and learn from it; to be comforted and made again significant, given an individual importance, by communication with it.

This is a long search. Man learns only a very little at a time, and often has to retrace his steps, and many times has to stop to find again the right direction, and the next step.

Brand Blanshard, Quaker, professor of philosophy at Yale University, said in a little talk about what he calls "The Great Commandment" some time ago: "In the mind of man there is an inner light that always throws enough illumination upon his path to make the next step possible; and what is important is that that step, however short, be taken."

That is it; it is exactly "the inner light." Of all creatures perhaps only man possesses the inner light, and the earth requires that he use it.

♣   ♣   ♣

We sat at the kitchen table late in the evening, drinking coffee, eating cheese and crackers, and thus hoarding the last few minutes of Nina's visit. In a little while she would have to go out to her car and return to the city. Nina has visited us on all our farms, and has also visited many cities in many countries.

"How will you like fish and algae farming, Dick?" she asked teasingly. "I read now that with the population exploding and five-sixths of the earth covered by sea, we may wind up getting our food and drinking water too from the ocean."

"I'd miss the cattle," he said.

"I'd miss the walks down to Monta's woods," I said, refilling the coffee cups.

It is not so much a future shortage of food I fear. We could probably feed the world a long time if we could distribute our nation's surplus better. And we could all eat less ourselves, to good advantage probably. What gives me cold chills is the thought of land shortage, of not having enough land for everyone to have a place to go to now and then for that healing touch of earth, and the feeling of not being pressed against, and for the solitude everybody has to have once in a while.

In Maple Grove we still follow the old-time farm

custom of seeing a departing guest all the way out to
the car. When we walked out into the yard with Nina the
night, merely by being there, was spectacular. It was the
time of full moon; under the big maples the shadows were so
distinct my first fanciful impulse was to gather up an armload to bring back into the house for kindling the morning
fire. The yard, beyond the maples, was drenched in moonlight. In the sloping field across the road the slopes formed
a trough and I could imagine the moonlight flowing down
out of the trough to be dipped up by cupfuls to drink. It was
a night of moonlight hyperbole; even so, lights in the distant
town thrust up a competitive reflection against the sky.

"My goodness," exclaimed Nina, "there's so much more
town light all around now than when you first came here!"

"And in the houses, too," Dick reminded her. "We didn't
even have electricity in Maple Grove then."

Now, from several of the neighboring farms the brilliance
of "farm safety lights" interrupted the moonlight. These
lights come on automatically at dusk, or in daytime hours
of exceptionally dark days, and burn with a cold, bleak,
blue light. Looking out toward the invisible highway (on
which Nina would presently be driving back to the city),
we could see the warm-looking glow made by traffic and in
the south horizon we could see the reflection thrust up
against the sky by the growing university town six and one
half miles away.

Urbanization has catapulted toward the community since we first knew Maple Grove. Steadily, like a crouching, bright-eyed cat, the town reaches out its furry, sharp-clawed paws deeper and deeper into the farmland, snatching a farm here, another there for a housing development, another for a shopping center, more for a school, for university needs, for roads, a lake. Now from Ralph Lewis's front yard on the hilltop near the Maple Grove church you can see the university's splendid new stadium looming up like a steamship about to come out across the treetops. Radio towers blink jewel-red eyes. Jet planes pass above the farm, unseen but felt, creating the sound of soft thunder and causing the small birds to scatter out of trees near the kitchen. The windows rattle in the farmhouse and the sound of the jets comes down magnified, through the fireplace and into the dining room. At night other planes go over above the farmhouse, showing their red and green lights and losing altitude in preparation for landing at the small airport a few miles beyond the town.

All these are the accessories of economic progress, into which farmers are steadily drawn. Both university and town provide welcome jobs for many small farmers who must have off-the-farm income in order to live on their farms. The economic change in the community has created a change in the geographic structure. The farms grow larger and fewer; there is a new kind of soil loss, erosion by concrete and asphalt as farms give up their fields to roads, houses, shopping centers, and essential services required by our modern industrial, luxurious society.

"How pleasant it is here, and how peaceful," murmured Nina, who has loved all the farms we have lived on. She got into the car and pressed a button which caused the windows to roll down with a little whir. Dick began to examine the windows with interest. Hearing our voices, the cattle came out to the fence and began to bawl softly as if to call our attention to the emptiness of the troughs there. From anonymous hidden places in the toolshed geese began to express their scorn of every word we had said. It seemed extremely pleasant to me: I was aware of a surge of deep love for this farm, to which I came rebelliously in the beginning, not wanting to leave the farm on which we were living at that time. Even with the addition of Monta's and Ira's 109 acres, this is still a small, family-sized farm.

The small family farm, I think, can be considered among our diminishing natural resources. It provides pleasant, anchoring memories for children who grow up on it or visit it frequently. It offers some feeling of peace and normalcy to adults. Its very smallness is a useful stimulus to farmers, compelling them to depend on their own ingenuity rather than expect all their problems to be solved for them.

Thinking this I added aloud, "But, of course, the basic philosophy of farming is opposed to the philosophy of the welfare state."

"I must go," exclaimed Nina suddenly. Dick stopped

leaning on the car window and we stepped back out of the way. "Take care now," she cried gaily, as always, and quickly drove away.

It is our family custom, when a dearly loved guest leaves, to stand at the back steps and watch until the car has reached the east road, the last possible glimpse. Then the guest sounds the car's horn, we wave, and the visit is over.

We came back into the house in that buoyant, lifted feeling that rises up behind a particularly happy visit like a swirl of autumn leaves in a wind. It is a feeling composed of many loves . . . love of people, love of the farm you have shared with them, love of the season, of the night, of life, of the earth and being able to walk about in it, and think and talk, and be still; a sense of overflowing cup which you cannot really explain; a strong feeling of kinship with the earth, knowing that the earth does not belong to man, but rather he belongs to the earth. And this perhaps is the real essence of it, for man has known since long ago that "the earth is the Lord's and the fulness thereof; the world, and they that dwell therein." Man dwells therein, therefore he is a part of the fulness and, like it, he is eternally important, eternally changing, and imperishable.